A GUIDE TO THE
VOLUNTEER
TRAINING CORPS
1914-1918

A GUIDE TO THE VOLUNTEER TRAINING CORPS

1914-1918

by Ray Westlake

The Naval & Military Press

For Iestyn Ellis who one day will create wonderful music

Thank you to my wonderful wife Claire for all her help and encouragement

© Ray Westlake 2020

Published by

The Naval & Military Press Ltd
Unit 5 Riverside
Bellbrook Industrial Estate
Uckfield, East Sussex
TN22 1QQ England

Tel: +44 (0) 1825 749494
www.naval-military-press.com

CONTENTS

Introduction ix

Chapter 1: A Short History of the VTC 1

Chapter 2: The Volunteer Training Corps Gazette 9

Chapter 3: Notes From the Volunteer Training Corps
           Gazette and Other Sources 19

Chapter 4: Higher Organisation 107

    Artillery 107

    Engineers 107

    Volunteer Regiments and Volunteer Battalions 108

    Transport and Supply Column Volunteers 132

    Medical Volunteer Corps 137

References 141

INTRODUCTION

A regular question during my fifty or more years writing and researching Britain's auxiliary forces has been, 'Where can I find a list giving details of the several Volunteer Training Corps units raised during the early months of the Great War?' True, the post-1915 years that saw the smaller companies merged into battalions, and later regiments, has been adequately covered in the several Volunteer Lists available. But what about the 'Citizens' corps, or the 'Fencibles', the 'Defence' organisations, the 'Village Guards'; those raised by shooting, cricket, golf or football clubs, or by railway companies, factories or athletes, businessmen or old school fellows? My answer must remain the same: 'I know of none.'

It will no doubt only be the tip of the iceberg but, before the higher organisation of the volunteers took a hold, many units would appear under their original titles as news items in the *Volunteer Training Corps Gazette*. Fortunate in having a complete run of this unique source of information to hand for the period 1914-16, I have in this book extracted such information relevant to unit existence and history. On occasion there will be delightful accounts submitted of when and where formed and by who, details of headquarters, commanding officers, secretaries and others responsible for running these all too often un-documented military formations. There will be information regarding route marches held and concerts to raise funds for equipment and other activity. But for some, intelligence would come in short doses ('The Secretary of ......VTC thanks the editor for Issue ...') and from such reports we must be content simply by knowing that such-and-such a corps existed.

I have provided a short history of the Volunteer Training Corps followed by a chapter dealing with the Volunteer Training Corps Gazette. Much has been drawn from these informative pages over the years resulting in articles by myself, one of which, dealing with advertisements placed by uniform suppliers, being repeated here. Regarding the corps themselves, I have placed the information into two sections: (1) that based on VTCG and other sources, (2) higher organisation details taken from Volunteer Lists and Army Orders. Although I have mentioned the badges worn by certain VTC units, this book in no way pretends to offer a complete record of this vast area of British military history.

CHAPTER 1
A SHORT HISTORY OF THE VTC

Quick to defend hearth and home were the Volunteers of the French Revolutionary and Napoleonic Wars. From stately homes, offices, universities, schools, factories and shops they came forward. They donned uniforms and found arms at their own expense and did regular drills and parades in their spare time. Much was the same when invasion from across the channel was probable once more. The time was the late 1850s; the Volunteers this time the sons of the previous generation of Volunteers. This was the Volunteer Force of Queen Victoria's reign and the origin of today's Territorial Army.

Within days of war being declared in 1914, Mr Percy Harris, in a letter to *The Times* dated 6 August 1914, proposed the formation of a 'London Defence Force.' 'Union is strength', wrote the Liberal member of the London County Council; 'all classes and all districts must stand together in face of the common danger… thousands of people desire to be of service to the State, but either because they belong to no Territorial unit or because of age and infirmities, they can be of no military value.' What we see here, of course, is a carbon copy of the situation that arose in the middle of the previous century. Storm clouds were gathering in 1859 perhaps, but in the first week of August 1914, indeed, it was already raining.

Mr Harris went on to suggest that units be raised within each London borough. Evening camps could be

The Norfolk Jacket and 'GR' arm band much in evidence in this photograph.

organised in parks and ex-soldiers too old for active service could help to drill and discipline recruits. Their charges, if they chose to do so, could then be drafted into the Regular or Territorial service, should they be required.

As for the funding of the scheme, Mr Harris envisaged this coming partly from the business ability of London and partly from local councils—the richer boroughs helping the poor. Committees would be formed for each borough with representatives '…not merely of the borough council, and the Poor Law authorities, but of the trade unions, and friendly societies who are in direct touch with their members.' In short, the Government would not be required to put its hand in its own pocket.

Within two days of Mr Harris's letter, a preliminary committee had been set up and on 8 August a meeting to discuss the idea of a 'Volunteer Force' took place at the offices of the Public Trustee, Sir Charles Stewart. Among those present, Sir O'Moore Creagh, VC who, having recently returned from his duties as Commander-in-Chief, India, was asked to act as Military Adviser to the new Defence Force.

At a further meeting, this time on 10 August and at the Cannon Street Hotel, Sir George Pragnell put forward several other names that he hoped would act as officers to a London-based 'Patriotic Association'. A committee was formed and, at offices taken over in the Exhibition Buildings in Aldwych, it was established that Lord Desborough should be President, Sir O'Moore Creagh, Military Adviser, Sir Charles Stewart, Treasurer, Mr Percy Harris, Honorary Secretary, Mr W Graham Everett, his assistant and Mr Master Bonner, Legal Adviser.

As in the cases of previous 'Citizen' forces there would be no immediate interest taken up by the Government, the main War Office belief in 1914, as in Victorian days, being that the existence of a part-time army would affect recruiting for the Regulars. Subsequently, at a meeting with Under Secretary of State for War, Harold John Tennant, Hon Secretary Harris would be persuaded to hold off for the time being any plans that his Committee may have for a Volunteer Force. But again, just as their fathers and grandfathers had done, they went ahead anyway.

VTC members on railway duty.

It would not be just from within London that thousands of individuals came forward with offers of service to some local Home, or Volunteer, defence organisation. The word had indeed spread and by early September many hundreds of requests had been received from cities, towns and villages outside of the Capital for some kind of association with the London movement. These places had already formed, or were about to do so, units for their own defence and protection. Some form of higher organisation—if the concept of a volunteer 'Home Defence Army' was to succeed—was certainly necessary and it was subsequently decided that London would provide the headquarters of what was to become known as the Central Association of Volunteer Training Corps (CAVTC). Here then, for the first time, we see the use of the overall term Volunteer Training Corps—the VTC.

Marksman's cloth arm badge.

From its first headquarters at the Royal Courts of Justice, the CAVTC, before the end of September 1914, would publish its aims together with a scheme for the formation and recruitment of VTC units throughout the country. In short, these echoed the ideas put forward the previous month by Mr Harris: '…military training in the form of regular drills for those unable to join the Army for various good reasons at present, but none-the-less would be willing to do so in any grave national emergency such as invasion.' It is of interest here to note (no conscription yet, remember) that each VTC unit was required to keep a register of all recruits which clearly showed the reasons why the men on the rolls had not joined the Regular Army.

Men from every walk of life were encouraged to join. The professions, institutions, sporting and rifle clubs, business houses, factories, would all form corps, a fact often reflected in the early titles of some units viz.: the Athletes Corps (branches throughout the country), Architects and Accountants Corps, the Chartered Institute of Secretaries Drill Club that met at St Botolph's Church, Bishopsgate in London, the Pharmacists VTC, which the *Daily Express* once referred to as the 'Anti Microbe Corps'. Also, in the Capital were the London Music Trade Volunteer Corps, and Allison's Piano Factory Corps which was at Kentish Town. In Sheffield there was the Chief Constable's Citizens Corps and, in the Midlands, formed from skilled workers within the city, the Birmingham Electrical Engineers.

Workers in businesses all over the country formed units: The Barclay and Perkins Brewery Corps in Southwark had its first inspection on its cricket ground in December 1914, while in Birmingham the tram drivers there organised themselves into the Birmingham and Midland Tramways Joint Committee Volunteer Corps. The Bowesfield Steelworkers Corps was drilling regularly by November 1914 and young men at the Bristol Coliseum out of working hours maintained a corps of horse riders, cyclists and motor cyclists. Other similar mounted corps were the Legion of Guides, in St John's Wood, NW London, the Leicester Motor Corps that took members of local units to drill and wore a uniform not unlike that of the Royal Flying Corps and the Surrey Corps of Guides which did much to assist Regular and Territorial Forces while training in their county. But the North Eastern Railway Company, for one, applied caution. See their Circular No

Ambulance Section cloth arm badge.

747 (dated 16 December 1914) that reminded employees of their commitment to railway work for military services: 'No servant of the Company, therefore, can, without the specific written permission of the Head of Department, allow himself to be bound to be at the disposal of any outside organisation, and any member of the staff who has already given such an undertaking should at once take steps to cancel it.'

Makers of soap at Fort Sunlight drilled after work—Alfred Bigland (their boss) upon joining announcing that he would 'make as good a stopper of German bullets as anyone else'. The Dulwich Defence League (not without objection, I'm sure) learnt how to dig trenches on Sydenham Hill Golf Course (there was a war on, you know) and how to shoot on an old skittle alley, while in Hampstead, composer Sir Edward Elgar drilled regularly alongside the illustrator of Peter Pan, Herbert Draper. Sir Arthur Conan Doyle helped get the Ilford Civilian Corps underway and with them, attended drills at the local skating rink.

There was a company of fit men prepared to provide physical training among volunteers, along with something that may come in handy if invaded, the Ju-Jitsu VTC being capably led by an expert preciously employed by the Paris Police and whose skills had also been put to good use in America 'when trapping the Apaches.' In Stratford-on-Avon, drills took place with broomsticks under the capable command of Major TH Bairnsfather, father of artist and journalist Bruce.

Although the Government was now aware of the existence of the various volunteer units springing up around the country, and had indeed giving a blessing of sorts, official recognition of the CAVTC and its affiliated corps would not come until November 1914. In that month, Lord Kitchener sent for Lord Desborough and from their meeting informed the CAVTC President of Germany's plans for an invasion. With very few trained troops in Britain—reinforcements had already left for France and the British Expeditionary Force—Kitchener was keen to make use of any available force then in existence. He would—and this came as good news to the Volunteers—now be prepared to give status to all units under the wing of the CAVTC and secure their efficient administration. Conditions for recognition were set out in a War Office Instruction dated 19 November (20/Gen. No. /3604 A.G.I) viz:

'In confirmation of the arrangements made with you in various interviews, I am commanded to inform you that the Army Council are prepared to grant recognition to the Central Association Volunteer Training Corps, as long as a responsible officer approved by the War Office is its adviser, and the Council will extend that recognition to such Volunteer Forces and Rifle Clubs, etc., as may become affiliated to your Association, and decide to abide by your rules.

The following rules have been framed as the conditions under which the Army Council are prepared to grant recognition to

The much disliked 'GR' armband.

your Association, and to those which may be affiliated there to:-

1. It is to be clearly understood that only the names of those can be registered who are not eligible through age to serve in the Regular or Territorial Army or are unable to do so for some genuine reason which is to be recorded in the Corps Register; in the case of the latter, they must agree in writing to enlist if specially called upon to do so.
2. No arms, ammunition or clothing will be supplied from public sources, nor will financial assistance be given.
3. There may be uniformity of dress among members of individual organisations provided that no badges of rank are worn, and provided that the dress is distinguishable from that of Regular and Territorial Units.
4. Members of recognised organisations will be allowed to wear as a distinctive badge a red armlet of a breadth of three inches with the letters G.R. inscribed thereon. The badge will be worn on the left arm above the elbow.
5. The accepted military ranks and titles will not be used or recognised, and no uniform is to be worn except when necessary for training.
6. No form of attestation involving an oath is permitted.
7. It will be open to Army Recruiting Officers to visit the Corps at any time and to recruit any members found eligible for service with the Regular Army whose presence in the Corps is not accounted for by some good and sufficient reason.

So, there it was. Britain would have its Volunteer Army. A force established to prepare young men for military service and allow those too old, or unable to join up, the opportunity to serve their country. One commentator would note that the absence of military ranks and titles, no uniform or weapons, suggested that the VTC was to take the form of '…bands of irregulars, and its duty in case of invasion, to carry on a form of guerrilla warfare.' A theory, in part anyway, that if not entirely true in 1914, certainly would be the case in 1939-45.

It was also suggested that the VTC had been created to assist those intent on shirking their duty— 'perhaps the ranks of the VTC would be filled with those desirous not to go on active service.' Paragraphs 1 and 7 of the War Office Instruction would take care of that, but throughout the history of the VTC there would be many, many cases in this respect that required a finer point of consideration. But the idea behind the system was good and, in general, a tremendous success.

Conditions of entry into the Regular forces changed as the war progressed, each time allowing for men hitherto excluded to enlist. The age limit increasing first from thirty-five to thirty-eight, then from thirty-eight to forty, would release thousands of men from the VTC, each with the advantage of being at an advanced stage of military training. Then there were the physical requirements. Tens of thousands of men below the required standard, when conditions changed, would also join the Regulars from the VTC, often as almost competent soldiers—certainly not raw recruits.

November 1914 also saw the introduction of a badge of proficiency. Designed by Soloman J Soloman of the Royal

Advertisement for the Cyclist Section badge.

Academy, the badge was given to all volunteers that had done the minimum of forty drills, passed through a test as a Second-Class Shot, and received a certificate of efficiency in drill and musketry. Worn in civilian clothing, the badge was a source of pride, along with being an indication that the wearer was not avoiding military service. It was recognised by the Army Council and an example in gold was presented to HM the King.

With hundreds of small local corps being formed throughout the country, the CAVTC then decided to concentrate on the formation of Volunteer Regiments. This, as was the case of the Victorian volunteer movement, would insure uniformity of training and a greater standard of efficiency. Lord-lieutenants of Counties were now to be involved and this would open many doors on the way to providing a greater selection of drill and shooting grounds.

Now seen was the smaller and independent corps merged into larger formations under county titles, e.g. Bedfordshire Volunteer Regiment—sad, indeed, was the loss at this time of those fascinating individual corps designations, e.g. 'Defence Corps', 'Civic Guard', 'Home Protection League', 'Patriotic League', 'Fencibles' (a term not in use for more than a hundred years) and 'Home Guard' (one that would become familiar again in a future war). Later, in 1918, these regiments were linked to county regiments and, as was the case with their Victorian predecessors, styled as, e.g. 1st Volunteer Battalion Bedfordshire Regiment.

Under the guidance of General Sir O'Moore Creagh, VC, the subjects of uniform and military rank were overcome. It was certainly proving difficult to install, within members of VTC units, that essential ingredient of military life: 'Regimental Pride' (this being easily, and usually automatically, obtained by the putting on of a uniform).

The clause '…there may be uniformity of dress among members…provided that it was distinguishable from that of Regular and Territorial Units…' in Paragraph 3 of the War Office terms was taken advantage of and in this way 1915 saw the introduction of a special green-grey uniform—frowned upon, of course, was the use of khaki—made of rainproof cotton drill. Officers' jackets, of a normal military pattern, were open

More armband fun.

at the throat to show shirt and tie. Those of other ranks were closed and of a 'Norfolk' pattern.

Also essential was a rank structure. With normal military ranks forbidden, the CAVTC adopted their own: Officers—County Commandant, Regimental Commandant, Commandant, Sub-Commandant, Company Commander and Platoon Commander. There would also Adjutants, Quartermasters, Chaplains and Medical Officers appointed on a regimental level. Non-Commissioned Officers—Regimental Sergeant Major, Regimental Quartermaster Sergeant, Battalion Sergeant Major, Battalion Quartermaster Sergeant, Company Sergeant Major, Company Quartermaster Sergeant, Platoon Sergeant, Section Commander and Section Corporal.

During 1915 the formation of Volunteer Regiments had taken place in almost every county. At the same time the general efficiency of the VTC had increased to a high standard and the Volunteers were keen to take on more responsible duties. This would have the effect of releasing other elements of the forces from general home duties. Soon the guarding by local Volunteers of munitions works, railway lines, bridges and other vulnerable points was commonplace. The digging and manning of trenches around large cities had also become the responsibility of the VTC.

The Volunteers now proving their worth on a daily basis, sanction was given by the War Office for the formation within the Volunteer system of arms of service other than infantry-styled units, and in this way Engineer, Signal, Field Ambulance and Transport services were formed.

All types of work were undertaken by the Volunteer Force: at airfields, Government building and installations, and in London even the Fire Brigade was augmented by men of the London Volunteer Rifles.

The value of the VTC was now well established, but with such success the need to be given the full status of soldiers grew. 'So long as they were refused the right to wear the ordinary uniform, and their officers denied His Majesty's Commission,' noted the CAVTC, 'they could not be assured of the right of taking their proper place in the fighting line.'

The CAVTC therefore decided to concentrate its efforts on forcing the Government to improve the status of the Volunteers. A long-time supporter of the Volunteer Movement, Lord Lincolnshire put forward a Bill with this purpose. But by the end of 1915, however, nothing had been achieved.

It was probably the great review of London Volunteers held in Hyde Park in June 1916 which brought home to the nation the value of its Volunteers. Seeing their work, as it were, close up, the Press were on their side and brought to the public's attention the fact that to date not a penny of public money had been spent on the VTC—uniform, equipment, rifles etc., all having been provided by public subscription or directly from the men themselves. Indeed, in some less well-off areas, a small number of men possessed no uniform whatsoever. At Hyde Park, however, their appearance was noted as being soldier-like and an example of good physical fitness. Lord French reviewed the troops and in his speech showered nothing but praise on the Volunteers. A speech that did much to convince the Government of their worth and subsequently place the VTC under the direct control of the War Office.

For what remained of the war, the Volunteers would prove their worth in a number of ways. For the emergency that arose in the spring of 1918, some ten thousand Volunteers were used to man for over three months important coastal defence posts, all available Regular troops and Territorials having been rushed to France to help hold back the advancing German army. Much was also done on coastal and anti-aircraft artillery work.

At the time of the Armistice the strength of the Volunteer Force stood at 234,800 officers and men and in a letter from the War Office dated 13 November 1919 it would be thanked for its work, 'so willingly rendered.' Grandad's Army, with its Captain Mainwarings, Sergeant Wilsons, Corporal Joneses—even its 'stupid boy' Pikes—had, for the time being, anyway, done its bit.

CHAPTER 2
THE VOLUNTEER TRAINING CORPS GAZETTE

Always fascinated by the names of the early 1914-18 Volunteer Training Corps formations (see my article 'What's in a Name' published in the *Bulletin of the Military Historical Society* (No 236, Volume 59, May 2009), and having spent a number of years attempting in vain to establish some listing of the many early units formed, it was with great delight that in 1980, tucked away on the bulging shelves of Maggs Bros Bookshop on the west side of Berkeley Square, London, I discovered two bound volumes of *The Volunteer Training Corps Gazette*.

It would not be necessary to glance beyond the contents page of issue No 1—that for Saturday 5 December 1914—to convince myself that the colossal amount being asked for these weighty tomes (I was in Berkeley Square, don't forget) was without doubt going to prove a good investment. Excitement indeed at the thought of delving deep into such features as: 'Meetings to Promote Corps' and 'Notes About Corps', in which we hear of who was present, where the meeting took place, how many enrolled, when and where training would take place, who was elected as commanding officer, secretary or treasurer and the 'We Hear' pages in which snippets of corps activity news found their way to the editor's desk.

Here, page after page, were unit names in abundance, all backed up with historical information—when and where formed, drill locations, officers and officials. News too regarding the VTC as a whole, a week-by-week commentary on the trials and tribulations experience in gaining recognition from the War Office, and biographical details of the several important individuals involved with the movement.

It would seem, having glanced through Issue No 1, that after just a few months of war having been declared things seemed to have been on the move and all were keen to do their bit. But not everyone, it would seem, was happy, the 5 December issue noting that in some places objections had been raised to the drilling and route marching of corps on Sundays. 'We doubt', remarked the editor, 'if the Germans, if they ever arrive here, will show much respect for the Sabbath.'

> **To VOLUNTEERS.**
>
> EVERY UNIT who desires his Corps to be **EFFICIENT** also has a **PERSONAL INTEREST** in its Tout-ensemble—**ON PARADE** or **ROUTE MARCH**.
>
> This can only be effected if each Unit has a Well-cut and Well-fitting Uniform. Some of the Uniforms supplied to Volunteers are too appalling for words.
>
> It is just as simple and easy to get the proper thing if you know **HOW AND WHERE**.
>
> **YOU** can be correctly fitted out at modest prices by experienced Military Tailors, if you apply to—
>
> **CASTLE & CO.** (Estd. 1889), *Naval & Military Tailors,*
> **37, PICCADILLY, LONDON, W.** (Facing St. James's Church).
>
> N.B.—The Committee have now passed the Cloth to be used, and this **IS BEING MADE**—deliveries are due in a few days, when Uniforms can be put in hand.
>
> CASTLE & CO., 37, Piccadilly, London, have made arrangements for securing the first outputs from the Mills of the **APPROVED CLOTH**.

In Issue 2 we find the *Gazette's* first single unit feature in the form of two complete pages devoted to the Optimists' National Corps. The accompanying photographs, in which we see a body of well turned out, equipped and uniformed troops, was for the time far from the norm. A diary column appears listing nation-wide meetings planned throughout the coming week, hardly a single day left free of gatherings held to promote the formation of corps. Readers were also brought up to date regarding the important, and controversial, subject of War Office recognition—'will the government's attitude hinder the formation of corps?'

And on come the advertisers, the publisher, Cassell & Co, Ltd, wasting no time in bringing out the first book aimed directly at the Volunteer.

Keen to associate the celebrities of the day with the Volunteer cause, the *Gazette*, in Issue 3, had approached novelist HG Wells (1866-1946) for an interview. But the apparently modest writer of *The Time Machine* and *The Invisible Man* declined on the grounds that the paper had overrated his importance, '… my proper place in the movement is merely that of a grade 3 or grade 4 private which is lowest in the unsound section of my local Corps.' Nonetheless, in a letter to the editor, he put forward several suggestions. Recommended was a steel dummy gun for drill and bayonet work available, he notes, at eighteen pence; the shot gun as a weapon in trench warfare, using buck shot as a means of stopping an advance; and the suggestion that VTC units on the east coast should have their defensive trenches ready or planned out now.

Not holding back in poking fun at the new 'Citizens Army', the *Gazette* published the first of many satirical cartoons in its Issue 3. But who could doubt the keenness of those involved? Even Christmas must not get in the way of important training, a camp having been arranged from 19 December to 2 January at Epping Forest at a cost of twenty-five to thirty shillings per head.

And more advertising. Rifles, real and dummy, are looking better, military tailors are warning Volunteers to steer clear of ill-fitting and shoddily-made uniforms, while companies with men's comfort in mind recommend their answer to soreness, with corns and blisters brought on through route marching. Reprinted here is an article of mine dealing with the subject:

Uniform, Badges, Equipment and Arms as Advertised in the Volunteer Training Corps Gazette 1914-1916: First published on Saturday 5 December 1914, it would be in issue No 2 of the weekly magazine for the new Citizens' Army, the *Volunteer Training Corps Gazette*, that the first advertisement regarding uniform appeared. The naval and military tailors, Castle & Co took a half-page headed 'Important Notice to Volunteers' in which they expressed their concern that the new VTC units may put at risk their efficiency by purchasing anything else but tailor-made and well-fitting uniforms, 'Factory-made and Contract Stuff", in their opinion, 'is no good—and never was—in the clothing way.' They (Castle & Co), of course, had the answer. Just pop along to their shop at 37 Piccadilly, London (opposite St James's Church) where 'you can be correctly fitted out at modest prices by experienced military tailors.' But don't rush. It would be another six weeks before the firm was in a position to announce, via the magazine, that the 'approved cloth' was being produced, and that 'deliveries were due in a few days.' As we know, the cloth in question was of the grey-green colour that had been settled upon for use by the volunteers.

Perhaps Castles were dealing with Frost & Son of 19/21 Heddon Street (just off Regent Street), who by the sixth week of the *Gazette* were advising all commanders of VTC units, and their appointed tailors, that they were purveyors of the regulation grey-green cloth. But competition was warming up; the same issue carried two competitors in the form of London firm Vince & Co (25 Wood Street, EC) and, no doubt closer to the mills themselves, C G Southcott, who could be found at Paragon Street, Hull, or Wellington Street in Leeds.

Prices still to be mentioned, Gerrish, Ames & Simpkins, Ltd of 63-67 Carter Lane in London would, however, be the first advertiser to go into any detail regarding what you could get for your money. Norfolk jackets were available both unlined, or check lined and the cotton Bedford cord breeches, with their laced knees, were on hand both in fine twills and woollen materials. But beware, those of you heeding Castle & Co's advice. Messes Gerrish, Ames & Simpkins were, it seems, manufacturers of the 'Contract Stuff' to be so avoided. The firm proudly boasted in its advertisement that they were 'The Largest Wholesale Tailoring Warehouse in the City of London', their factory being the North Hants Clothing Works in Basingstoke. As much 'off the peg', I imagine, was the product supplied by the East London Rubber Co which offered 'Quick Delivery' of 400 jackets within fourteen days.

By the beginning of January 1915, tailors and military outfitters were falling over themselves to get in on this great boom to their trade, their advertisements now appearing on almost every page of the *Gazette*: plenty to see at the Little St Andrew's Street (off St Martin's Lane) showrooms of M Wanda, or Hawes Bros, who were keen for you to have the 'Correct' uniform and Fox & Co in Shoreditch, already 'Clothing Contractors to HM Government'. So proud of their service to

OUR CITIZEN ARMY.

It should be particularly noted by the Commandants of the various Volunteer Training Corps and also the Tailors appointed by them that the Central Association cannot undertake to supply the new Grey-Green Cloth necessary for the Uniforms, but all Enquiries and Orders for same should be sent direct to

FROST & SON
19/21, Heddon St., Regent St., London, W.

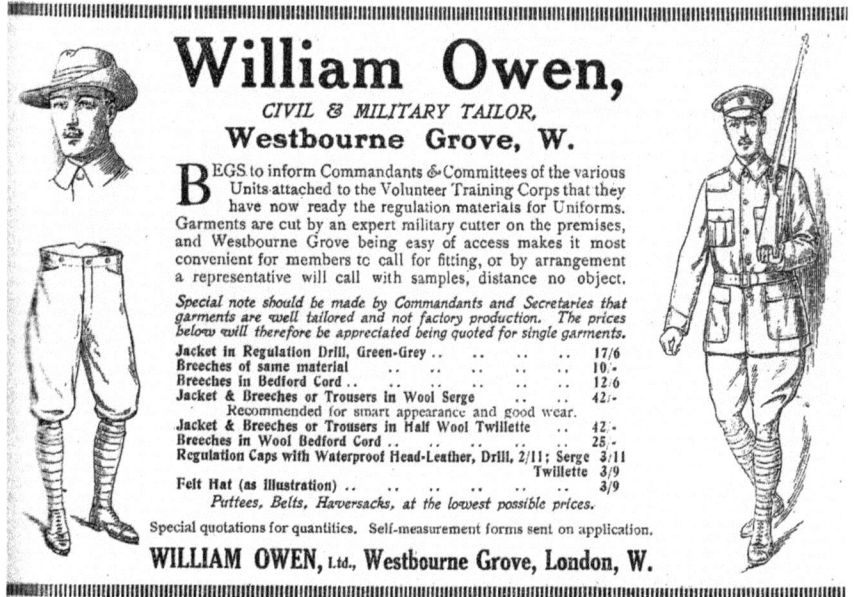

the 'VeTeCy', as they would have it, Samuel Brothers of Ludgate Hill and Oxford Circus took out a full-page advertisement in March 1916 which quoted from letters sent in from already satisfied customers—'We have had a week-end under canvas and during part of the time the weather was atrocious...our uniforms appeared to stand the test' (Blackburn VTC), and after a sample had been sent to the South Tottenham and Harringay Volunteer Company for approval: 'Please send your measurer on Tuesday at 7pm, as we wish to get Company in uniform as soon as possible'. Samuel Bros also offered, as an incentive to purchase their products, a 'Free for the Asking' copy of Kit Hints and Don'ts, extracts of which were included in another full-page insertion. The 'Kit Hints' part naturally steered the reader towards their good selves, while the 'Don'ts' section offered invaluable advice to volunteers on, eg, saluting and how not to rile the Sergeant-Major. Officers, at the same time, were advised not to stand men to attention in the sun for long periods, that 400 yards of road is taken up by a battalion in fours, and to be aware that men on the march like to whistle and sing—'if they get bored, they begin to weary'.

In business since the year of Waterloo, Hazel & Co. in Nile Street, Shoreditch included in their advertisements delightful cartoons of men in uniform, one in particular illustrating the point that uniforms made out of lesser material than their own were unlikely to stand up to barbed wire. They were also keen to push home the point that their tailoring always fitted the client; from their 13 May 1916 insertion: 'When Hazel's execute a contract Brown's uniform fits Brown, and Jones's uniform fits Jones'.

But in business, an eye must always be kept on stiff competition, and the all-important magnet of keen prices which must be carefully considered: 'Get Your Uniforms at Very Moderate Charges' was the carrot dangled by M Nanette of 26 Church Street—their workshops by the side of the Palace Theatre in Shaftesbury Avenue—or better still, providing you were prepared to cross the river to South London, a keener deal could be got at Peckham's Josiah Messent where 'Our prices are considerably lower than those ruling in the West End or the City'.

In a recent television programme featuring the several tailoring emporiums to be found in London's Savile Row, one shop owner, when asked by the interviewer about prices, remarked that 'pounds, shillings and pence' have never been mentioned in this establishment since it opened its doors almost two centuries ago'. What, I wonder, would he have thought about Bickerton & Son, whose 16 January 1915 advertisement in the *Gazette* was the first to mention cash—'promptly supplied' Norfolk jackets in waterproof twill at 16/11, trousers to match at 9/6; Bedford cord breeches, 11/6; an assortment of puttees: ordinary, 2/11, the 'non-fray' variety costing an extra shilling, the pattern known as 'Four-wind', luxury surely at 4/6 or 5/6; leggings, brown hide, 8/6 and 12/6, all could be obtained from their premises at 61 Cheapside, London, EC.

An actual illustration of uniform, albeit just the lower half, first appeared on 16 January 1915 in the form of the Bedford Riding Breeches Co's small add offering a selection of their products—'Cut to measure and Tailored by Experts', at 10/6, 13/11 and 15/11. Do write off for their free 'Patterns and Self-measure Chart'. Isaac Walton and Co, Ltd, on the other hand, provide good full-length sketches of what was worn by both officer and private, while Robinson & Cleaver's illustration of the latter included the much despised 'GR' armlet.

And, of course, there were those little extras essential to the well-turned out volunteer: to keep dry, 'The Parade Drill Mac', grey-green in colour and offered by Tepson's, just off the Strand in Essex Street, at 23/9—Colletts of Queen Victoria Street going one step better, perhaps, with their 'Colmac Featherweight Waterproof', an early version of the pac-a-mac which came complete with its own pouch. For 'Hot Drinks and Shaving Water' (there were thousands already in use at the front, noted the supplier) the 'Little Kitchener Cooker' would be a good investment at 1/-. There were Sam Brown belts (single strap) from Bickerton & Son at 6/6, the latest leather belt, pouch and frog from Birmingham's Edward Jones at 12/6, Knitted Cardigan Jackets for 5/-, 'necessary for wear under tunics', according to Morris of 7 King Street, EC, and if you really want to get ahead, an outlay of 3/9 would have secured you from William Owen of Westbourne Grove, one of their felt hats. Oh, and while you're considering headgear, why not invest in the 'Trencher's Sun Shield' with its little secret pocket tucked away out of sight—Gamages could supply at 6½ each—or, just the job for those clandestine exercises in the Home

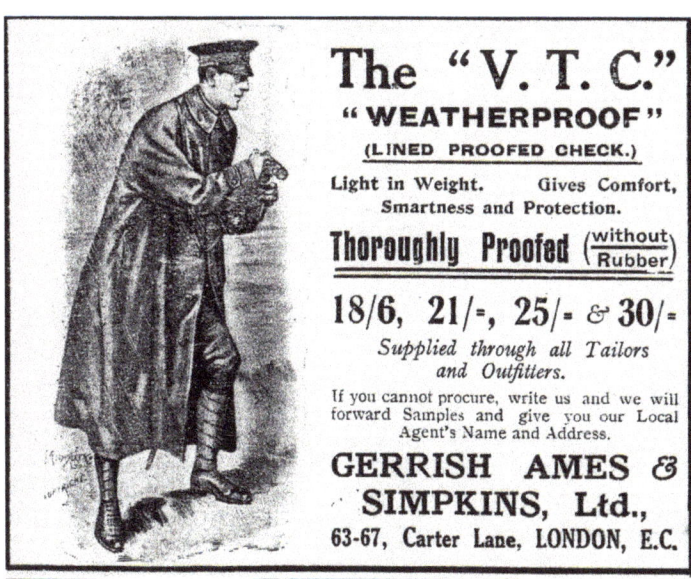

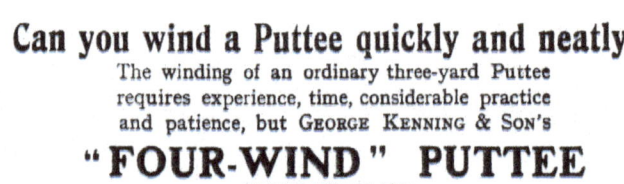

Counties, the new 'Scout Helmet' with its matching gloves.

Footwear is mentioned for the first time by Gardiner & Co (Commercial Road, London, E.), who offered 'Tan Russet Calf Boots' from 12/6. Perhaps a pack of 'Red Star Infantry Foot Dressing' (see *Gazette* advertisement on 16 January), which 'Comforts and relieves at once the route marcher', was available from the same supplier. And don't forget the band; Besson & Co Ltd, on 2 October 1915 offered their instruments 'All British Made and Guaranteed', with catalogues being available from 196-8 Euston Road, London, NW.

Quick on the heels of the uniform and equipment suppliers were badge manufacturers. Fattorini's of Bolton showed as an example of their wares the star-shaped cap badge of the Middlesex Volunteer Regiment, while JA Wylie & Co at 62 Holborn Viaduct, who offered 'badges of every description', illustrated two examples of their lapel-badge work: one, for the West Ham National Reserve Rifle Club, the other that made for the Great Eastern Railway. The Birmingham firm of JR Gaunt illustrated the circular badge worn by, local to them, the Birmingham Rifle Reserve (the ciphered letters BRR in the centre, with the title in full around the edge). Gamages, 'which catered for the volunteer's every need' from entrenching tools (3/3) to wickless oil stoves (10/6), also offered in their advert of 5 June 1915 the regulation cloth Marksman's Badge which had only just been approved. Also approved by the Central Association for Volunteer Training Corps, and again in cloth, was the badge for Ambulance Sections, Gamages offering these at 9d each, or cheaper by the dozen at 8/6. Shoulder titles were not forgotten, the embroidered type for tunic or overcoat being priced from 4d per pair, metal making an appearance for the first time in August 1916 when 'hand cut' pairs (Gamages again) went on offer at 2/-.

To end with, just a brief look at two of the many firms that solved the scarcity problem of drill rifles—the real thing being unavailable for this purpose, as not uncommon are photographs of men on parade with broomsticks, pitchforks or pickaxe handles. Summers had the answer, this Cheapside firm turning out, as they did, wooden dummy rifles of 'correct balance and weight'. But, at 48/- per dozen, they looked like dummy rifles made of wood. Tepson & Co in Essex Street off the Strand, on the other hand, could provide an 'Exact copy of the Short Lee

Enfield', correctly weighted and balanced, with bolt, magazine, trigger, sights, sling and piling swivel, at 10/6 each.

So here, in this small space, are details of just a few of the many hundreds of advertisements set to attract the early members of another 'Dads' Army'. After a time, recognition by the War Office brought permission to wear a more army-style uniform, so, as far as the advertising departments of the Gamages, Samuel Brothers, JA Wylie & Co's, etc were concerned, it all had to start again.

****

An interview—his photo on the front cover, nonetheless—with General Sir O'Moore Creagh, VC, begins Issue 4. Out just in time to ponder over after Boxing Day lunch, full of enthusiasm, the winner of the Victoria Cross during the Second Afghan War tells how he had 'heard of the movement almost at once... I thought the idea an excellent one...and soon found myself in the thick of it.' The General held the position of Military Advisor to the Central Association of Volunteer Training Corps. Still in civilian clothes, the Willesden and District Defence League are seen on parade in the playground of Leopold Road School, while further on there is much to be said regarding uniforms (or the lack of them), and the first of a series of articles by FAM Webster concerning the VTC's part in home defence. Regarding the Christmas Camp, well, there is still time to get down to Epping Forest, the request to let the caterer, Mr William Riggs, know by 'noon next Thursday (24th)', coming, I fear, a little too late.

And so, with Issue 5, the new, and second, year of the war begins. But what has been said regarding the VTC so far? The editor reserved the front page for a selection of comments under the heading 'What They Have Said'. 'At a time like this no one ought to shirk his duty', so says 'Mr Asquith at Alderley', the Liberal Prime Minister between 1908-16 almost anonymous in his signature; while Sir William Lever from his Port Sunlight soap empire reminds readers that 'the object of forming a corps is to enable those who are older to join the younger ones in preparing themselves to defend their country.' Percy Harris, of the CAVTC, expresses the opinion that the general public were not yet aware of 'what a great movement has been going on in their midst'. But are we to believe that the editor was short of comments to the extent that he felt it necessary to draw on something that the thirty-four-years dead Benjamin Disraeli had said back in 1879 about another Citizens' Army? — 'the British Army is the guardian of our Empire, but the Volunteer Force is the garrison of our hearths and homes.'

As the *Gazette* progresses, there seems to have been no shortage of authors willing to contribute good advice. In Issue 6, for example, General Sir O'Moore Creagh, VC has been allotted a whole page in which he deals with 'The Work of the Volunteer Corps in Case of Invasion', while 'The Problem of Corps Organisation' is covered from the editor's desk. There is news of the recently introduced Proficiency Badge too: one shilling each, if brought separately, but at eleven shillings, cheaper by the dozen. Forty drills and a second-class pass in shooting will give you entitlement to wear it. Dated 24 December 1914, a letter

received from the War Office giving HM the King's approval of the badge is reprinted.

The front page of Issue 7 is devoted entirely to the recruitment of cyclists: 'Cyclist Volunteer Battalions for the Army and Territorials'. Colour and style having been decided upon, tailors the length and breadth of the country, it seems, were working flat out, this week seeing no less than eighteen separate advertisements for VTC uniform. In Issue 8, advertising has now taken over the front page, Gamages offering everything required by the Volunteer from their Holborn store.

Just five months in and the larger units are growing even larger, the Optimists National Corps taking up the whole of the front cover of Issue 9 with an advertisement for its Motor Transport Battalion. The Athletes' Volunteer Force, however, make do with the corner of page 149 for its Cyclist Battalions. The Bradford City Force is featured, a photograph taken on a recent field day showing that uniforms had not yet arrived.

The extent to which any project has flourished is reflected in the amount of commercial advertising that it attracts. Things, then, must be looking good for the new Volunteer Movement if its weekly organ is anything to go by. Now, typical without a doubt, Issue 10 is made up of twenty pages, more than half of which are dedicated to selling uniforms, equipment, weapons, badges and the occasional instruction manual. In the correspondence section this week, the editor regrets that a complete list of corps is impractical. After all, there are over 1,000 affiliated to the CAVTC alone.

Three nice illustrated advertisements from badge companies in Issue 11: London-based JA Wylie & Co shows a good example of their wares in the form of a lapel badge to the West Ham National Reserve Rifle Club, while JR Gaunt illustrates a circular pattern to a local corps, the Birmingham Rifle Reserve. But first prize for design, in my opinion, must go to Thomas Fattorini of Bolton for the enamelled lapel badge produced for the Mount Pleasant Rifle Club at the General Post Office. Badge manufacturers, uniform suppliers, all still doing their best to relieve the Volunteer of his cash. But, just for a change, the 'AG' cigarette paper company try their luck.

Two nicely illustrated unit features are in Issue 12, the men of both the Lewisham Division Defence League and Royal Courts of Justice VTC photographed in civilian clothing still. And a new advertisement. Robert De Lacy of 182 Euston Road, London assures prompt delivery of his instruments for bugle, fife and brass bands.

Issue 14 treats us to two nicely illustrated reports on recent inspections: one at Deptford, the other, Bristol. Off on a tangent, however, is the feature by Mr A van Someren on Switzerland and its part-time military.

Still comparing serving conditions to overseas non-regular forces, A van Someren in Issue 15 finds himself in the United States of America and Australia, while Issue 16 sees the ubiquitous reporter in Russia. Closer to home, weekly features continue to delight, the Post Office Engineering Volunteer Corps impressing General Sir O'Moore Creagh, VC with their telegraph and telephone expertise in Hyde Park (Issue 15) while Issue 16 takes a look at the Northamptonshire VTC and its busy army boot making members. Birmingham almost takes over Issue 17, with its closer looks at the city's Electrical Volunteers, East Birmingham VTC, Aston Defence Corps and Small Heath Home Defence Corps, the latter numbered as

No 1 in the hopes that more will follow. To London and Issue 18 for the Southgate VTC, then up to Yorkshire, where a 'memorable weekend' was had by the Bradford City Volunteers (Issue 19). In Issue 19 we also have the first illustration of the special badge designed for marksmen.

Plenty to read about in Issue 20 regarding recent Easter camps at Hainault Forest and Shenley. Local authorities come under scrutiny in regard to the help, or lack of it, given to volunteer corps—Bradford coming out on top. And memories of the Victorian Volunteer Movement as we read in Issue 21 of the King's Norton Rifle Corps and the Birmingham City Rifle Volunteers. 'Slackers' in the ranks are dealt with on the editor's page, along with a length item on 'Corps Discipline' by a writer going under the name of 'GVR'. Among the ever-growing crop of advertising in Issue 22, most welcome I'm sure, would have been the publication of Regulations for the VTC, sixpence direct from the publisher (the Clerkenwell Press) or through any newsagent or bookseller. And corps themselves are getting into advertising, the last page of Issue 23 offering souvenirs of the Bombardment of Whitby—paperweights made of German shell—at one to three guineas each, all authenticated by Mr Louis Tracy, Company Commander of the Whitby and District Company, North Riding Regiment. In his article 'We Want an Ideal', the commandant of the Putney VTC, however, is more concerned with general slackness, slow recruiting and bad attendances at drill. Other contributors, on the other hand, are more concerned with the forthcoming Whitsun camps.

Slowly but surely the authorities are noticing the worth of the Volunteers. Several news items in Issue 25 report call outs riots, the guarding of vulnerable points and interned aliens. Issue 26, unfortunately, is missing from my bound volume.

Much news of the Whitson camps appears in Issue 27, along with a handy list of some twenty Yorkshire and Lancashire volunteer corps recently inspected by Colonel Dundonald Cochrane, CB. Lots on badges, too. Of great interest is a complete listing of ranks and badges of rank, while the CAVTC points out that proficiency badges are specifically to be worn in mufti, but may be worn in uniform with the sanction of regimental commandants, and when so worn they will be on the right breast on the same level at medals. It is recommended, suggests the CAVTC, that corps specify, when ordering, the number of badges required with brooch pins for attaching to uniforms. But only one badge must be issued to each man. Badges for marksmen and first-class shots are to be worn on the right sleeve below the elbow whether in uniform or in mufti, while those authorized for members of signalling section will wear them on the right sleeve above the elbow. Cap badges bearing a similarity to those worn by Regular regiments are forbidden.

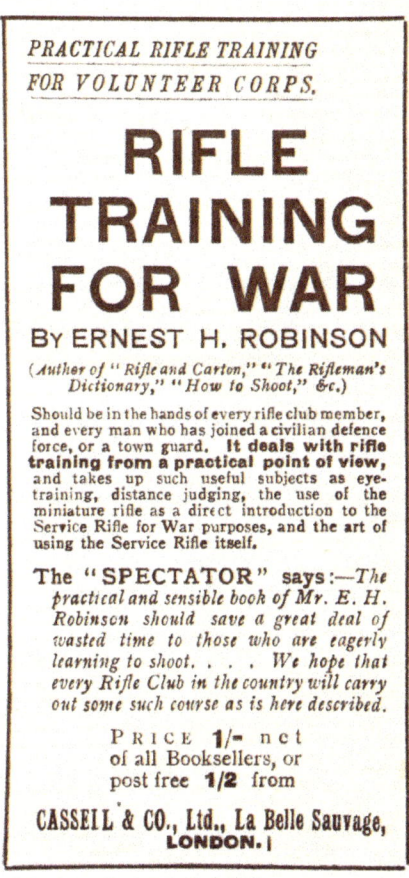

In Issue 31's first feature, 'Be Ready', the Southgate VTC put forward its scheme for rapid mobilisation; the 'Zeppelins have paid us their first visit here in London, and it is an open secret that members of Volunteer Training Corps rendered prompt and valuable assistance to the police and fire brigades during and after the visitation.' And something for the book and ephemeral collector to look out for, the Practical Press placing a full-page advertisement for seven of its publications: Practical Points in Musketry (price 3d), Guard and Sentry Duty Simplified (2d), Practical Points for Sentries (1d), Practical Points in Infantry Drill

(1d), Section Attendance Books (large, 5/- per dozen) and Parade State Forms (3/6 per dozen pads). Printers again, this time in the form of Hill, Siffken & Co who from their Grafton Works in Holloway, London, will produce lithographed posters advertising your corps. A sample of their work in Issue 31 shows members of the Northern Polytechnic VTC skirmishing.

As more and more individual corps become swallowed up into the fast growing county regiment scheme, the old titles appear few and far between within the pages of the *Volunteer Training Corps Gazette*. But a report of a recent inspection of Irish corps (generally known as the 'Veterans' Corps') brings forth a sizable crop of new names. Issue 33 and much talk of Summer Camp, the advertisers, of course, wanting to miss nothing in the way of a sale: Gardiner & Co offer holdalls containing knife, fork, spoon, razor, hussif, tooth brush, shaving brush and comb complete for six shillings and sixpence. [I am recently informed that hussif actually means 'housewife' – as in a small case for needles, thread and other small sewing items.] And tents, too. William Pope & Son—'Sole Contractors for Government Part-worn Tents' promising the largest stock of first class tents in the kingdom. Mentioned in the editor's column are a number of publications recently issued by corps. Worth looking out for now would be: *The National Guard*, the monthly magazine of the City of London National Guard; Regimental Orders of the 5th Battalion Surrey VTC, an excellent pamphlet, in the editor's view, published by the 2nd Battalion Southampton VTC, and a detailed report of its work so far from the Colwyn Bay Corps. Seen for the first time in Issue 40 is the badge to be worn by ambulance section members who have passed the qualifying examination. A neat, full size. illustration comes complete with detailed description. Advertising again, this time in the form of a private sale: 'Rudge 1915 Motor-Cycle, 5-6 hp, 3-speed Gear, coach built Sidecar with hood and screen, Lucas Lamps, Watford Speedometer and all Accessories; splendid appearance and condition—not done 2,000 miles: cost over £100; accept £65 for cash, quick sale—Sub-Lieut. Courtena, 12 Green End Road, Bedford Park, W.'

More and more mergers into county regiments are taking place resulting in fewer and fewer new corps appearing in the Gazette. But the pages remain full, the editorial staff now, however, concentrating on subjects general to all such as 'Infantry Drill'. In 'Wisdom for Warriors', wise words from 'Spontaneous' who deals with medical matters, keeping up members' interest, recruiting and raising funds, while another author, not wishing his identity known, 'Nero', takes up whole pages, over several issues, on the subject of 'Digging Trenches (Somewhere in England)'. Issue 46 includes a whole page concerning the recent availability form Vickers of a model machine gun. This is a most important addition to any Volunteer corps in the opinion of the editor who, on a second page, offers one as a prize to the corps sending in the largest number of half-yearly prepaid subscriptions. The *Gazette,* now getting on for a year old, in Issue 50 begins a series of features entitled 'Our County Regiments.' The introduction to No1 (Buckinghamshire) notes that already there are some forty regiments in England and Wales. And some of the corps themselves are completing their first year's service, bringing news of many first annual general meetings. And so to Issue 52 which includes a nice illustration of the recently introduced Cyclist Section badge—bronze, to be worn on the left uniform sleeve below the elbow, and comprising a cycle wheel superimposed upon crossed rifles with the letters VTC in the centre.

CHAPTER 3
NOTES FROM THE VOLUNTEER TRAINING CORPS GAZETTE AND OTHER SOURCES

Alleyn Volunteer Training Corps

In his Society for Army Historical Research article dealing with VTC uniform (Vol 17, 1938) Mr EJ Martin illustrates a circular lapel badge inscribed with this title around the edge. In the centre are the arms of Alleyn's School which show three cinquefoils and a chevron on the shield, and an arm holding a heart issuing from flames. Alleyn's School is in Dulwich, SE London.

Alleyn's Grammar School (Stone) Cadet Corp

Recognised on 28 September 1918 (Army Order 373) and affiliated to the 1st Volunteer Battalion North Staffordshire Regiment.

Anerley Company National Volunteer Reserve

An item published in the *Volunteer Training Corps Gazette* on 8 May 1915 reported that this company was to meet at the bottom of Stratham Common on Sunday 10 May for a route march to Warlington. On the southwestern side of Penge in Surrey, resident in Anerley throughout the First World War was the poet Walter de la Mare.

Architects' Volunteer Training Corps

Soon after war was declared in August 1914 the Council of the Surveyors' Institute urged its members to join the Architects' Corps, so reported the *Volunteer Training Corps Gazette*. Colonel JW Marsden Newton had been elected as colonel commandant and headquarters were being set up at the Architectural Association, 18 Tufton Street, Westminster, London. Mention was also made in the *Gazette* for 13 February 1915 of an Epping Forest Company which was then drilling at Loughton.

The edition for 6 March 1915 went on to report that at a meeting held the previous week at the United Arts Force headquarters in Burlington House, London it was decided to merge the following corps under the title of Central London Regiment: United Arts, Optimists, Architects, Old Boys and Inns of Court OTC. As the 4th Battalion of the Central London Regiment, the Architects Corps is also on record as maintaining detachments at Dulwich College, the Mercers' School in Holborn and at the Architectural Association Sports Ground, Boreham Wood, Hertfordshire. Headquarters were later taken over at Chester House, Eccleston Place in SW London.

Argyllshire National Guard Volunteer Corps

The badge of this corps (illustrated) featured a boar's head in the centre of a strap inscribed Argyllshire NGVC.

Arlington Volunteer Training Corps

The *Gloucestershire Journal* for 23 October 1915 reported that this corps had recently been formed.

Ashwell Volunteer Corps

Former officer of the Bedfordshire Yeomanry, Major WA Fordham, is credited with the formation of this Hertfordshire corps in the middle of October 1914. Drills were carried out every evening for an hour at a local school.

Aspley Guise and District Volunteer Corps

The *Volunteer Training Corps Gazette* for 2 February 1915 reported that Colonel RA Sargeaunt (Royal Engineers retired) was president of this Bedfordshire unit and that Mr CE Macfarlane (formally of the Royal Scots) was commandant. Mr SG Wilkinson of St Neots had been made second-in-command and Mr F Crosbie Roles of Aspley Guise, the Hon Secretary. The first drill took place on 29 December 1914.

Associated Volunteer Training Corps, 1st (Dublin) Battalion

Mr Steven Hurst writes in *The Bulletin of the Military Historical Society* (No 250, November 2012) how in July 1915 arrangements had been made to organise the several Dublin volunteer corps then in existence into a single battalion. He gives the initial organisation as: 'A' Company (Irish Rugby Football Union VTC), 'B' Company (Dublin Veterans VTC), 'C' Company (Glasnevin VTC), 'D' Company (Great Northern Railway and North City VTC). Also recorded by Mr Hurst is the battalion structure as listed in Battalion Orders (No 28) of 17 February 1916: 'A' Company (Irish Rugby Football Union and St Andrew's VTC), 'B' Company (Dublin Veterans), 'C' Company (Glasnevin), 'D' Company (Great Northern Railway, Great Southern Railway, North City and South City).

Aston Home Defence Corps

The *Volunteer Training Corps Gazette* reported that the Ashton Home Defence Corps was the only affiliated and recognised corps in Aston, Staffordshire and that it had held a church parade on 28 March 1915. Afterwards it toured the district headed by the Aston Prize Band. The corps, it was hoped, was soon to have uniforms and its own band. Instruments had already been purchased.

Associated Accountants Training Corps

The *Volunteer Training Corps Gazette* for 13 February 1915 reported that this corps had recently been inspected by Colonel Francis A Lucas, VD [Volunteer Decoration]. No location was mentioned.

Athletes' Volunteer Force

Having formed several hundred branches throughout the country, the Athletes' Volunteer Force introduced an oval lapel badge (illustrated) for use in civilian clothing. With crossed rifles in the centre, around the edge of the badge on a blue enamel ground were the words and date, Athletes' Volunteer Force 1914. The same badge, this time with a scroll placed at the bottom inscribed Med Officer, has also been noted.

Babbacombe and St Marychurch Civil Rifle Club

This corps in Torquay, Devon was formed on 27 August 1914 and began with a membership of just twenty, its strength growing to 120 before the end of the year. General CH Spragge, CB was appointed as president, Colonel CR Burn, MP (who was later to serve on the staff at the War Office) became Lieutenant-Colonel, J Gordon Geddes (who would go on to command the 25th Brigade, RFA in France) and FH Grinlington, CMG (late of the Ceylon Light Infantry) were vice presidents. Drills were carried out on Tuesday and Friday nights, musketry practice being held on an indoor range at Homelands and Coysh Ltd, a local business belonging to secretary of the corps, Mr WC Coysh. The Coysh Stores were at No 1 Redden Hill Road.

Baildon Military Training Corps

Hon Secretary Mr A Robinson reported in the *Volunteer Training Corps Gazette* for 26 December 1914 that this corps had been formed on the previous 4 September and now comprised 238 members. Headquarters, he noted, were at a local council school and drills were being held three evenings each week. Baildon is now part of the Bradford Metropolitan District. A circular lapel badge was worn showing crossed rifles, a crown and the date 1914.

Balham and Wandsworth Home Defence League

To set up an equipment fund for this South London corps, a concert was given at the Balham Hippodrome (illustrated) on 19 December 1914. On London's Balham Hill (corner of Yukon Road), the Hippodrome was known as the Royal Duchess Theatre until 1909.

Baltic, Mincing and Mark Lane Volunteers

The History of the City of London National Guard by AE Manning Foster (1920) records how in July 1916 this corps was absorbed into the 6th (National Guard) Battalion of the City of London Volunteer Regiment. The first parade had taken place at the Baltic Exchange, Saint Mary Axe (illustrated), in October 1914. To the south of the Baltic Exchange, Mincing Lane included the Rubber Exchange. After severe damage by an IRA bomb in 1992, the Baltic Exchange was demolished and replaced by the building now called The Gherkin.

Barclay, Perkins Brewery Volunteer Training Corps

This Southwark in South London firm, which provided beer for the Army for many years, was quick to form a Volunteer Corps from within its work force. It was inspected by General Sir Ronald Bertram Lane at the brewery cricket field in Green Lane, Dulwich on 12 December 1914. Founded in 1616 by James Monger, the firm occupied premises just yards from Southwark Cathedral—the Anchor Brewery—and could also be found between Park Street and Anchor Terrace and on the River Thames at Princes Wharf, Anhalt Road, Battersea.

Barnet Volunteer Training Corps

It was reported by the *Volunteer Training Corps Gazette* on 19 December 1914 that the recently formed corps at Barnet in Hertfordshire then comprised some ninety members and that Mr G Gurnett of 10 Carnarvon Road was its secretary.

Barrow and North Lonsdale Volunteer Training Corps

The cap badge (illustrated) comprised a crowned circle with the name of the corps around the edge and the intertwined letters VTC in the centre.

Barrow-in-Furness Volunteer Training Corps

The *Volunteer Training Corps Gazette* for 26 December 1914 reported that at a meeting held at the town hall on 2 December it was decided to form a corps. The Mayor of Barrow, Alderman Alfred Barrow, took the chair. Those present included Colonel GH Huthwaite, Lieutenant-Colonel W Williams, QMS J Pearson Postlethwaite (who was elected as secretary), Mr W Lacey, Mr Tulley and the Town Clerk Mr Hewlett.

Beckenham Volunteer Training Corps

Formed by November 1914 with Mr Alfred T Carter as secretary. Since formation the District Council had provided an orderly room in the Municipal Buildings, three school playgrounds for drill and the Croydon Road Recreation Ground for parades. Shooting took place at the Beckenham Rifle Club. The corps was recently called out after a heavy fall of snow to clear the roads, reported the *Volunteer Training Corps Gazette*. A membership of 307 was drawn from residents of Beckenham, West Wickham, Shortlands and Kent House. A photograph published in Issue 19 of the *Volunteer Training Corps Gazette* and taken at a recent inspection by Colonel Dundonald Cochrane, shows the whole parade in uniform. There is an enamelled lapel badge in the form of an oval strap bearing the name Beckenham with, in the centre, the letters VTC.

Bedford Volunteer Defence Corps

Moves to form this corps begun in November 1914. Mr CS Gibson of 2 Clarenden Street, Bedford was appointed as acting secretary.

Bedford Volunteer Training Corps

A solid shoulder title (illustrated) exists with the wording Bedford VTC.

Belfast Volunteer Defence Corps

The cap badge of this corps featured a shamrock within a crowned eight-pointed star. Mr Steven Hurst writes in *The Bulletin of the Military Historical Society* (No 250, November 2012) that the strength of the unit stood at 917 in November 1915.

Berkeley Volunteer Training Corps

The *Gloucestershire Journal* for 7 April 1915 reported that a corps by this name had been formed.

Berkhamsted Volunteer Training Corps

Formed on 9 November 1914 and by the end of the year comprised 140 Volunteers. The elected president was General R Pine-Coffin, and the commandant Captain JH Girling. Instruction in drill and musketry was provided by former military personnel, as well as the Berkhamsted School OTC and members of the Inns of Court OTC then billeted in the town from London. Born at Berkhamsted, Herts, the writer Graham Green would have been ten-years-old at the outbreak of war in 1914. His father was headmaster at Berkhamsted School. From its headquarters at Stone Buildings, Lincoln's Inn, London, the Inns of Court

OTC (TF) had moved to Berkhamsted for war service on 28 September 1914.

Bermondsey Volunteer Training Corps

In January 1915 the Bermondsey VTC in South London and members of the Optimists Corps took part in an official reception to welcome home to Bermondsey Corporal Frederick William Holmes who had been awarded the Victoria Cross for his gallantry at Le Cateau, France on 26 August 1914. Headquarters by August 1916 were located at Yalding Road.

Bethnal Green Volunteer Training Corps

Formed in December 1914, the strength of this East End of London corps by the following February stood at more than 350. Drills were carried out at the Bethnal Green Council Depot.

Bexhill-on-Sea Volunteer Training Corps

This corps held its first parade at the York Drill Hall, Bexhill on 13 October 1914. Some 220 had come forward from the town as a direct result of a recruiting campaign organised by the local Commercial Association. Its chairman was Mr AG Wells. Appointed as acting commandant was Mr Percy Webber, the corps by December 1914 being divided into four platoons under the command of Messrs Webber, Stearns, Duncan and Wise. Elected as Hon Secretary was Mr JH Morton of 29 Linden Road, Bexhill-on-Sea. Built by the landlord for the local Victorian Volunteers, York Drill Hall was situated behind the York Public House in London Road.

Bideford and District Emergence League

Men of the Devonshire market town and seaport of Bideford were quick to respond to the call for Volunteers in 1914, some eighty in number coming forward within days of war having being declared.

Bilston and Willenhall Volunteer Training Corps

Reported in 1915 was the unit's recent activities at Whitson Camp. Both Bilston and Willenhall form part of Wolverhampton.

Birdlip Volunteer Training Corps

The *Gloucestershire Journal* for 11 January 1916 reported the recent formation of this corps.

Birkenhead and District Volunteer Training Corps

The *Volunteer Training Corps Gazette* for 2 January 1915 reported that a meeting had been held regarding this corps at St Peter's Hall, Rock Ferry on 18 December 1914. The Mayor of Birkenhead, Alderman AH Arkle, presided. Sir William Lever of the soap manufacturing family addressed the meeting and told how he was to join a corps being formed at Port Sunlight. Two shields feature in the centre of the cap badges, that from the arms of Birkenhead on the left, another bearing a rampant lion to the right.

Birmingham Electrical Engineers

Formed at the end of November 1914 from, what the *Volunteer Training Corps Gazette* for 27 March 1915 refers to as, 'everyone who counts in the electrical world in the Midlands.' Two companies were in existence at this time, 'A' Signal Company (wireless, cable

and airline) and 'B' Company which had searchlight, fortress, works and transport platoons. Drills were being carried out at Messrs. Caves' Repository and at the large Birmingham Wholesale Market Hall.

Regular lectures took place in the City's Technical College. Volunteers paid a two-shilling subscription for artisans and five for non-manual workers. Honorary members paid ten-and-six. Of the original officials elected, on record are: Mr RA Chattock, MIEE (president) who was the Birmingham City Electrical Engineer and Manager, Mr David Shanks, JP (chairman), a Major Vickers (military advisor), Mr TH Hunter (treasurer), Mr WTB Bartram (recruiting officer), Dr Russell Green (surgeon) and the Rev JW Pyddoke, MA (chaplain). Hon secretary of the corps was Mr WE Milns of 14 Dale End, Birmingham.

The Birmingham Electrical Engineers had a white metal cap badge (illustrated) made up of a hand grasping streaks of lightning extending from a sphere. The name of the unit appears on scrolls passing across the sphere and below.

Birmingham Home Defence Corps, No 1 Small Heath

Formed as a result of a meeting presided over by Alderman Jephott at Small Heath on 9 November 1914. Some 369 members enrolled on the first day, each of them paying an entrance fee of one shilling and a weekly subscriptions of three pence. Evening drills took place at local council schools.

Birmingham Rifle Reserve

An item in the *Volunteer Training Corps Gazette* for 12 December 1914 noted that the Birmingham Rifle Reserve has special sections devoted to signalling, map reading, field sketching, military hygiene and the machine gun. There was also an ambulance corps. Weekly lectures given by officers of the Regular Army have been taking place, the subjects dealt with included: Characteristics of Fighting Troops, Obstacles, Elementary Musketry, The Mechanism of the Rifle, and Fire Control. Transport seemed no problem as at the beginning of December some sixty motor cars transported the corps twenty miles from their headquarters for drill. Practice in entrenching taking place on waste ground six miles from headquarters.

Bishop's Stortford Volunteer Corps

After a combined route march held by the VTC and Special Constables of Bishop's Stortford, Hertfordshire on Saturday 28 November 1914, those taking part were given refreshment and hospitality by Mr and Mrs Robert L Barclay (of the banking family) on the lawn of Gaston House, Little Hallingbury. Perhaps some of the marchers chose to make the three-mile return journey via close-by Spelbrook Station and the old Great Eastern Railway.

BLRB

Illustrated on page forty-eight of *The Bulletin of the Military Historical Society* for August 2012 under the title 'More VTC Badges', is a circular badge bearing these initials, crossed rifles and the date 1914.

Blackburn Unit Athletes' Volunteer Force

Formed by November 1914 with Mr J Isherwood as secretary.

Blackheath Defence League

Mentioned in the *Volunteer Training Corps Gazette* for 20 March 1915.

Blackheath Unit National Volunteer Reserve

The *Volunteer Training Corps Gazette* for 24 April 1915 reported that this corps, commandant Mr Leslie Jenkins, had opened a new rifle range at Greenwich on 17 April. The issue for 1 May 1915 also noted that a church parade had been held a fortnight before at St Alphage Church in Greenwich, the unit first assembling in the courtyard of the Royal Naval School before marching to the church. Another report on 22 May 1915 told that the unit had recently marched to Lewisham Station where they entrained for Hayes to take part in an exercise—'The Fox Hotel', reports the *Gazette*, 'was successfully captured.'

Blackpool Volunteers, 1st Battalion

Formed in 1914, the battalion wore a cap badge (illustrated) which featured the arms of Blackpool.

Bletchingley and Godstone Cadet Corps

Recognised on 15 July 1918 (Army Order 307) and affiliated to the 2nd Volunteer Battalion Queen's (Royal West Surrey Regiment).

Blythe Bridge Volunteer Training Corps

The unanimous decision to form a VTC unit at Blythe Bridge in Staffordshire (Mr Harber proposed, Mr Woodward seconded) was taken at a meeting held at the Church Schools on Tuesday 1 December 1914. Mr AT Abell took the chair and noted that members of the corps should pay a fixed subscription of five shillings. Youths between the age of seventeen and nineteen, however, would pay just two shillings and sixpence.

Borough Polytechnic and District Volunteer Training Corps

Formed 21 November 1914 and soon comprised 150 members. Former Boer War veteran and one of the governors of the Polytechnic, Mr Basil Williams, was appointed as commandant. The drill instructor was Sergeant H Davies, late of the Rifle Brigade and now Gymnastic Instructor to the Borough Polytechnic. At the Polytechnic, which was located at 103 Borough Road, Southwark, SE London (illustrated), the corps used the Edric Hall and the Gymnasium for drills. Also used for parades was the Polytechnic Sports Field at Dulwich.

Bournemouth War Emergency Corps

An enamel lapel badge exists which consists of a crowned circle inscribed with the name of the corps and the words For King and Country around the edge. In the centre, a rose.

Bowsfield Steelworks Training Corps

Started on the initiative of the works manager, Mr Howard Harris, more than 30% of the work force enrolled in the first weeks. Several lads of seventeen were allowed to join on the understanding that they enlisted into the Regulars when of age. A generous supply of instructors was available from within the works, the men having previously served with the Regular Army, Territorials and even the Volunteers of 1859-1908. The Bowsfield Works was an important employer in Stockton-on-Tees.

Boxgrove School Cadet Corps

Recognised 3 June 1918 (Army Order 240) and affiliated to the 3rd Volunteer Battalion Queen's (Royal West Surrey Regiment).

Brackley Volunteer Training Corps

Brackley in Northamptonshire was quick to take interest in the Volunteer Movement, steps being taken to raise a corps during the first weeks of the war. Things would not, however, be finalised until November when at a meeting chaired by the mayor, Councillor J Coles, at the Town Hall on the 30th, plans were drawn up. The corps were to have the use of a number of old Regular and Volunteer soldiers as instructors, and from the local rifle club and Magdalen College School who provided ranges and weapons. Early members were the Rector of Whitfield, the Rev CH Coles, Messrs EF Humphries, FG Partridge who was agent to the Earl of Ellesmere, and from the rifle club, Mr JD Smart. Mr AJ Kay of Lloyds's Bank was appointed as secretary.

Bradford (Wiltshire)

The *Volunteer Training Corps Gazette* for 5 December 1914 reported that efforts to form a corps at Bradford in Wiltshire had so far been unsupported by the local authority.

Bradford (Yorkshire)

The *Volunteer Training Corps Gazette* reported that a corps formed at Bradford in Yorkshire had enrolled some 3,000 members by November 1914.

Bradford Volunteer Cadet Battalion

Recognised 8 July 1918 (Army Order 307) and affiliated to the Bradford Groupe West Riding Volunteers.

Bradwell Training School Cadet Corps

Recognised 7 November 1917 and affiliated to the 4th Battalion Cheshire Volunteer Regiment.

Bray Volunteer Training Corps

This Irish corps was inspected by General Sir John Maxwell on Saturday 16 May 1916. The strength, according to the *Irish Times* for 6 November 1915, was sixty-two.

Brecknell, Munro and Rodgers Cadet Engineer Field Company

Recognised 23 September 1918 and affiliated to the Bristol Volunteer Battalion. This Bristol company was occupied in shell production during the 1st World War.

Brentford Volunteer Training Corps

This Middlesex corps was in existence by December 1914.

Bridlington Volunteer Force

An enamel lapel badge exists to this corps which features the arms of the town (illustrated).

Bristol Athletes' Volunteer Force

Formed in September 1914, this corps was composed of four sections: North (Central Bristol), South (Totterdown, Ashton), East (Easton) and West (Clifton). All became part of the Bristol Volunteer Regiment in April 1915.

Bristol East Training Corps

Formed as a result of a meeting held at the Church Boys' School in the St George's area of Bristol on 2 December 1914. Mr WH Butler, JP took the chair and fifty-two names were taken. Mr Raymond Jones was appointed as secretary and a range was later set up at the local Conservative Club. Later formed part of the 2nd (Coliseum) Battalion Bristol Volunteer Regiment.

Bristol Rugby Football Club Training Corps

Formed in January 1915, there is a circular badge to this corps which has the word Committee in the centre of a circle inscribed Bristol Rugby Club Rifle Section.

Bristol Tram and Carriage Company Ltd Volunteer Force

Formed November 1914 and, notes Daniel Brinson in his book of Gloucestershire military insignia, in the following month became part of the Athletes Volunteer Force.

Bristol University Officer Training Corps Reserve

Formed in November 1914 and in the following year became part of the Bristol Volunteer Regiment.

Bristol Wheelers Training Corps

Noted as being formed in November 1914 with a membership restricted to 120 and with a circular lapel badge showing the title and crossed rifles.

Bristol Volunteer Regiment

Formed from existing Bristol VTC units after a meeting held in April 1915, the regiment was made up of three battalions: 1st (University), 2nd (Coliseum), 3rd (Athletes). Daniel Brinson's book on Gloucestershire military insignia illustrates three badges, the first of which features the arms of Bristol complete with supporters. Crossed rifles and the date 1915 appear within a crowned wreath in a second cap badge. Also shown is the bronze shoulder title BVR.

Bristol Women's Volunteer Corps

Daniel Brinson in his book *Military Insignia of Gloucestershire* mention how this corps was formed in October 1916 and later became known as the Khaki Corps.

British Legion

In his article dealing with the uniforms of the VTC (*Journal of the Society for Army Historical Research,* Vol 17, 1938) Mr Ernest J Martin shows an oval enamel lapel badge to this corps which features in its centre a soldier holding a rifle. At the top of the oval is a shield charged with the Union flag, the outer edge being inscribed with the title of the unit and the date 1914 (illustrated). Mr Martin notes that the British Legion was a similar, but much smaller, organisation than the Athletes. He also points out that there is no connection with the ex-servicemen's organisation founded in 1921, now the Royal British Legion.

Brixton Rifle Club

Formed before the end of 1914 and held drills and musketry training in a disused brewery and a cinema.

Brixton Volunteer Defence Corps

The *Volunteer Training Corps Gazette* for 5 December 1914 refers to this corps as the Brixton Volunteer Training Corps and records that it consisted of some 250 members with a drill ground at the rear of the Town Hall and a well-constructed miniature rifle range with ten targets under the parish church. The information had been supplied to the *Gazette* by Captain F Barnes of 55 Brixton Hill, SW. Brixton parish church is St Matthew's at the bottom of Brixton Hill which was opened in 1823 having been built to celebrate the victory at Waterloo eight years earlier. The *Gazette* for 16 January 1915 refers to this corps as the Brixton Volunteer Defence Corps and this is the title on two lapel badges in the Mike Jackson collection: one silver with blue enamel, the other gilt with blue enamel. Both consist of a crowned oval, with crossed rifles in the centre and the words Volunteer Defence Corps around the edge. The name Brixton is on a scroll below.

Brockley Defence League

Mentioned in the *Volunteer Training Corps Gazette* for 20 March 1915.

Buckinghamshire Volunteer Defence Corps

A report in the 12 December 1914 edition of the *Volunteer Training Corps Gazette* noted that the Marquis of Lincolnshire had been appointed as commandant of the Volunteer Force in Buckinghamshire. There was, at the time, three battalions (each 1,000 strong) corresponding with the county's parliamentary divisions. The issue for 26 December also gives Captain Lloyd (late 1st Gloucestershire Regiment) as Staff Commander and the following organisation details:

North Bucks Battalion: Headquarters Wolverton, Commander Colonel Bowyer, RE, propose company centres, (1) Bletchley, (2) Buckingham, (3) Newport Pagnell, (4) Wolverton.

Mid Bucks Battalion: Headquarters Aylesbury, Commander the Earl of Buckinghamshire, proposed company centres, (1) Aylesbury, (2) Chesham, (3) Princes Risborough, (4) Wendover.

South Bucks Battalion: Headquarters High Wycombe, Commander, Colonel Pope (late 4th Dragoon Guards), proposed company centres, (1) Eton, (2) Gerrards Cross, (3) High Wycombe, (4) Slough.

A swan, the ancient badge of the Dukes of Buckingham (illustrated) and the main charge of the county arms, featured in the badges of this corps.

Burnham and Berrow Volunteer Training Corps

Formed early in November 1914, a public meeting presided over by Mr Sydney Peel held in the Town Hall, Burnham to support the corps was held at the end of the month. The chairman was Major Archdale and some 150 enrolled at the meeting. Headquarters were at the Town Hall; Mr Clement Gardiner, secretary.

Burnley Cadet Corps

Recognised 12 April 1918 (Army Order 173) and affiliated to the 1/11th Lancashire Volunteer Regiment.

Burnley Volunteer Training Corps

The Bishop of Burnley attended the first drill of this corps which took place at Todmorden Road Council School early in December 1914. The Bishop in 1914, Henry Henn, had served as a private in the old Inns of Court Volunteers. The arms of the

Borough of Burnley featured on the enamel lapel badges worn in civilian clothing (illustrated) and the cap badges.

Burton-on-Trent Athletes' Volunteer Force

Recently inspected, reports the *Volunteer Training Corps Gazette* in 1915, at the Burton Cricket Club.

Burton-on-Trent Cadet Corps

Recognised 22 April 1918 (Army Order 173) and affiliated to the 2nd Battalion Staffordshire Volunteer Regiment.

Burton-upon-Trent Volunteer Training Corps

Formed and commenced training towards the end of August 1914, membership of the corps was close to 250 by the following November. Members, who pay a one shilling entrance fee, had the use of an outdoor rifle range belonging to the Legion of Frontiersmen and held parades at the Old Drill Hall in Meadow Road. There were signalling, ambulance and cyclist sections and the men are on record as having adopted a Scottish Collie dog as mascot. Hon Secretary of the corps was Mr PF Ashby-Norris, headquarters being at 65 Union Street, Burton-upon-Trent.

Burslem Volunteer Training Corps

The town is well known for its pottery production; evidence of this can be seen in an enamel lapel badge which shows the town's arms (illustrated).

Camberwell and Peckham Athletes Volunteer Force

The *Volunteer Training Corps Gazette* for 30 January 1915 reported that although this corps had been in existence for less than two months its enrolled strength was already 320. The item went on to say that headquarters had been set up at Caxton Hill, Warner Road, Camberwell and that the corps had the use of two drill grounds—one in a school, the other in a park—both in the immediate area. A temporary miniature rifle range was being used, but plans were well advanced for the acquisition of an open-air range at Nunhead. A recent church parade taken by chaplain to the corps, the Rev Dr Porte, was held at St Matthew's Church, Denmark Hill. Drills took place on Tuesday and Thursday evenings and Saturday afternoons. The *Gazette* for 10 April 1915 reported that a new rifle range had been opened at Station Road, Camberwell New Road.

Camberwell Battalion Volunteer Training Corps

The *Volunteer Training Corps Gazette* for 26 June 1915 reported that this battalion had decided to form an Allies' Legion, to be attached, which had already enrolled many prominent Italian residents in London and several Belgians. The issue for 18 September 1915 mentions a Camberwell and Peckham Battalion of the South London Volunteer Regiment. Another issue has 3rd (Dulwich, Camberwell and Norwood) Battalion.

Camborne Volunteer Training Corps

Hon Secretary of the corps, Mr Sidney L Pain, reported in December 1914 that the Camborne VTC had been formed and that when detachments at Troon and Illogan had been completed its membership would include agriculturists, gamekeepers, chauffeurs, grooms and mining men. The area at the time employed a number in its numerous tin mines. He also acknowledged the assistance and encouragement so far received from leading landowners and gentlemen from the district. Named was a Major Lidgey, VD—this would have been W Lidgey who was commissioned into the 1st Volunteer Battalion Duke of Cornwall's Light Infantry in April 1896—and Captain Tyack, another former officer in the Victorian Volunteer Force. At Illogan, on the road from Redruth to Camborne, the Tehidy Rifle Range was put at the disposal of the Volunteers, as was another at Gwithian.

Cambridge Civilian Drill and Rifle Club

Hon Secretary of the club, Mr PA French of 9 St Andrew's Hill, Cambridge, reported to the *Volunteer Training Corps Gazette* on 5 December 1914 that already membership of the corps stood at almost 600. Detachments were also at the time being formed from many of the villages surrounding Cambridge. His note in the next issue (12 December) gives the club as having been affiliated to the Athletes' Volunteer Force. Both the town and university were of great assistance to the volunteers. The OTC provided instructors, the Town Council granting the use of the Corn Exchange and Guildhall for drills. Glynis Cooper in her book *Cambridge in the Great War* mentions that further companies were set up at close by Chesterton and Cherryhinton. The OTC referred to was the Officers' Training Corps contingent formed in 1908 from the Cambridgeshire University Rifle Volunteers Corps.

Cambridge Volunteers

A cap badge exists bearing the title Cambridge Volunteers and featuring the arms of Cambridge (illustrated).

Campbeltown Grammar School Cadet Corps

Recognised 3 July 1918 (Army Order 307) and affiliated to the 1st Battalion Argyllshire Volunteer Regiment.

Campsie Cadet Company

Recognised 4 September 1917 (Army Order 360) and affiliated to the 1st Battalion Stirlingshire Volunteer Regiment.

Cannock Volunteer Training Corps

A report in the *Volunteer Training Corps Gazette* mentioned that the Cannock Volunteer Training Corps was now guarding railways, bridges and canals.

Canterbury Volunteer Training Corps

Former Indian Army officer, Lieutenant-Colonel CE Baynes, was appointed as military advisor to the corps early in December 1914.

Cardiff Coal Exchange Volunteer Corps

Formed as a result of a meeting held on 7 August 1914, Hon Secretary of the corps was Mr HJ Heath of Kingston House, Barry. The Cardiff Coal Exchange in Mount Stuart Square (illustrated) was where the first million-pound cheque was signed in 1909.

Cargo Fleet Iron Company Cadet Corps

Recognised 21 February 1918 (Army Order 149) and affiliated to the 1/1st North Riding Volunteer Regiment.

Carlisle Grammar School Cadet Companies

Recognised 11 December 1917 (Army Order 11 of 1918) and affiliated to the 1/1st Battalion Cumberland Volunteer Regiment.

Carmarthenshire Volunteer Training Corps

The cap badge of this corps featured crossed rifles, the letters VTC and the date 1915 in the centre of a crowned wreath.

Carnarvonshire Volunteer Regiment

The regiment wore a crowned pear-shaped cap badge featuring the arms of Carnarvon Borough Council (illustrated).

Carrickfergus Athletes Volunteer Force

Mr Steven Hurst writes in *The Bulletin of the Military Historical Society* (No 250, November 2012) that this corps had been founded in late August 1914 by local rowing, football and rugby clubs.

Catford Defence League

This London corps was mentioned in the *Volunteer Training Corps Gazette* for 20 March 1915.

Central London Volunteer Regiment

The *Volunteer Training Corps Gazette* for 6 March 1915 reported that a meeting held the previous week at the United Arts Force headquarters, Burlington House, had decided to merge the following corps under the title of Central London Regiment: United Arts, Optimists, Architects, Old Boys and Inns of Court Reserve. General Sir Bindon Blood, KCB, later accepted position as Regimental Commandant. The United Arts became 1st Battalion. Old Boys, 3rd Battalion, Architects, 4th Battalion and the Optimists, 5th Battalion. The *Gazette* for 27 May 1916 states that the Architects' Corps and London County Council Staff Corps were amalgamated to form the 4th Battalion, Central London Volunteer Regiment, which is now linked up with the Engineering Institutions Volunteer Engineer Corps to form the 1st London Engineer Volunteers. The services of the corps have been offered to the King as a battalion of twenty officers and 479 NCOs and men, containing as it does numerous professional surveyors, electrical and mining engineers. Headquarters were at Chester House, Eccleston Place, SW. The issue for 8 July 1916 states that the regiment is also known unofficially as the Professional and Business Man's Regiment and that the organisation comprises: the United Arts, Inns of Court Reserve, the Old Boys' Corps, London Volunteer Rifles and the Pharmacists' Corps. Headquarters are given as 26 St Pancras Road, NW.

Chartered Secretaries' Drill Corps

The *Volunteer Training Corps Gazette* for 23 January 1915 reported that this corps attended a special service in St Botolph's Church, Bishopsgate on the previous Sunday. Over 600 members were present under the command of Sir Ernest Clarke. After the service the corps marched to Custom House where it was inspected by the Lord Mayor. A strength of over 800 is reported in the *Gazette* for 6 February 1915.

Cheadle Heath Civilian Volunteers

Formed as the result of a meeting held on 2 September 1914 at a local council school. Members were nearly all Manchester and Stockport businessmen. Some 100 joined on the first day and membership by the end of the year stood at 200 which included a signalling section and bugle band. Local farmers provided fields for drills, the Stockport Education Committee allowing the use of the school. Mr Henry Mainwaring of Manchester donated £20 towards the purchase of rifles shortly before he died. Mr Harry Wood, and Mr AE Buckland were early drill instructors. The corps was divided into four companies which drilled respectively on Mondays, Tuesdays, Thursdays and Fridays. The whole corps met on Saturdays for drill, skirmishing and route marching. Mr James R Nuttall of 16 Swythamley Road was secretary.

Cheam Volunteer Training Corps

Three miles north-east of Epsom, the headquarters of this Surrey company were at the Cheam Rifle Club and applications for membership were to be made to the Hon Secretary, Mr WR Hodgson at Avondale, Salisbury Avenue, Cheam.

Chelmsford Branch Old Boys' Corps

Formed in London, membership of the Old Boys' Corps was strictly confined to former Public School and University men and their friends. No unmarried man under thirty-eight was admitted, except those that are exempt from Regular or Territorial service. The Chelmsford Branch was formed before the end of 1914 and soon had a membership of some 160 Volunteers. Every man was expected to put in at least three drills each week. Mr JE Seager, who was the originator of the movement in Chelmsford, was appointed as commanding officer. This corps, it was reported, was mainly composed of men employed in firms engaged on government contracts and who had been refused permission to enlist into the Regular or Territorial forces. Some 160, it was noted, had already enrolled into units formed in surrounding areas. In 1914, the Marconi's Wireless Telegraph & Signal Company was located in Hall Street, Chelmsford, Essex, the employees there certainly being occupied on essential work.

Chelsea Volunteer Training Corps

The cap badge of the corps comprised a crowned wreath with crossed rifles, the letters VTC and date 1915 in the centre. The name Chelsea was on a scroll below. The Chelsea VTC later became a battalion of the West London Volunteer Regiment with the metal shoulder title, West London Regt over VTC over Chelsea.

Cheltenham Cadet Corps

Recognised 17 December 1917 (Army Order 111 of 1918) and affiliated to the 3rd Battalion Gloucestershire Volunteer Regiment.

Cheltenham Rifle Association

Raised in August 1914, this corps held its drills in the yard at Cheltenham Police Station, Clarendon Street under the supervision of one of the police instructors.

Chertsey and Lyne Emergency Force

Originated and organised by Lieutenant-General Sir Edward Hutton at the end of August 1914 with headquarters at the Lyne Club, this corps had sections at Lyne (29 men, under the command of Sergeant J Southerton), Thorpe (19, Captain N Brettell), Longcross (17, Mr G Copland), Ottershaw (35, Mr H Baker) and Chertsey (96, Colonel Lawson)—in command, Major Sir Edward Stern. A range was set up at Lyne Recreation Ground, the Chertsey men drilling at the Drill Hall belonging to 'G' Company 6th Battalion East Surrey Regiment (Territorial Force). Lieutenant-General Sir Edward Hutton had retired from the army, but in 1914 was recalled to command the recently formed 21st Division.

Cheshire Volunteer Regiment

The cap badge of this regiment (illustrated) featured the three garbs (wheat sheaves) from the county arms on a crowned shield.

Chief Constables Civilian Corps Sheffield

The arms of Sheffield featured in the centre of an enamel lapel badge (illustrated).

Chippenham Civilian Reserve Corps

The Mayor of Chippenham issued a proclamation in September 1914 calling on men from the town to enrol as volunteers. Appointed as organising secretary was Mr Edgar Reade. Some 250 came forward within two weeks.

Chiswick Emergency Defence Corps

The *Volunteer Training Corps Gazette* for 13 March 1915 reported that on Tuesday 2 March the corps had been inspected by Colonel Stanley Bird the Chief Recruiting Officer of the Hounslow District. Headquarters are noted as No 287 High Street, Chiswick and the commanding officer as Colonel Willoughby Wallace, CMG. In the issue for 18 September 1915, Colonel Wallace reported that on 8 September the corps celebrated its first anniversary and that since formation some 472 have passed through its ranks. There exists a brass badge comprising the intertwined initials CEDC above a scroll inscribed Chiswick Emergency Defence Corps.

Chorley Volunteer Training Corps

President of the Chorley VTC was former lieutenant-colonel of the 3rd Lancashire Artillery Volunteer Corps, WJ Thom, his committee including Messrs PE Middleston (chairman), JB Bennett, H Brindle, T Brindle, W Brindle, WM Gillibrand, W Harper, JB Hide, HS Hollings and R Shaw. Mr JH Neville was appointed as secretary with JH Yates the assistant secretary and RC Greenwood, the treasurer. Both 'G' and 'H' Companies of 4th Battalion Loyal North Lancashire Regiment (Territorial Force) were located at Chorley and their drill hall was put at the disposal of the local volunteers for parades and rifle practice on two miniature ranges. Corps headquarters were at Chorley Town Hall.

Cinderford Volunteer Training Corps

The *Gloucestershire Journal* for 31 June 1915 reported that this corps had been formed.

City of Edinburgh Volunteer Regiment, 1st Cadet Battalion

Recognised on 29 November 1917 (Army Order 51 of 1918).

City of Exeter Athletes' Volunteer Force

This corps had a bronze cap badge featuring the arms of Exeter (illustrated) within a wreath of laurel and oak.

City of London Civic Guard

An enamel lapel badge with this title exists which features the shield from the city arms.

City of London National Guard

The *Volunteer Training Corps Gazette* for 26 December reported that a corps with this name was being raised under the presidency of the Rt Hon Sir Charles Johnston, Bart, the Lord Mayor of London. The object behind the Guard was to provide a force of actively engaged professional men, business men, artisans, and others, who are not already rendering service to the country, are physically fit and of the age forty and upwards. Each member was asked to pay an entrance fee of £1 and to provide his own uniform and weapons. Applications for membership were to be sent to the secretary at 99 Gresham Street, EC. The *Gazette* for 13 February 1915 reported that seventy-seven-year-old Field Marshal Sir Evelyn Wood, VC had recently joined. The *Gazette* for 27 March 1915 mentions a Stock Exchange Platoon and at a recent parade grey-green uniforms were being worn and that some forty-seven officers and 2,046 men had taken part. The *Gazette* for 15 May 1915 mentions an Engineer Unit and Marylebone Section of the Guard. The issue for 18 December 1915 notes that the veteran members of the Guard are acting as guides for soldiers arriving at Waterloo and Victoria Stations on leave, changing their French money and arranging connections. The Guard soon consisted of three battalions and there were five Station Companies: 'Victoria', 'Euston', 'Waterloo', 'King's Cross' and 'St Pancras'. The Guard later formed the 4th, 5th and 6th Battalions of the City of London Volunteer Regiment. The arms of the City, complete with supporters, formed the unit's cap badge, the metal shoulder title having the letters C.L.N.G in a straight line above V. Unmentioned by the *Volunteer Training Corps Gazette* is the existence of the Scottish Company of the City of

The Cyclists' Section *Central Press Photos Ltd*

London National Guard. Following is an article of mine regarding this company that was published by the Military Historical Society:

The Scottish Company City of London National Guard: In the City of London, six battalions were raised and later organised into the City of London Volunteer Regiment. The regiment was split into two groups: Group A, containing the 1/1st, 2/1st and 2nd Battalions; Group B, the 4th, 5th and 6th Battalions. It was from within Group B, or as it was also know, The City of London National Guard, that a company consisting entirely of Scotsmen resident in the London area was formed. The idea of a Scottish section of the National Guard had been conceived almost from the very beginning of its conception—Colonel GTB Cobbett, Commanding Officer, inviting Mr Kenneth Barclay-Brown at the Guildhall on Boxing Day, 1914, to get things under way.

Following in the traditions of the Victorian/Edwardian Volunteer Movement (1859-1908), meetings were soon set up to discuss formation. A Recruitment Committee was established with much help and support coming from Mr (later Sir) John Ferguson, of the National Bank of Scotland, and Mr Francis Bannerman who donated a cash grant for the purpose of purchasing equipment. Late of Dundee, and then living in New York, Bannerman was the proprietor of the famous Bannerman's Catalogue—a mail order business specialising in surplus military items.

At Brighton—The Work of the Ambulance Section *Central Press Photos, Ltd.*

Originally styled as the Scottish Detachment, the unit assembled for its first drill on 6 February, 1915 at the Buckingham Gate headquarters of the 14th London Regiment (Territorial Force)—the 'London Scottish' which had its origins in the 1859 revival of the Volunteer Movement, a not unexpected association, as Barclay-Brown and many members of the new Scottish Volunteers had gained military experience with this famous regiment as far back as the 1870s.

In April 1915 the detachment was organised into two platoons (numbered 11 and 12) under the commands of Mr Barclay-Brown and Mr JC Hamilton

THE CITY OF LONDON NATIONAL GUARD BAND *[Miles & Kay]*

ST. PAUL'S CATHEDRAL, JUNE 9th, 1915
"The National Guard is making boys of you all again," said the Bishop of London. "And it is a step in the direction of the necessary organisation of the nation for service."

Greig (he also held a commission in the London Scottish) and allotted to 'C' Company of the 5th Battalion. The union of the Scots with 'C' Company would, however, have several drawbacks, the main being that both units had by this time set themselves up with their own drill premises throughout the London area. The Scots, in addition to the Buckingham Gate drill hall, also held parades in the moat of the Tower of London.

The strength of the Scottish Detachment grew rapidly and in November 1915 was sufficient to be formed into an independent company. In the same month, and as 'E' Company of the 5th Battalion, the Scots were inspected by Lord Kitchener. Passing down the ranks, the Field Marshal stopped and spoke at some length to Private HR Stimson, the topic of conversation being Stimson's impressive display of medals—the China Medal of 1860, Meritorious Service Medal and Long Service and Good Conduct award being among them. Later, Private Stimson was the centre of interest. The several members of the Press present made much, in the next day's papers, of the fact that he had served at Peking in 1860 and was still 'soldiering on' some fifty of more years later. In fact many of the company's members that day wore medals gained for service in both the Egyptian and South African campaigns.

Popularly known as the London Kilties, the company, which had transferred to the 6th Battalion in September 1916, was in 1917 at full strength despite the fact that many of its elder and original members had fallen out due to the work proving to be too severe. Recruiting campaigns were usually quite successful though, and on one instance practically all the men working in the London offices of Scottish banks were enrolled. A special effort, however, was made in April, 1918, as a direct result of the loss to the Army of many members now qualifying (under the new age limit stipulations) for military duty. The raising of the age limit for service in the armed forces in fact was to deprive the Company of their Commanding Officer Captain R Stewart, who had replaced Barclay-Brown in June 1917.

The duties of the company included the guarding of several main-line London railway stations, the Post Office power station at Blackfriars, and the Central Telephone Exchange. A Lewis gun post was also manned at Blackwell as part of the barrage defence of London.

The company's uniform followed basic army pattern but would include certain Scottish refinements. The headdress was a plain Glengarry cap upon which was worn a badge comprising the star of the Order of the Thistle superimposed with the Arms of the City of London. Tunics were cut-away at the front according to Scottish style, bronze thistles decorating the collars (the officers wore the letter V below these) and the letters (also in bronze) CLNG over V on the shoulder straps. It would seem, however, that in the early part of the Company's service no special efforts were made to adopt the kilt as part of its dress. Captain Barclay-Brown did not in fact even apply for permission and is on record as saying that '....to adopt the kilt is inadvisable and permission unlikely to be granted.' In May, 1915, however, a pipe band was inaugurated, its members wearing kilts of Macdonald of the Isles tartan. Pipe banners bearing the rampant Lion of Scotland embroidered in gold were at the same time presented by Barclay-Brown's mother.

It was shortly after Robert Stewart's appointment as Commanding Officer in 1917—and largely due to his efforts—that the Scottish Company was later that year given permission to adopt the kilt as a whole. The tartan of the Argyll and Sutherland Highlanders was chosen (said to have been 'readily available') together with Atholl hose and sporrans bearing four tassels and the City arms. These items members were expected to purchase for themselves, but an issue of khaki aprons and hose tops for service purposes was made via a donation to the Company by a 'well-wisher'. The new uniform was first worn at the St. Andrew's Day service held at St. Columba's Church in 1917.

The Scottish Company, City of London National Guard, was just one of the many hundreds of home-front units that served with great enthusiasm and distinction during the Great War. It served its country well and without doubt the duties it performed enabled other men to serve overseas.

The three Scottish Company individuals illustrated are: J T E Rees (photo), Captain Barclay Brown (1st cartoon) and QMS James Weir (2nd cartoon).

City of London Volunteer Corps

A report in the *Volunteer Training Corps Gazette* for 12 December 1914 tells how on 8 August 1914, four days after war broke out, a letter had been addressed to the Press by Mr Ernest W Phillips which, as a result, the City of London Volunteer Corps sprang into existence. The total number of members, noted the report, stood at over 1000, this figure including names at the time being held on a 'waiting list'. Signalling, medical and transport sections had been

formed, while each platoon had its own section of motor cycle scouts.

The CLVC was under the distinguished patronage of the Right Hon Sir Charles Johnston, Lord Mayor of the City, and Sir T Vansittart Bowater, Bart. By the courtesy of the Chief Commissioner it was privileged to use the City of London Arms as its badge. The address of the CLVC is given by the *Gazette* as c/o Messrs Alpe & Ward, 3, Serjeant's Inn, Temple, EC. A concert to raise funds for arms was held at the King's Hall, Holborn Restaurant on 17 December 1914. Alpe & Ward were a firm of solicitors. An oval lapel badge exists bearing the City arms in the centre and the title of the corps around the edge. *The C.L.V.C* by John Quebec was published by W Knott in 1917.

City of Westminster Volunteers

The *Volunteer Training Corps Gazette* for 13 February 1915 reported that a meeting had been held with a view to the formation of this corps at Caxton Hall on 5 February. Two cap badges have been noted, both having the arms of Westminster, one with City of Westminster Volunteers inscribed upon a scroll, the other with the Westminster motto, *Custodi Civitem Domine*. There is a button bearing the arms in the centre with the title City of Westminster Volunteers around the rim and the metal shoulder title, C of W over Volunteers. The corps became a battalion of the West London Volunteer Regiment with the metal shoulder title West London Regt over V.T.C. over Westminster.

Clapham Home Defence League

Mentioned in the *Volunteer Training Corps Gazette* for 20 March 1915. There is a round gilt and enamel lapel badge bearing the title Clapham Branch Home Defence League and the Union flag in real colours.

Clapham Volunteer Corps

The *Volunteer Training Corps Gazette* for 17 July 1915 reported that this corps under the command of Captain HH Gethen had carried out exercises on Clapham Common the previous 26 June. Another issue refers to the corps ground in Aristotle Road, Clapham.

Clapton Volunteer Training Corps

The *Volunteer Training Corps Gazette* for 8 May 1915 reported that No 1 Platoon of the Clapton VTC, together with the Hackney VTC, had taken part in a march to aid the recruitment of the 17th (Service) Battalion King's Royal Rifle Corps (British Empire League). Clapton's commanding officer, Lieutenant-Colonel L Whitehead, had been appointed to command the 17th.

Cleator Moor Athletes' Volunteer Force

Enrolment and first drill was held in the Market Hall on 1 December 1914. Cleator Moor on the River Eden is just over four miles from Whitehaven in Cumberland. The hall was destroyed by fire (illustrated) in April 1966.

Coliseum Training Corps

Formed 1 November 1914, this Bristol corps had a lapel badge showing the city arms in the centre of a circle inscribed Bristol Volunteer Regiment. A scroll below has Coliseum Volr Corps. The corps had become part of the Bristol Volunteer Corps in April 1915, that name changing to Bristol Volunteer Regiment in the following month. Another circular mufti badge had the letter C in the centre of a circle inscribed Coliseum Training Corps.

Co-operative Wholesale Society Rifle Club and Defence Corps

An enamel lapel badge was worn consisting of a crowned oval inscribed with the title of the corps. In its centre, crossed rifles and the letters CWS.

Cork Volunteer Training Corps

The cap badge of this Irish corps featured the arms of the city (illustrated). Mr Steven Hurst writes in *The Bulletin of the Military Historical Society* (No 250, November 2012) that the strength of the corps stood at 223 in November 1915.

Cornwall, 1st Cadet Battalion of

'H' Company of this battalion was recognised on 21 March 1918 (Army Order 149) and affiliated to the 1st Battalion Cornwall Volunteer Regiment.

Cornwall Volunteer Training Corps

The fifteen bezants from the arms of the Duchy of Cornwall featured on the badges of this corps.

Corps of Citizens

The *Volunteer Training Corps Gazette* for 9 January 1915 reported that this corps, referred to as the Corps of Citizens of London, was now well under way and had started drilling in the grounds of the Botanic Gardens, Regent's Park. Colonel and Alderman Sir W H Dunn is Hon Colonel, with Colonel H H Tasker and Major F Rose-Innes, KC as second in command. A later edition notes that the corps was formed shortly after war was declared in August 1914. Permission was given by the Court of Common Council to use the Guildhall as headquarters. The Corps of Citizens was made up of Liverymen, Freemen and other well-known and prominent City men. The Adjutant was Mr WH Champness and the Commandant, Colonel HH Tasker. Headquarters, 14 Serjeant's Inn, Fleet Street.

By the end of April 1915 the Citizens Corps had been merged with the St Paul's Company which became 'C' Company Corps of Citizens. During 21 to 25 May 1915, the corps carried out exercises in Amersham, using the Griffin Hotel as headquarters. There exists a button displaying the shield from the City of London Arms together with, on either side, the letter C.

Corps of Volunteers Artillery Regiment

Under this title, authors Arthur Kipling and Hugh King (*Head-dress Badges of the British Army*) include the following details of a badge to this unit in their VTC section: 'Within a laurel-wreath a shield. On this in chief a label inscribed *Corps of Volunteers*. On the shield a wheel with the letter *V* in the centre and inscribed *Protect the populace,* in the top left-hand corner a small shield inscribed with the letter *A*, and in the top right a similar shield inscribed with the letter *R*. In the bottom left- and right-hand corners guns with the barrels raised.'

County of London Volunteer Regiment

Noted is a cap badge to the 14th (Wandsworth) Battalion which features the borough's arms. Similar is another to the 19th (Kensington) Battalion.

County of London Volunteer Training Corps

Just a short walk from South Kensington Station at 54 Sussex Place was the headquarters of this corps. There was also a central office at 5 Henrietta Street, Covent Garden. Drills were held on Mondays, Wednesdays and Fridays in the evenings, members being required to pay a one shilling subscription each quarter. There were signalling and ambulance sections. An Associate of the Society of Accountants and Auditors, Mr Walter Mason was Hon Secretary.

Courts of Justice Volunteer Training Corps

The *Volunteer Training Corps Gazette* for 30 January 1915 reported that His Honour Judge Cluer of Shoreditch County Court has joined the Maidenhead Division of the Courts of Justice Corps.

Cows Rifle Club

Hon Secretary of the club Mr EE Vincent reported on 5 December 1914 that members were drilling regularly at the Territorial drill hall belonging to 'H' Company of the Isle of Wight Rifles (8th Battalion Hampshire Regiment) on Monday and Thursday evenings. Strength at the time stood at 145, some twenty-one of which had recently passed the National Rifle Association standard of efficiency—254 points minimum in a possible 300.

Crewe Cadet Corps

Recognised on 22 November 1917 (Army Order 51 of 1918) and affiliated to the 4th Battalion Cheshire Volunteer Regiment.

Crewkerne School Cadet Company

Recognised on 14 March 1918 (Army Order 149) and affiliated to the 3rd Battalion Somerset Volunteer Regiment.

Crouch End Volunteer Rifle Club

Under the title 'More VTC badges' an item in the August 2013 *Bulletin of the Military Historical Society* shows an enamel lapel badge with Crouch End Volunteer Rifle Club on a scroll below a shield charged with crossed rifles and a target.

Crouch End Volunteer Training Corps

The *Volunteer Training Corps Gazette* for 20 March 1915 reported that this corps had been inaugurated towards the end of September 1914 and now had a membership of 600. Headquarters were at Park Road Schools, Crouch End. In the issue for 22 May 1915 mention was made that the corps was to assist in keeping guard at the Alexandra Palace, then being prepared for the reception of a 'large number of aliens.' The *Gazette* for 26 June 1915 reported that the Crouch End Detachment of the Horsey Motor Transport Corps had took part in a mobilisation exercise on 8 June. The issue for 9 October 1915 refers to the corps as the Crouch End Detachment of the Middlesex Volunteer Regiment.

Croxley Green Volunteer Training Corps

Hon Secretary MW Raggett reported in the *VTCG* for 26 December 1914 that the Croxley Green Corps of about sixty members had formed without any knowledge at the time of the VTC's existence. He also noted that the company was fortunate in that it enjoyed the services of Messrs Dickinson's military band, which was under the direction of a Mr Walsh, late of the Royal Dublin Fusiliers. Mr John Dickinson provided free of charge the use of the Dickinson Institute Hall for drills, headquarters of the corps being at the Dickinson Institute. Drills were held each Tuesday and Friday evening. President of the corps was Mr C Barton Smith, the manager of Croxley Mills. Sergeant Denton, late of the Army Service Corps, was appointed as instructor.

Cumberland Volunteer Regiment

The regiment wore a bronze cap badge featuring the arms of Carlisle.

Darlaston Volunteer Training Corps

An item in the *VTCG* reported that this Staffordshire corps had held its first annual meeting recently, the membership at the time being 120.

Darlington Civilian Rifle Club

The Hon Secretary of the Darlington Civilian Rifle Club, Mr EC Howe of 10 Vane Terrace South, Darlington, wrote in the *Volunteer Training Corps Gazette* of 12 December 1914 how the club, with its membership of 260 men over age for military service and embracing leading professional, commercial and working men, had come into existence on 12 September 1914 as the result of a meeting of gentlemen 'greatly moved by the state of unpreparedness and want of knowledge of and in handling a rifle.' The meeting had been held at Darlington's Temperance Institute and was presided over by Mr WL Taylor, headmaster of the local Grammar School. A Committee was formed, and the officers elected were Mr Taylor (chairman), Mr WD Foster of Lloyds Bank (treasurer), Mr TC Howe and Mr. JJ Wedgewood (joint secretaries). Members of the club were to pay an annual subscription of five shillings. The club had received substantial offers from a number of gentlemen to provide a rifle range, one being the Darlington Motor Garage Company in Crown Street through their manager Mr Hill who offered a site adjoining their premises. A contingent of some seventy boys and Old Boys of Darlington Grammar School formed part of the club. Opened in 1909, the Darlington Temperance Institute was in Gladstone Street.

Denbighshire Volunteer Regiment

The badge of the regiment had in its centre a lion rampant upon a shield, part of the arms of Denbigh Borough Council.

Deptford Volunteer Training Corps

Formed 24 December 1914 after a meeting held at the Municipal Buildings, Deptford. The *Volunteer Training Corps Gazette* for 30 January 1915 reported the opening by the Mayor of Deptford (Councillor WA Wayland) of a new rifle range for use of the corps at the Laurie Grove, New Cross Swimming

Bath (illustrated). In his opening speech, the Mayor remarked that there were now 600 enrolled members and that it was hoped shortly to bring this number up to 1,000. Drills were taking place on Monday and Thursday evenings, Saturday afternoons and Sunday mornings. The *Gazette* for 6 March 1915 reported that the corps had assembled on 21 February at Penn's disused ironworks and from there marched to Blackheath. Over 800 men organised into four companies took part. An enamel lapel badge exists which consists of a crowned circle inscribed with the title of the corps, in its centre the White Horse and motto *Invicta* of Kent.

Derby Physical Training and Rifle Club

A circular enamel lapel badge exists which has crossed rifles behind the Union flag.

Derbyshire

The *Volunteer Training Corps Gazette* for 2 January 1915 reported that a meeting had been held with a view to forming a corps for the County of Derbyshire, Colonel H Brooke Taylor of Bakewell acting as secretary. Another report mentions that a meeting chaired by the Duke of Devonshire was also held by the County Justices.

Derbyshire Volunteer Regiment of Home Guards

One of the regiment's cap badges featured a Tudor Rose with crown above. Another had a stag within the centre of a Maltese Cross.

Devonshire Regiment, 1st and 2nd Volunteer Battalions

Cadet companies were formed for each of these battalions in 1918.

Dorsetshire Volunteer Regiment

The cap badge included the three lions from the arms of Dorset County Council (illustrated) and the date 1915.

Dover Volunteer Training Corps

Formed as a result of a meeting held at the Connaught Hall, Dover (illustrated) on 28 November 1914. Connaught Hall in Biggin Street was opened in July 1883 by HRH Prince Arthur, Duke of Connaught.

Dublin Motorcycle Volunteer Corps

Mr Steven Hurst writes in *The Bulletin of the Military Historical Society* (No 250, November 2012) that the strength of this corps stood at nineteen in November 1915.

Dublin Veterans' Volunteer Training Corps

Formed in 1914 from dons and graduates of Trinity College, Dublin. Author Tom Wylie mentions this corps (*The Bulletin,* Military Historical Society, No 194, November 1998) and tells how it '…entered the pages of history during the Easter Rising, 23rd-26th April 1916.' Marching home after field exercises on Monday 24 April along Haddington Road, the men were 'fired on by Irish Volunteers, five Veterans were killed including Frank H Browning, their commanding officer.' Browning is commemorated on a memorial at the Wanderers Rugby Football Club, Dublin. Forty-six other members of the corps were wounded. The cap badge worn comprised a crowned seven-pointed star displaying in its centre the arms of Dublin (illustrated). Around the arms is a circle inscribed Dublin Veterans' Corps. Mr Steven Hurst writes in *The Bulletin of the Military Historical Society* (No 250, November 2012) that the Dublin Veterans VTC was formed on 2 October 1914 and within a week mustered some 150 members who were drilling twice a week.

Dublin Volunteers, Loyal

On 23 February 1915 the Loyal Dublin Volunteers took part in a march to the Fowler Memorial Hall in Rutland Square. Tom Wylie (*The Bulletin,* Military Historical Society, No 194, November 1998) writes that this unit was in the main composed of men recruited from Orange lodges and other Protestant fraternities in the city centre, South County Dublin and North County Wicklow. He also records that during the march to the Fowler Memorial most of the men were in khaki and wore on their shoulder straps the letters LDV.

Dudley Cadet Corps

Recognised on 24 May 1918 (Army Order 209) and affiliated to the 1st Volunteer Battalion Worcestershire Regiment.

Dudley Volunteer Training Corps

Located for correspondence at Chaddesly House in Wolverhampton Street, Dudley, reported the *VTCG,* this corps numbered some 160 before the end of 1914. Secretaries were Messrs John Dobson and J Hetherington. Chaddesly House at 196 Wolverhampton Street is now offices and flats.

Dulwich Defence League

The *Volunteer Training Corps Gazette* for 6 February 1915 reported that several members had objected to the recent affiliation to the Central Association for Volunteer Training Corps. The *Gazette* for 20 March 1915 noted that founder of the Dulwich Defence League, Mr RG Newton, had organising a meeting at the Lordship Lane Hall, Forest Hill on 7 September 1914 at which some 1,000 were present. The Dulwich Division, records the *Gazette*, regards the Lordship Lane Hall as it headquarters. Drills and shooting took place at the Lordship Lane end of Dulwich Common. The range, formally a large skittle alley, is a 'two decker', twenty-five yards long. Another range was being constructed on Sydenham Hill Golf Club where trench digging was also taking place. Skirmishing and open order work took place on Hayes Common. The *Gazette* was informed that this South East London corps had been formed on 7 December 1914 by Mr RG Newton and two colleagues.

Dulwich and District Defence League

A bronze cap badge has been noted comprising a large solid shield bearing crossed rifles with bayonets fixed and the motto 'Defend our liberty'.

Dumfries-shire Volunteer Regiment

The regiment wore a bronze cap badge featuring the winged figure of Victory standing on a dragon from the burgh arms (Illustrated).

Durham Volunteer Training Corps, 3rd Battalion

The cap badge featured crossed rifles with the letters VTC and number 3 superimposed. The 3rd Battalion was from Auckland.

Ealing Volunteers

Commandant of the Ealing Volunteers, former Volunteer of the Victorian period, Colonel WR Haughton, reported in December 1914 that some 670 men were then on the muster roll and that to date over 100 from the corps had already joined the Regular or Territorial Forces. The corps was formed as a result of a campaign led by the Mayor of the West London suburb that had begun on 15 August 1914. Rifle practice took place in Walpole Park—much assistance given in this direction by the Ealing and Perivale Rifle Clubs. Colonel Haughton was a holder of the Volunteer Decoration.

Earls Court Volunteers

There exists a circular enamel lapel badge with this tile, in the centre of which are displayed the Union and French crossed flags crossed. Earls Court is in the district of London's Kensington.

East Ham Division Athletes' Volunteer Force

The East Ham branch of the Athletes' Volunteer Force was started at Boleyn Castle by its Hon Secretary, Mr WS Pennett of 134 Masterman Road, East Ham on 1 October 1914. The first drill of twelve men took place within two weeks, notices placed in several local newspapers later swelling the ranks to more than 600. Signal, ambulance, scouting and despatch riding sections were later introduced. Boleyn Castle, the name given to a red brick Tudor mansion demolished in 1955, formed part of an estate at the junction of Green Street and Barking Road. West Ham Football Club was a neighbour from 1904.

East Ham Volunteer Defence Corps

The bronze cap badge featured the three seaxes from the arms of Essex on a crowned shield.

East London Volunteer Regiment

The *Volunteer Training Corps Gazette* for 23 October 1915 reported that there were elements of the regiment in Bethnal Green, Stepney, Mile End, Whitechapel and Limehouse. The issue for 25 March 1916 also noted that the originally there was only four small corps with a total membership of 368, now there are three battalions: Bethnal Green, Poplar and Stepney with a total membership of 1,000.

East Yorkshire Cadets Royal Engineers

Recognised on 14 August 1918 (Army Order 342) and affiliated to the East Riding Volunteer Engineers.

Ebbw Vale Volunteer Corps

An oval lapel badge exists with the letters 'WSC' in its centre.

Eccles Battalion Athletes' Volunteer Force

By December 1914, this corps numbered 900 men divided into four companies. Regular drills were carried out, one early route march taking the Volunteers through Stretford, Sale, Altrincham, Bowden, Bollington,

Lymm, Warburton, Portington and Flixton. At Sale a detachment of the Altrincham VTC accompanied by the Broadheath Military Band marched with the battalion as far as Altrincham. One report made in December 1914 noted that all officers of the battalion had previous military training, at least four being in possession of the medal for the South African War. The Hon secretary was Mr CW Tonge of 15 Granville Road in Pendleton.

Ellastone Volunteer Training Corps

The existence of this Staffordshire corps was notified in the *Volunteer Training Corps Gazette*.

Eltham Defence Company

The *Volunteer Training Corps Gazette* for 13 February 1915 reported on a recent inspection of this corps by Major General Sir Desmond O'Callaghan, KCVO. The company was noted as a strong one of eleven officers and 506 men. The inspection took place in the grounds of Lemonwell, the residence of the Commandant, Major Sir Harry North.

Engineer Volunteer Training Corps

The *Volunteer Training Corps Gazette* for 17 April 1915 reported that formation of this corps was in hand within the London area. Members were to be from the engineering profession and would train others in field and fortress work (including telephones, telegraphs and searchlights) with a purpose to aid recruiting for the Royal Engineers. Recruits were expected to provide their own uniforms and equipment.

Engineering Institution Volunteer Engineer Corps

The *Volunteer Training Corps Gazette* for 27 May 1916 stated that the 4th Battalion Central London Volunteer Regiment had now linked up with the Engineering Institution Volunteer Engineer Corps to form the 1st London Engineer Volunteers. The services of the corps have been offered to the King as a battalion of twenty officers and 479 NCOs and men, containing as it does numerous professional surveyors, electrical and mining engineers. Headquarters were at Chester House, Eccleston Place, SW.

Essex Regiment, 11th Cadet Battalion

Recognised on 18 July 1918 and affiliated to the 6th Volunteer Battalion Essex Regiment.

Essex Volunteer Regiment

Two cap badges have been noted, one displaying the arms of the county on a crowned shield, another with crossed rifles and the date 1915. Later provided the 1st to 7th Volunteer Battalions Essex Regiment.

Essex Volunteer Training Corps

The cap badge featured crossed rifles with the letters VTC superimposed, the date 1915 and a scroll inscribed Essex.

Exeter Athletes' Volunteer Force

The arms of the City of Exeter formed the centre of a bronze cap badge.

Exeter Volunteer Regiment

The cap badge was formed of crossed cartridges on a scroll inscribed with the motto *Pro aris et focis* (For altars and hearths).

Fakenham Volunteer Training Corps

Formed as a result of a meeting held at the Assembly Room, Fakenham in Norfolk (Sir Lawrence J Jones, Bart in the chair) on Thursday 3 December 1914. About seventy enrolled that evening. The Corn Exchange and Assembly Rooms were in Oak Street.

Faringdon Volunteer Training Corps

With its fine views of the Thames Valley, Faringdon in Berkshire lies nine miles north-west of Wantage, the VTC there being noted in November 1914 as giving 'quite a military appearance' at their Sunday afternoon drills in Faringdon Park.

Feltham and District Volunteers

Hon Secretary, Mr F Sanders of 5 High Street, Feltham, Middlesex in December 1914, gave the formation date of his corps as 5 November. It had come about, he notes, as a result of the largest ever public meeting held in the town. Whereas as 'little, or none', he pointed out, 'had been held or was forthcoming in some areas, it would seem that all in and around Feltham were keen to assist the Volunteers.' Major Knox, the Governor of the Feltham Borstal Institute, gladly allowed eleven of his officers to act as drill instructors, while the local Council granted the use of several schools for their use. Messrs Pritchetts and Gold Ltd, who had recently moved its operations to Dagenham in Essex, gave the use, free of any charge, of its old factory buildings. Mr AW Smith, another local businessman, at the same time providing his largest packing shed. Drill nights were Mondays, Wednesdays and Fridays. By the end of 1914, the corps comprised three companies, each of about 120 men, some as young as seventeen, others as old as sixty-five. Pritchetts & Gold produced accumulator batteries from their Feltham factory from 1887, the new Dagenham works where the firm moved to in 1914 was at Chequers Lane, Dagenham Dock.

Finchley (Church End) Training Corps

The *Volunteer Training Corps Gazette* for 16 January 1915 reported that this corps was inaugurated in September 1914 and that its membership now stood at well over 500. Headquarters was at Christ's College where drills were carried out using rifles supplied by the cadet corps. There were signalling, ambulance and transport sections. Church End (St Mary's Church), N3 is located in central Finchley. Christ's College is in Hendon Lane. A circular, enamelled lapel badge exists with the words Training Corps on a shield and Finchley Church End around the edge.

Finchley, Friern Barnet and New Southgate Volunteer Training Corps

By November 1914 sufficient Volunteers had come forward from these three London suburbs to form a unit of battalion size. Mr A van Someren, from Melbourne Place, Strand, reported in December 1914 that Finchley and Friern Barnet were first off the mark, these to form 'A' and 'B' Companies respectively. It would be at the Lecture Hall in Bellevue Road that a meeting attended by, among others, Captain Pretyman-Newman, Mr A Lord and the Chaplain of 'B' Company, the Rev Edward Gage Hall, that some seventy New Southgate men came forward. Thus began 'C' Company. Lord Ronaldsay presided over 'A' Company which numbered some 100 men, Mr Sydney Simmons commanded 'B' Company of eighty. The *Volunteer Training Corps Gazette* for 26 December noted that Mr C Cosgrove had been elected as chairman of the New Southgate Company, its strength now 100, and that a church parade had recently been held at Christ Church Congregational Church.

Finsbury Volunteer Training Corps

The *Volunteer Training Corps Gazette* for 18 December 1915 reported that this corps was about to be formed, the Mayor of the borough, Alderman HB Barton, being the first to enrol.

Fishponds and District Training Corps

Mentioned by Daniel Brinson in his book on Gloucestershire military insignia as having been formed in October 1914. The name was changed to Fishponds Volunteer Training Corps in March 1915 and in the following June became No 16 Platoon of the 2nd (Coliseum) Battalion Bristol Volunteer Regiment. Mr Brinson illustrates a lapel badge worn by the corps which has a crown on draped Union flags and the title Fishponds Training Corps.

Fleet Street Company Athletes' Volunteer Force

The *Volunteer Training Corps Gazette* for 12 December 1914 reported that this corps was being formed, its members to be confined to those associated with the Press. Mr Harry Young of the Press Club was acting as Hon Secretary. The *Gazette* for 6 March 1915 gives numbers as now being about 200 and that applicants for membership should apply to the Press Club at St Bride's House, Salisbury Square. Fleet Street, of course, for many years the centre of London's newspaper industry, runs eastwards from Temple Bar to Ludgate Circus.

Folkestone Volunteer Training Corps

A report in the *Volunteer Training Corps Gazette* of 5 December 1914 noted that this corps then stood at over 140 strong and comprised members of all classes of society from the town. Included in the ranks were a number of ex-non-commissioned officers who were proving to be a valuable asset to training.

Forest Gate Company Citizens' National Reserve

This east London corps was formed for the convenience of men residing in Forest Gate, Upton Park, and the surrounding districts. Headquarters were at Sandringham Road Schools in Katherine Road. Mr J Moore, a former sergeant in the Essex Regiment, was appointed as commanding officer and he was assisted by Mr AC Rogers and Mr FJ Godfrey. Mr G Norris acted as orderly room sergeant, Mr N Butcher, orderly room corporal. Drills took place every evening except Saturday, company parades being held every Sunday with the Ilford Division CNR. Forest Gate, South Essex is just over five miles by rail from London's Liverpool Street Station.

Forest Hill Company National Volunteer Reserve

The *Volunteer Training Corps Gazette* for 8 May 1915 reported that this company had rendezvoused at the bottom of Stratham Common on Sunday 10 May for a route march to Warlington. The *Gazette* for 26 June 1915 reported that the corps, together with the Lewisham Volunteer Training Corps, have now become a unit of the National Volunteer Reserve and was now part of the National Volunteer Reserve Battalion of the South-East London Regiment.

Fowey Volunteer Training Corps

The *Volunteer Training Corps Gazette* form 26 December 1914 noted that Professor Sir AT Quiller Couch of Cambridge, better known as 'Q', was taking an interest in the formation and organisation of the corps at Fowey.

Friern Barnet Volunteer Training Corps

Kipling and King describe a badge to this corps as follows: 'An oval inscribed *Friern Barnet VTC Esse quam videri* [To be, rather than to seem] surmounted by an Imperial crown with the letter "B" in the centre. Gold on blue-enamel oval, gold-and-red crown, initial in white-edged gold on gilt ground.'

Fulham Volunteer Training Corps

The *Volunteer Training Corps Gazette* for 17 July 1915 reported that this corps had started in November 1914 and as the Fulham Battalion of the West London Volunteer Regiment was inspected at the Peterborough School, Clancarty Road on 8 July. The metal shoulder title, West London Regt. over V.T.C. over Fulham, was worn and a cap badge bearing the arms of Fulham.

Gawdy Hall Volunteers

So keen to make some contribution to the war effort, Mr I Sancroft Holmes of Gawdy Hall, Harleston in Norfolk, raised a squad of sixteen Volunteers from tenants and employees on his estate. Forming the nucleus of a local corps, the workers gave up part of the dinner break for drill and shooting.

Giggleswick Village Guards

Here at the North Yorkshire village of Giggleswick, where a two-arched bridge takes you across the Ribble into Settle, here at the end of November 1914, the following notice appeared in the parish magazine: 'VILLAGE GUARDS. The duty of some of us is to keep things going at home. The age or condition of others of us prevents us "joining the colours", yet we feel we ought to know enough of drill and musketry to make us feel within ourselves the power efficiently and honourably to take our place in the firing line should this village of ours be invaded. I ask those who agree with the imperative need of preparation to meet me, fine or wet, at The Bungalow on Sunday afternoon at half-past two o'clock on 29th November. Theodore P. Brocklehurst, Vicar.'

It is not on record how many attended the Rev Brocklehurst's meeting, but the eventual Giggleswick Village Guards were to have at their disposal for drill, a field belonging to Mr Thomas Scambler and the use of, thanks to Headmaster Mr Robert N Douglas, the covered playground at Giggleswick School. The school was also pleased to provide drill and musketry instruction in the form of one of their OTC officers, Lieutenant, ED Clark. The Rev Theodore Percy Brocklehurst was vicar of Giggleswick's St Alkelda's Parish Church.

Gillingham Volunteer Training Corps

A meeting to discuss the possibility of forming a Volunteer Corps in Gillingham, Kent was held by the Mayor and Town Council on Monday 30 November 1914. The motion was carried unanimously, and recruiting began immediately.

Glamorgan Volunteer Training Corps

The cap badge of this corps comprised a circle inscribed with Glamorgan VTC with in its centre a shield bearing three chevrons. The county used the arms (three red chevrons) of the De Clares who held the Lordship of Glamorgan from 1217 to 1317.

Glasnevin Volunteer Corps

This Irish corps was inspected by General Sir John Maxwell on Saturday 16 May 1916, Mr Steven Hurst writing in *The Bulletin of the Military Historical Society* (No 250, November 2012) noting that its strength was 96 in November 1915.

Gloucester Civil Training Corps

Daniel Brinson notes in his book *Military Insignia of Gloucestershire* how this corps had held its initial meeting on 9 January 1915. He also mentions the brassards issued to each man were individually named.

Gloucestershire Volunteer Regiment

Organised by 5 June 1915 with four battalions: Berkeley Vale, Gloucester, Forest and Cheltenham. A 5th Battalion was soon added. The regimental badge was the arms of Gloucester complete with supporters.

Golders Green Training Corps

Hon Secretary, EH Burgess of 47 Woodstock Avenue, Golders Green, wrote in December 1914 that the corps formed in this North-West London suburb had been started on 3 September and that some 735 had enrolled since that date. Of that number, about twenty-two had already left to join the Regulars or Territorials. Journalist and member of the Victorian Volunteer Movement, Mr Sidney E Eynon was orderly room quartermaster sergeant.

Goole North East Railway Company Volunteer Training Corps

Formed within days of war being declared with Captain WH Featherstone in charge of recruiting.

Gosport and District Volunteer Training Corps

Towards the end of 1914 those interested in joining a VTC unit then forming in the Gosport area were invited to contact either of the joint Hon Secretaries, Mr CEF Parker, of 88 High Street, Gosport, or Mr S Rogers at 86 North Street, Gosport.

Grantham Volunteer Training Corps

Formed as a result of a meeting held at Grantham Town Hall (illustrated) on Wednesday 2 December with Major Sir Arthur Priestley in the chair. Some 100 joined and a committee was formed which included Sir Arthur, Chief Constable of the town, Lieutenant Colonel RF Morseby White, and Mr T Norton.

Gravesend and District Volunteer Training Corps

By the end of 1914 this corps was already some 500 strong. The Mayor of Gravesend, Councillor H Huggins, had been made president, headquarters being at the Town Hall in the High Street. Drills took place every Monday to Thursday evenings in the Market Hall, open training was also held in a field (Dashwood Meadow) belonging to Mr JH Cooper. Regular route marches were held each Sunday which were preceded by a short service at St Mary's Church in Rochester Road. In a building put at the disposal of the corps by the Canal Coal and Building Materials Company, a miniature rifle range was set up and opened during the last weeks of 1914. Hon Secretary of the Gravesend VTC was Mr HR Cox of 158 Darnley Road, Gravesend, and the corps possessed a band directed by Associate Member of the Royal College of Organists, Mr HR Shirley.

Great Northern Railway Volunteer Training Corps

Mr Steven Hurst writes in *The Bulletin of the Military Historical Society* (No 250, November 2012) that the strength of this Irish corps stood at 46 in November 1915.

Great Southern and Western Railway Volunteer Training Corps

Mr Steven Hurst writes in *The Bulletin of the Military Historical Society* (No 250, November 2012) that the strength of this Irish corps stood at 51 in November 1915.

Great Yarmouth Volunteer Training Corps

Formation of this corps came about as the result of a meeting held at Great Yarmouth Town Hall on Monday 30 November 1914. Those present included the Rev George McLuckie, the Rev W Booker, a Colonel Lucas, Fleet Surgeon Miller, Commander Prickett, RN, Major CJ Wiltshire, who had served with the Victorian Norfolk Volunteers, and Doctors W Wyllys and H Potts. Doctor Wyllys of 25 King Street undertook the duties of Hon Secretary.

Green Hammerton Volunteer Training Corps

The *Volunteer Training Corps Gazette* for 26 December 1914 reported that Dr JA Benson of Green Hammerton and a former member of the Edinburgh University Company of the Queen's Edinburgh Volunteer Brigade, had been drilling some sixty men from his area since 14 October 1914. Major Dent of Ribston Hall had been appointed as president and military advisor.

Green Park College Cadet Company

Recognised on 4 May 1918 (Army Order 209) and affiliated to the 2nd Volunteer Battalion Somerset Light Infantry.

Greenock Citizen Volunteers

News was received by The *Volunteer Training Corps Gazette* that a corps had been formed at Greenock in Renfrewshire and that requests for local men to enrol were appearing in newspapers by November 1914. Those interested were advised to contact Mr FA MacBrayne at 122 Wellington Street, Greenock.

Greystones Volunteer Training Corps

This Irish corps was inspected by General Sir John Maxwell on Saturday 16 May 1916. Mr Steven Hurst writes in *The Bulletin of the Military Historical Society* (No 250, November 2012) that the strength of the corps stood at 54 in November 1915.

Grimsby and Cleethorpes Citizen Army

Within three weeks of its formation in September 1914, the strength of this corps stood at over 800. By the end of the year four companies are on record as drilling regularly at Doughty Road Barracks in Grimsby, the Cleethorpes company then comprising about 200 Volunteers. There were also detachments at Waltham, Scartho, Caistor, Tetney, Immingham and Great Coates. The *Volunteer Training Corps Gazette* for 26 December 1914 reported that the corps had been armed with shot guns. The Doughty Road Barracks referred to was that occupied in 1914 by the 5th Lincolnshire Regiment (TF). The Grimsby arms, with its three boars' heads, forms the centre of an oval enamel lapel badge worn by the corps in civilian clothing.

Grove Academy Cadet Company

Recognised on 18 June 1918 (Army Order 307) and affiliated to the City of Dundee Volunteer Regiment.

Guernsey Volunteer Corps

A bronze cap badge was worn consisting of a crowned circle inscribed Diex Aie Guernsey Volunteer Corps. In the centre of the circle, the arms of Guernsey.

Guild Street Cadet Corps

Recognised on 18 June 1918 (Army Order 240) and affiliated to the 2nd Battalion Staffordshire Volunteer Regiment.

Guildford Volunteer Training Corps

Formed in November 1914 and by the end of the year membership stood at some 130. Drills were held at the local Territorial Force Drill Hall, musketry practice taking place at the local rifle club. The Hon Secretary was located at Hopefield, St Catherine's in Guildford.

Hackney Athletes' Volunteer Force

The *Volunteer Training Corps Gazette* for 28 August 1915 noted that this corps was now part of the 5th Battalion North London Volunteer Regiment.

Hackney Volunteer Training Corps

The *Volunteer Training Corps Gazette* for 17 April 1915 reported that there are now well over 250 members in this corps and that the commanding officer was Captain Thomas. Drills were taking place at King's Hall, Lower Clapton Road. The cap badge featured the tower from the borough arms. The corps later became the 5th (Hackney) Battalion of the North London Volunteer Regiment.

Hale End Volunteer Training Corps

The *Volunteer Training Corps Gazette* for 16 January 1915 reported that this corps in London E4, just to the east of Epping Forest, was under the command of Commandant AJ Pearce. A recruiting meeting had been arranged for Saturday 23 January at the Church Room, Church Avenue, Higham's Park. The issue for 3 July 1915 noted that the present strength of the corps was less than 200. Later became a company of the 5th Battalion Essex Volunteer Regiment.

Halifax Volunteer Corps

A triangular-shaped enamel lapel badge exists with this title and crossed rifles.

Ham Volunteer Training Corps

This Surrey corps was reported as being in existence by December 1914.

Hammersmith Volunteer Training Corps

Became a battalion of the West London Volunteer Regiment wearing the metal shoulder title, West London Regt. over V.T.C. over Hammersmith.

Hampstead Volunteer Reserve

The *Volunteer Training Corps Gazette* for 23 January 1915 reported that this corps had been initiated on 9

 August 1914 by Colonel Sheffield and Mr T Hancock Nunn, its first meeting being at the 1st Cadet Battalion Royal Fusiliers drill hall at 25 Pond Street on Thursday 13 August. Enrolled strength was over 600 divided between three companies. There was a subscription of two shillings and sixpence per month. Drills were also carried out at the University College School, St Stephen's Parish Hall in Rosslyn Hill, the County Council Elementary School in Fleet Road and on Hampstead Heath. The *Gazette* for 20 March 1915 noted that the corps included among its members many men 'well known in the world of letters and art', among them Hugh Riviere, Mouat Loudan, FH Townsend and Lewis Baum (both of *Punch*), Arthur Rackman, George Hillyard Swinstead, John Masefield and DC McColl. The *Gazette* for 24 April 1915 reported that Sir Edward Elgar and the painter Maurice Griffenhagen had also recently enrolled. A drawing by FH Townsend of *Punch* was featured in a recruiting circular and also published in the 1 May issue of the *Volunteer Training Corps Gazette*. The corps later became part of the 1st (Hampstead) Battalion of the North London Volunteer Regiment. The issue for 2 September 1916 mentioned the 'reincorporation' of the corps as part of the Forces of His Majesty under the Volunteer Act of 1863 and that the official designation is now 7th (Hampstead) Volunteer Battalion County of London Regiment.

Hampstead Volunteer Training Corps

Mentioned in the *Volunteer Training Corps Gazette* for 24 April 1915, later becoming part of 1st (Hampstead) Volunteer Regiment. A bronze cap badge is described by Kipling and King as follows: 'A circlet inscribed *Central Assocn VTC* surmounted by an Imperial crown and with oak sprays either side. In the centre a shield bearing the arms of Hampstead. Below the shield a scroll inscribed with Hampstead's motto *Non sibi sed toti* (Not for oneself but for all).

Handsworth Athletes' Volunteer Force

A note in the *Volunteer Training Corps Gazette* referred to this corps.

Hanley Drill and Training Corps

Formed at a meeting held by the Old Hanliensian Club (the Old Boys of Hanley Municipal Secondary School) in the school hall on 14 November, its strength, 500. A Mounted detachment was also formed. The school, originally called the Higher Grade School, was renamed in 1905 and was located between Old Hall Street and Birch Terrace.

Hanley Volunteer Training Corps

Hanley resident, Mr Louis Taylor, reported at a meeting held at the Staffordshire village of Blythe Bridge on Tuesday 1 December 1914 that at that time Hanley had already enrolled some 400 men, some of whom, in addition to undertaking infantry drill and training, were also engaged in cyclist and ambulance work. This, noted Mr Taylor, had taken just nine days to achieve.

Harringay, South Tottenham and Wood Green Volunteers

The *Volunteer Training Corps Gazette* for 9 October 1915 stated that this corps had only been formed a matter of months and now had a membership of 126, all over military age. Headquarters were at Downhills, West Green, Tottenham.

Harrogate Volunteer Training Corps

By November 1914 the Harrogate corps had passed some 600 of its members on to the Regular or Territorial Forces, about 100 of these having joined the University and Public Schools Battalion of the Royal Fusiliers. Hon Secretary of the corps, Mr J Lomas-Walker, could be contacted at Westminster Chamber, Harrogate. Two Territorial Force units, the Yorkshire Hussars Yeomanry and 5th Battalion West Yorkshire Regiment, were represented in Harrogate.

Haswall Volunteer Training Corps

Formed at the Cheshire village of Haswall in November 1914 by Mr R Pardoe who became commandant. Sixty members had enrolled by the end of the year at the Concert Hall, part of the Victoria Hotel. Rifle practice took place on property belonging to Mr Thomas Broklebrook. Hon Secretary and deputy commandant were Captain GE Martindale, the treasurer, Mr Charles Anderson. Other members of the committee were Messes Anchterlonic, Graham, Parr, Miles, Forwood, RH Hooper and Sergeant Tarbuck.

Hastings and St Leonards Division Athletes' Volunteer Force

Drills were held at various locations in Hastings, including the University School and Hastings Rifle Club, and in St Leonards at the Hatherly Road Drill Hall, and the Middle Street Drill Hall. Membership by the end of November 1914 stood at about 170. Secretary of the corps was Mr S Overton of 1 Grosvenor Crescent, St Leonards. Drill halls in the two towns were occupied by the Sussex Yeomanry (St Leonards), 2nd Home Counties Brigade, RFA (St Leonards), the Home Counties Divisional Engineers (St Leonard's) and 5th Battalion Royal Sussex Regiment (Hastings).

Haydock Volunteer Training Corps

Hon Secretary Mr Charles Dickinson reported on 19 December 1914 that consequent upon the endeavours of Doctor Dowling, JP, a meeting had been held at the Council Offices on the previous 18 November at which it was decided to raise a VTC unit in Haydock. Appointed to the committee at the time were: Councillor Lloyd (chairman), Mr J Dickinson, Doctor Dowling (commandant) and several town councillors.

Haywards Heath Volunteer Training Corps

Formed in November 1914, the Haywards Heath corps drilled every weekday evening and comprised over 100 members within two weeks of its formation. Instruction, notes another report, was given by sergeants from Territorials quartered in the town. Both the Sussex Yeomanry and 4th Battalion Royal Sussex Regiment had Territorials at Haywards Heath.

Heacham Volunteer Training Corps

This Norfolk corps was formed on 15 November 1914 and held parades each Monday and Friday in the Old School (then the property of Mr CE Strachan) and on Sundays in the park. One Sergeant Major Jelly (late of the Norfolk Regiment) was employed as an instructor, Hon Secretary of the corps being Mr Bellerby

Lowerison. *Norfolk's War: Voices of the First World War* by Fran Meeres mentions that 'Scoutmaster Bellerby Lowerison is engaged in Coast Watching services under the Admiralty, which necessitates his visiting the beach at Heacham and elsewhere at all times of the day or night.'

Hednesford Volunteer Training Corps

Mentioned in the *Volunteer Training Corps Gazette* as being employed guarding railways, bridges and canals.

Hendon Rifle Club Drill Section

Five officers and 174 other ranks from this corps were present at a review attended by General Sir O'Moore Creagh, VC at Hendon Park on Saturday 12 December 1914.

Hendon Volunteer Training Corps

The *Volunteer Training Corps Gazette* for 3 April 1915 mentions this corps and gives its commandant as Mr G Edgar Morris. Another issue refers to a Hendon Battalion of the Middlesex Volunteer Regiment.

Hendon and Cricklewood Rifle Club

Forty-eight members were present at a review held at Hendon Park attended by General Sir O'Moore Creagh, VC on Saturday 12 December 1914. The club was inaugurated at Childs Hill by Field-Marshal Earl Roberts, VC in 1906. Both Hendon and Cricklewood are north-west London districts.

Herefordshire Regiment, 1st Cadet Battalion

Recognised on 30 April 1918 (Army Order 209) and affiliated to the 1st Volunteer Battalion Herefordshire Regiment.

Hertfordshire Cadets, 12th

Recognised 17 December 1917 (Army Order 149 of 1918) and affiliated to the 3rd Battalion Hertfordshire Volunteer Regiment.

Hertfordshire Cadets, 13th

Recognised 17 December 1917 (Army Order 149 of 1918) and affiliated to the 3rd Battalion Hertfordshire Volunteer Regiment.

Hertfordshire Cadets, 14th

Recognised 30 September 1918 (Army Order 342) and affiliated to the 2nd Volunteer Battalion Hertfordshire Regiment.

Hertfordshire Volunteer Regiment

The Hart lodged from the county arms above a scroll inscribed Herts V R formed the cap badge

High School Cadet Company

Recognised 19 February 1918 (Army Order 307) and affiliated to the 2nd Volunteer Battalion Black Watch.

Himley Fire and Red Brick Co Ltd Volunteer Training Corps

Started in November 1914 and consisted mainly of employees. Managing Director, Mr GRL Chance was organiser and secretary.

Hitchin Volunteer Training Corps

The *Volunteer Training Corps Gazette* for 5 December 1914 reported that plans for a Volunteer Corps at Hitchin in Hertfordshire were 'hanging fire' for some unexplained reason. Hitchin, however, would later provide No 2 Company of the 1st Battalion Hertfordshire Volunteer Regiment

Hither Green Defence League

Mentioned in the *Volunteer Training Corps Gazette* for 20 March 1915.

Hoddesdon Volunteer Training Corps

Four miles south-east of Hertford, Hoddesdon began recruiting towards the end of 1914. Acting Hon Secretary Mr Lumley Clery of Riverdene, Broxbourne made it known in December that he hoped to raise a corps of at least 200 men. Together with Ware, Hoddesdon would later provide No 4 Company of the 1st Battalion Hertfordshire Volunteer Regiment

Holborn Volunteer Training Corps

The *Volunteer Training Corps Gazette* for 8 May 1915 reported that this corps had taken part in exercises with the Post Office Engineer VTC in Hyde Park on Saturday 1 May, the Holborn Corps band leading the march back to Grays Inn Square. Later became a battalion of the West London Volunteer Regiment.

Honour Oak Defence League

Mentioned in the *Volunteer Training Corps Gazette* for 20 March 1915. Honour Oak forms part of the London borough of Lewisham.

Hornsey and Harringay Athletes' Volunteer Force

Mentioned in the *Volunteer Training Corps Gazette* for 28 August 1915 and in the issue for 2 October 1915 a report announced that the Horsey Volunteers were to be amalgamated with the Muswell Hill, East Finchley and District VTC to form a battalion of the Middlesex Volunteer Regiment. The new battalion would be known as Hornsey. The issue for 9 October refers to a Horsey Athletes' Volunteers as being part of the Hornsey Battalion.

Hornsey Motor Transport Corps

The *Volunteer Training Corps Gazette* for 20 March 1915 reported that the Crouch End Detachment of this corps had taken part in a mobilisation exercise.

Hornsey Volunteer Training Corps

The *Volunteer Training Corps Gazette* for 6 March 1915 reported that steps were now being taken to form a regiment out of the three corps already in the borough. The issue for 2 October 1915 followed this up with the announcement that there was to be an amalgamation with the Muswell Hill, East Finchley and District VTC to form a battalion of the Middlesex Volunteer Regiment. The new battalion was to be known as Hornsey.

Hounslow and District Volunteer Training Corps

Mr JJ Bonmett (chairman). Mr JJ Arathoon (secretary). Address of corps, Myrtle Cottage, Bath Road, Hounslow, Middlesex.

Hove Battalion Home Protection Brigade

The channel swimmer, Jabez Wolefe (illustrated), was employed by this corps as physical instructor.

Hove Volunteer Corps

A circular lapel badge exists for this unit which includes crossed rifles, a crown and the date 1914.

Howth and Sutton Volunteer Training Corps

Mr Steven Hurst writes in *The Bulletin of the Military Historical Society* (No 250, November 2012) that the strength of this Irish corps stood at 54 in November 1915.

Hucclecote Civil Training Corps

The *Gloucestershire Journal* for 19 March 1915 reports the formation of this corps.

Huddersfield District Volunteer Corps

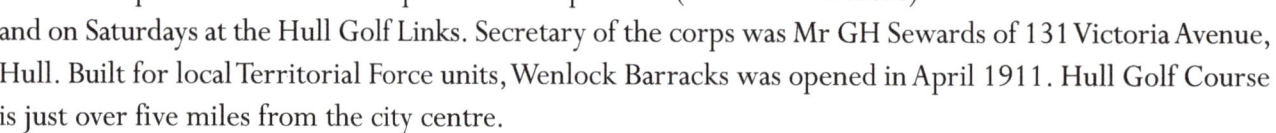

The bronze cap badge to this corps featured the arms of Huddersfield.

Hull Golfers Volunteer Force

Former officer of the 5th Battalion Yorkshire Regiment, Captain WS Walker, commanded the Hull Golfers corps which, by November 1914 had a membership of 300. Drills took place at headquarters (Wenlock Barracks) and on Saturdays at the Hull Golf Links. Secretary of the corps was Mr GH Sewards of 131 Victoria Avenue, Hull. Built for local Territorial Force units, Wenlock Barracks was opened in April 1911. Hull Golf Course is just over five miles from the city centre.

Hull Home Defence League

Hon Secretary of the corps Mr A Newton of 41 Dock Road, Hull, reported on 26 December 1914 that the League had been formed at the instigation of Mr A Newton as the result of a mass meeting held at the Grosvenor Hotel in Hull on 19 October. Strength at the time was 145 members.

Hunstanton Drill Club

Adjutant of the club Mr HC Barber wrote in December 1914 that the Hunstanton Drill Club had been formed on Tuesday 6 October and then comprised some 180 members. The original commandant was former 20th Hussars colonel, Sir Horace Beauchamp, Bart, but upon his appointment as commanding officer of the 5th Battalion Norfolk Regiment, his place was taken by Colonel GFA Cresswell, CVO, VD. The colonel was a former member of the old 3rd Norfolk Rifle Volunteer Corps. President of the club was Mr Hamon le Strange, DL, and the vice president, another old Norfolk Volunteer from Victorian days, Major W Pattrick, VD. Drills were held on Tuesday and Thursday evenings at the Town Hall and at Johnson's Garage. Late of the Norfolk Regiment, Sergeant Major Jelly was employed as instructor to the club.

Hythe Volunteer Defence Corps

Moves to form a corps by this name were reported as having begun in November 1914. The locality is uncertain, there being a Hythe in Kent, Essex, Surrey and Hampshire.

Ilford and District Civilian National Reserve

This corps notified the *Volunteer Training Corps Gazette* that a parade and inspection by Lieutenant General Sir Henry Settle was to take place at 3pm on 20 December 1914: if fine, on Wanstead Flats, if wet, at the Ilford Skating Rink. The issue for 2 January 1915, however, reported that due to a serious accident to the general, the inspection had to be called off. A parade did take place, the Ilford companies under Captain Wheeler, and, headed by the Ilford Military Band and drums and bugles belonging to the corps, left Ilford Skating Rink at 2 pm for Wanstead Flats. On the way they were joined by companies from Manor Park, Barking and Forest Gate. Total on parade, 820.

Ilford Civic Guard

Formed as a result of a meeting held on 11 August 1914 and soon constituted a double company drilling, among other places, at the Ilford Rink owned by Mr F Leighton. Hon Secretary was Mr AL Parks of 124 High Road, Ilford.

Ilford Rifle Club

An enamel lapel badge exists which consists of a circular strap inscribed 1st V.B. Essex – Ilford Rifle Club. In the centre, crossed rifles and a target.

Ilfracombe Volunteer Training Corps

A public meeting to inaugurate a VTC corps in Ilfracombe, Devon was held early in December 1914 at which Mr FH Pollen was appointed as commandant and Mr L Parsons, secretary. Some forty enrolled.

Imperial Service Corps

The *Volunteer Training Corps Gazette* for 2 January 1915 noted that the commanding officer of this corps was Lieutenant-Colonel Harold E Butcher and that at a recent field day the cavalry was under Captain Margetts, the infantry under Lieutenant De Vane. From headquarters, a train was taken to Barnet from where the corps marched to Potters Bar. The operations were under the command of the assistant adjutant Captain L Stafford Shallard. The issue for 6 February 1915 reported that the officers of the Imperial Service Corps had recently entertained Corporal Frank Holmes, VC, MM to dinner in their Mess. During the evening Lieutenant-Colonel Harold Butcher announced that Corporal Holmes had received a commission in the Imperial Service Corps.

Inns of Court Officer Training Corps

The *Volunteer Training Corps Gazette* for 6 March 1915 reported that a meeting held the previous week at the United Arts Force headquarters, Burlington House, had decided to merge the following corps under the title of Central London Regiment: United Arts, Optimists, Architects, Old Boys and Inns of Court OTC.

Inns of Court Reserve Corps

The *Volunteer Training Corps Gazette* for 20 March 1915 reported that this corps will leave the 'somewhat confined area' of the rectangle in King's Bench Walk for the more spacious ground provided in Arundel Park at Easter. Later became a battalion of the Central London Volunteer Regiment. The four shields from the Inns of Court Arms within a wreath formed the unit's cap badge.

Inverness Volunteer Training Corps

The cap badge worn was a representation of the town arms and motto.

Irish Rugby Football Union Volunteer Corps

The cap badge of this corps (illustrated) features in its centre, a shamrock within a crowned wreath. Mr Steven Hurst writes in *The Bulletin of the Military Historical Society* (No 250, November 2012) that this corps was the first to be raised in Ireland and how the governing body of the Irish Rugby Football Union had invited representatives of the several member clubs to attend a meeting to discuss the formation of a volunteer unit on 10 August 1914 at Lansdowne Road, Dublin. Membership was made open to other sporting clubs and a week after commencement of training on 24 August some 250 were present at an inspection by Lieutenant-Colonel Sir Bryan Mahon. Within a month, some 800 had enrolled.

Irthlingborough Volunteer Training Corps

Irthlingborough, Northamptonshire, lies on the River Nene and formed its Volunteer Corps as a result of a meeting held on Wednesday 2 December 1914. Some 150 of those present at the gathering, including its Chairman, Mr CA Hazeldine, JP, enrolled.

Isle of Wight Volunteer Training Corps

On 12 December 1914 it was reported that at a meeting held on the previous Saturday presided over by Lord Tennyson, it was decided to affiliated all corps on the island to the Central Association of Volunteer Training Corps. The cap badge featured the tower from Carisbrooke Castle.

Islington Rifle Volunteer Force

Mentioned in the *Volunteer Training Corps Gazette* for 18 September 1915.

Islington Volunteer Training Corps

Mentioned in the *Volunteer Training Corps Gazette* for 24 April 1915, this corps had a rifle range in Penton Street. Later became 3rd (Islington) Battalion of the North London Volunteer Regiment.

Ju-Jitsu Volunteer Training Corps

The *Volunteer Training Corps Gazette* for 26 September 1914 reported the formation of this corps, its object being to promote the physical training of volunteers after the Japanese Ju-Jitsu method. Applications for membership were to be sent to the Hon Secretary, Edgar P Rathbone on the third floor of Salisbury House, London Wall, EC2. Salisbury House is close to Circus Place which leads into Finsbury Circus. In the *Gazette* for 6 March 1915, Mr Rathbone pointed out that members enrolled so far were being given Ju-Jitsu instruction by an expert previously employed by the Paris Police who had found his skills very useful when trapping the Apache Indians in America.

Judd School (Tonbridge) Cadet Corps

Recognised 31 December 1917 (Army Order 111 of 1918) and affiliated to the 3rd Kent Volunteer Regiment.

K' Division Defence League

Formed by November 1914 from leading citizens resident at Beddington, Carshalton and Wallinton. Strength before the end of the year stood at 700. Hon Secretary of the League, Mr EH Farr, noted that the corps included many former members of the Regular and Volunteer forces. A disused chalk pit was used as a rifle range and drills were held at various school premises. Headquarters were in the High Street, Carshalton.

Keele Volunteer Training Corps

The north-west Staffordshire parish and village of Keele lies some three miles west-south-west of Newcastle-under-Lyme and it was at the Assembly Rooms there that the Keele Volunteer Training Corps set up its headquarters after formation in the early months of the war. Drills were carried out twice weekly at 7 pm on Mondays and Thursdays, two-hour route marches taking place each Saturday afternoon. Early members of the corps were: Mr JS Scott, who was appointed as captain, Messrs HW Adams and A Chew, who became lieutenants, Colour Sergeant WJ Bates, General Manager at the Silverdale Collieries, and Sergeants E Dix, A Goodwin, R Bloor and H Summerfield. A former member of the Militia, Mr GK Downing, acted as instructor.

Keighley Volunteer Training Corps

A letter from the corps requesting financial aid was read out at a meeting of the Keighley Town Council early in December 1914. It was suggested that one or more of the profit-making concerns, such as the Gas or Tramways Committees, could devote a portion of their profits.

Kensington Athletes' Volunteer Force

The *Volunteer Training Corps Gazette* for 6 March 1915 noted that this corps was an offspring of the Kensington Rifle Club and had been in existence since the beginning of the war. Drills were taking place on Barnes Common.

Kensington Rifle Club

The *Volunteer Training Corps Gazette* for 8 May 1915 mentions that this corps had a rifle range at Fenelon Road, Kensington.

Kensington Volunteer Training Corps

The *Volunteer Training Corps Gazette* for 5 December 1914 noted that the weekly subscription to this corps was sixpence and that two shillings and sixpence was payable upon joining. Drills were carried out each weekday evening at various locations around Notting Hill Gate, including on Mondays the Victoria Memorial Hall, Kensington Place off Church Street near Notting Hill Gate Station. Open-air parades took place on

Saturdays at ground owned by Sir Robert Perks adjoining Kensington Gardens. Rifle practice took place every Monday and Wednesday at a miniature range provided by the Borough Council at Kensington Baths (illustrated), Lancaster Road, Notting Hill. Applicants for membership were invited to contact Mr Arthur J Jacob, c/o London City and Midland Bank, Ltd, 92 High Street, Notting Hill Gate. The shield and motto from the arms of Kensington were used as a cap badge by the Kensington VTC.

Kent Volunteer Fencibles

Had a white metal cap badge which featured the white horse and motto, *Invicta*, of Kent.

Kent Volunteer Regiment

From the county arms, the White Horse and motto *Invicta* formed the regiment's cap badge.

Kettering Volunteer Corps

A bronze badge has been noted to this corps which features crossed keys in the centre of a crowned oval.

Kidderminster Cadet Company

Recognised 13 April 1918 (Army Order 173) and affiliated to the 1st Volunteer Battalion Worcestershire Regiment.

Kilburn Volunteer Reserve

The *Volunteer Training Corps Gazette* for 21 August 1915 reported that through the hospitality of the Kodak Company, the Kilburn Corps of the North London Regiment had spent three days at their premises during the recent Bank Holiday. Corps headquarters are noted as being at Netherwood Street Schools.

Kimbolton Grammar School Cadet Corps

Recognised 8 November 1917 (Army Order 51 of 1918) and affiliated to the 1st Huntingdonshire Volunteer Regiment.

King's Lynn Volunteer Training Corps

A corps at King's Lynn was formed as a result of a meeting called by the Mayor at the beginning of December 1914. Members enrolled at the local Police Station and a Colonel Everard was appointed commandant.

Kingston, Surbiton and District Athletes' Volunteer Force

By the end of 1914 the strength of this Surrey branch of the Athletes' Volunteer Force stood at 269. Mr EC Hartnell was in command, assisted by Mr GF Preston. Hon Secretary of the corps was Mr C Coombes of 21 Queen's Road, Kingston-on-Thames. Drills took place each Saturday and Sunday afternoon and on Mondays, Wednesdays and Fridays.

Kingstown and District Volunteer Corps

The badge of this corps featured the arms of Kingstown in the centre of an eight-pointed crowned star. Kingstown in Ireland reverted to the old Gaelic name of Dun Laoghaire in 1920. Mr Steven Hurst writing in *The Bulletin of the Military Historical Society* (No 250, November 2012) noted that the strength of this corps stood at 60 in November 1915.

Kingswood Training School Cadet Corps

Recognised 18 December 1917 (Army Order 111 0f 1918) and affiliated to the 2nd City of Bristol Volunteer Regiment.

Kingswood Volunteer Corps

Formation was proposed early in 1915. First known as a rifle club, the corps later became part of the 2nd (Coliseum) Battalion Bristol Volunteer Regiment.

Knottingley Civilian Defence Corps

Hon Secretary Arthur Berry wrote in December 1914 that this corps had been formed on 30 October 1914 with a membership of fifty. This was increased to 150 by December. Drills were held in council schools three nights each week, members being required to attend at least eight each month.

Lancashire Volunteers, 1st Battalion

In the VTC section of *Head-dress Badges of the British Army* by Arthur L Kipling and Hugh L King, the authors describe a bronze cap badge to this unit as follows: 'A heart-shaped plate surmounted by a coronet. Below this a shield bearing the Arms of England with a label of three points. On either side a Talbot holding an ostrich feather. Below the shield the Red Rose of Lancaster. Scrolls either side of the Rose inscribed *Lancashire Volunteers*. A further scroll at the base of the design inscribed *1st Battalion 47A*. Sprigs of laurel at both ends of the scroll.'

Lee Defence League

Mentioned in the *Volunteer Training Corps Gazette* for 20 March 1915.

Leeds Volunteer Cadet Battalion

Recognised 1 July 1918 (Army Order 307) and affiliated to the Leeds Group West Riding Volunteers.

Leeds Volunteer Training Corps

The bronze cap badge to this corps featured the arms and motto of Leeds.

Legion of Guides

The *Volunteer Training Corps Gazette* for 10 April 1915 published a letter from TH Pentony, Hon Organising Officer of the North London Squadron Legion of Guides, stating that this organisation was forming mounted squadrons in several London districts. The corps was intended to appeal to any with previous training in a mounted corps or had used horses. Applicants should apply to Mr Pentony at 37 Avondale Avenue, Woodside Park, North London. The issue for 1 May 1915 includes a letter from TH Pentony, now Hon Organising Officer North London ('A') Squadron, Legion of Guides, stating that headquarters had been secured at Wellington Hall, St John's Wood, North West London.

Leicester Citizens Training League

A round enamel lapel badge exists to this corps which has the initials 'LCTL' in the centre. Perched on the top of the circle is the dragon from the Leicester arms.

Lewes Volunteer Training Corps

Formed in December 1914 after a meeting held at the Town Hall. The Mayor of Lewes, Councillor TG Roberts, was elected as chairman, Captain Selby Ash of the Royal Navy, vice chairman, Mr DH Evans, secretary and Mr Edmund White, treasurer.

Lewisham and Forest Hill Volunteers

The *Volunteer Training Corps Gazette* for 16 October 1915 refers to the Lewisham and Forest Hill Battalion South London Regiment Volunteers. It states that the corps was formed in the first week of the war from the overflow of the Lewisham National Reserve.

Lewisham Defence League

Formed 8 October 1914 by Mr HE Hollay of 1 Ardoch Road, Catford. In four weeks, over 1,000 men from the London borough had enrolled, he reported to the *Gazette,* the volunteers drilling regular in eighteen different locations throughout the area. Those associated with the early development of the league included Major Sir Edward Coates, MP, the Mayor of Lewisham, who acted as president, Lieutenant-Colonel BW Pigott, commanding officer, and Alderman R Gordon Brew, JP. Headquarters were at Lewisham Town Hall. Under the heading of 'Borough of Lewisham Defence League', the *Volunteer Training Corps Gazette* reported that a recent resolution had been passed by this corps to the effect that a strong protest should be made against the rules laid down by the War Office for the recognition of Volunteer Associations for National Defence. A circular, enamelled, lapel badge exists which displays the arms of Lewisham in its centre.

Lewisham Volunteer Training Corps

The *Volunteer Training Corps Gazette* for 5 December 1914 recorded that the Lewisham Civilian National Reserve had been formed early in August and was then in possession of a headquarters provided by the African Bank's Cricket Club—many employees of the bank were its first recruits. Total enrolled, about 350, those joining being made honorary members of the Lewisham Battalion National Reserve, along with the use of its club and range. Permission had also been obtained to use the 20th London Regiment's Drill Hall at Holy Hedge House, Blackheath for parades and drills. An annual subscription of four shillings was set. The *Gazette* for 20 March 1915 reported that the corps has changed its title to Lewisham Volunteer Training Corps.

Leyton and Leytonstone Volunteers

The *Volunteer Training Corps Gazette* for 9 October 1915 reported that this corps had published its first monthly magazine under the name of the *Leyton and Leytonstone Volunteer Gazette*. The same issue mentions that the corps is now the 11th Battalion Essex Volunteer Regiment.

Leytonstone National Volunteer Reserve

The *Volunteer Training Corps Gazette* for 17 April 1915 reported that a 'spy from this corps' had been arrested by the guard during a recent camp held at Foxbarrow Farm, Hainault Forest by the Wanstead Volunteer Reserve, Woodford Volunteer Training Corps and South London Battalion National Volunteer Reserve. A surprise night attack by Leytonstone followed.

Lincoln Cadet Battalion, 4th

Recognised 19 July 1918 (Army Order 307) and affiliated to the 4th Volunteer Battalion Lincolnshire Volunteer Regiment.

Lincoln Unit Volunteer Training Corps

Formed within days of war being declared and was soon noted as drilling three to five evenings each week. Colonel JG Williams was elected as chairman, Mr JG Parsons, secretary. Membership, which included the Dean of Lincoln, stood at almost 400 by the end of 1914.

Liverpool Athletes' Volunteer Force

By the end of November 1914 the strength of this corps stood at more than 300 members. Drills were taking place on Tuesdays and Thursdays at the Corn Exchange, on Wednesdays and Thursdays at St Francis Xavier's College Hall in Salisbury Street and on Saturdays at the College Grounds in Shaw Street. A company was in the course of formation at Garston. Chairman of the corps was J McKenna, President of the English Football League. Other Committee members included Charles E Pugh (Chairman of the National Cyclist Union Champions Committee), Charles E Snowdon (President of the Northern Swimming Association), AG Nicholson (President of the Northern Cross Country Association), the English Channel swimmer Ted Heaton, JA Dean of the Boxing Association and the Liverpool footballer JS Gomersall.

Liverpool Training Corps

Formed by November 1914 with Mr WP Withered elected as secretary.

Liverpool Volunteer Guard

The cap badge of this corps featured, upon an eight-pointed star, the Liver Bird of Liverpool.

Liverymen and Freemen of the City of London Volunteers

A meeting was held in December 1914 to consider the formation of a corps made up exclusively of Liverymen and Freemen of the City of London. Colonel Sir W Dunn presided and was elected as president.

Llandaff and Ely Drill and Rifle Club

Formed in September 1914, the strength of this Glamorgan, South Wales corps stood at 130 by the end of November. Mr W Davies was appointed as commandant, Alderman Illtydd Thomas, JP, chairman, Mr EU David, JP, treasurer, Mr JH Thomas of Pentwyn, secretary. Headquarters were at the Parish Hall, Ely.

London Chamber of Commerce

The *Volunteer Training Corps Gazette* for 12 December 1914 reported a recent meeting held by the Naval and Military Defence Committee of the London Chamber of Commerce.

London County and Westminster Bank Volunteer Training Corps

The *Volunteer Training Corps Gazette* for 27 May 1916 reported that in the early days of the war the staff of the bank flocked to join the VTC. Many have since joined the army resulting in a decline in numbers. Therefore it has been decided to amalgamate 'A' (LC and W Bank) Company with 'B' (Old Whitgiftians) Company of the 2/1st (Croydon) Battalion Surrey Volunteer Regiment, 'A' Company to become No8 Platoon of 'B' Company.

London County Council Staff Volunteer Training Corps

Mr TF Hobson, a former member of the Inns of Court Volunteers, was appointed as commandant. Drills were held in the basement of County Hall on the south side of Westminster Bridge (illustrated). The *Volunteer Training Corps Gazette* for 10 April 1915 reported that this corps, which is made up of LCC employees, is

making good progress and it is hoped before long to make up a complete battalion of 1,000. The *Gazette* for 27 May 1916 stated that the corps had been amalgamated with the Architects' Corps to form the 4th Battalion Central London Volunteer Regiment and is now linked up with the Engineering Institutions Volunteer Engineer Corps to form the 1st London Engineer Volunteers. The services of the new corps have been offered to the King as a corps of twenty officers and 479 NCOs and men, containing as it does numerous professional surveyors, electrical and mining engineers. Headquarters were at Chester House, Eccleston Place, SW.

London Volunteer Regiment, 1st Cadet Battalion 10th Battalion

Recognised 6 May 1918 (Army Order 209).

London Volunteer Regiment, 1st Cadet Battalion 14th Battalion

Recognised 6 December 1917 (Army Order 149 of 1918).

London Volunteer Regiment, 1st Cadet Battalion 15th Battalion

Recognised 7 February 1918 (Army Order 149).

London Volunteer Regiment, 2nd Cadet Battalion 15th Battalion

Recognised 24 April 1918 (Army Order 209).

London Volunteer Regiment, 1st Cadet Battalion 17th Battalion

Recognised 6 March 1918 (Army Order 173).

London Volunteer Regiment Cadet Corps, 20th Battalion

Recognised 7 December 1917 (Army Order 111 of 1918).

London Volunteer Rifles

A bugle-horn with a lion carrying a banner on which are inscribed the letters LVR set within its strings features as the unit's cap badge.

London Wall Volunteer Training Corps

The *Volunteer Training Corps Gazette* for 9 January 1915 included a letter from a Mr RF Henderson of the London Wall Corps.

Longhope Civil Volunteer Corps

Mentioned in the *Gloucestershire Journal* on 6 February 1915 as having been formed.

Lord Mayor's Own (Bristol) Cadet Corps

Recognised 18 March 1918 and affiliated to the 1st City of Bristol Volunteer Regiment.

Louth Volunteer Training Corps

Mr Steven Hurst writing in *The Bulletin of the Military Historical Society* (No 250, November 2012) noted that the strength of this Irish corps stood at 70 in November 1915.

Ludham Home Defence Corps

A meeting was held on 2 December 1914 at the Church Room, Ludham in Norfolk to discuss the formation at Ludham of a detachment of the Home Defence Corps. Mr W England proposed that recruiting for the corps should also include the neighbouring villages of Horning and Potter Heigham. This was seconded by the Rev GAB Boycott. On the subject of a rifle range, Mr Kirby England said he was willing to provide a site, the vicar at the same time offering a spotting telescope and waterproof ground sheet. Some thirty enrolled at the meeting, Mr G Hayhurst being appointed as secretary, and former veteran of the war in South Africa, Mr Haningham, drill instructor. Drills were held in the Church Room.

Lydney Volunteer Training Corps

The *Gloucestershire Journal* for 19 May 1915 reported the formation of this corps.

Lynton and Lynmouth Volunteer Training Corps

A photograph (illustrated) exists to this corps dated February 1916. Only the two officers seated at the front have uniform, the image also showing GR armbands and lapel badges being worn and several men with dummy wooden rifles.

Lytham Volunteer Training Corps

Crossed rifle, the letters VTC and the date 1915 featured on the cap badge.

Macclesfield Citizens Defence League

The centre of an enamel lapel badge worn by the corps displays the lion and garb from the town's arms.

Maidenhead Town Cadet Company

Recognised 3 May 1918 (Army Order 209) and affiliated to the 1st Battalion Berkshire Volunteer Regiment.

Maldon Grammar School Cadet Corps

Recognised 14 November 1917 (Army Order 51 of 1918) and affiliated to the 1/2nd Essex Volunteer Regiment.

Malmesbury Volunteer Training Corps

Answering the call for volunteers, the Wiltshire market town of Malmesbury in the southern Cotswolds called a meeting to discuss the matter at the Council Chamber on 10 March 1915. Here it was

overwhelmingly decided to go ahead with the formation of a volunteer corps, Mr FGT Goldstone being appointed as company commander, the names of the mayor and several councillors being among those appearing on the first muster roll. Cap Badge: Upon crossed rakes and surmounted by a crown, a barrel with crescent moon below. At the base, a scroll inscribed Malmesbury VTC. In bronze, the badge reflects that old Wiltshire legend of before 1787, the Moonrakers. In possession of several barrels of smuggled French brandy, and to defeat the customs men, some local people hid their contraband in the village pond. Caught while trying to retrieve one of the barrels at night, the excuse given was that they were in fact raking in a round of cheese. The cheese was the moon's reflection in the water.

Manchester Athletes' Volunteer Corps

A circular enamel lapel badge exists with this title. In its centre crossed rifles and the words Ready For The Call.

Manchester Volunteer Regiment

The cap badge of the regiment included crossed rifles, the Lancashire Rose and the arms and motto of the City of Manchester. An enamelled lapel badge is illustrated.

Manchester Volunteer Defence Corps and Rifle Club

This corps, which had been formed by November 1914 with Mr FW Wood of 62 Market Street as Hon Secretary, confined its membership to Manchester businessmen. The *Volunteer Training Corps Gazette* for 26 December 1914 reported that the corps had held a smoking concert at the Balmoral Café in Deansgate and that organiser of the corps, Captain F Oldfield announced that membership then stood at 2,100, the majority being manufacturers, agents, clerks etc in the drapery trade. Some 400 had been passed on to HM Forces. An enamel lapel badge exists showing in its centre a soldier carrying a rifle.

Manchester Volunteer Regiment

The arms of Manchester featured in an oval enamel lapel badge to this corps. The title of the regiment appears around the edge together with the date 1915. The same device was also used in the cap badge, crossed rifles being placed behind.

Mangotsfield and District Home Defence Corps

Daniel Brinson in his book *Military Insignia of Gloucestershire* notes how this corps was formed in February 1915 and by the following month had changed its name to Mangotsfield and District Volunteer Training Corps. He also notes how in June 1915 the unit had become No 13 Platoon 2nd (Coliseum) Battalion Bristol Volunteer Regiment.

Mansfield Woodhouse Athletes' Volunteer Force

Hon Secretary of the corps, Mr Albert Dennett of Park Road, Mansfield Woodhouse, reported in December 1914 that the company then stood at eighty members and that to date some thirty-two had already joined Kitchener's New Army. Drills were taking place regularly on Tuesdays and Thursdays in the Drill Hall belonging to the 8th Sherwood Foresters, shooting outdoors on Wednesday and Saturday afternoons.

Market Drayton

A corps at Market Drayton comprising some 150 members was formed under the command of Colonel Francis Randle Twemlow, DSO by November 1914. Colonel Twemlow, of the 4th North Staffordshire Regiment, was awarded his DSO while serving in the South African War.

Metropolitan Railway Volunteer Training Corps

Formed from employees of the Metropolitan Railway and numbered some 500 by the end of November 1914. Drills were held on the company's land at Wembley, Mr Oliver Onions, the well-known novelist, being a private in the ranks.

Metropolitan Water Board Volunteer Training Corps

Kipling and King describe the bronze cap badge worn by the corps as follows: 'A circlet inscribed *Metropolitan Water Board 1914* surmounted by a scalloped border. A scroll above the circlet inscribed *Volunteer* and a two-part scroll below the circlet inscribed *Training Corps*. In the centre a female figure with a pitcher in her right hand and a watering pot in her left hand. Water gushes from a rock on the right and flows before the female figure. Top left, the Houses of Parliament and, top right, St Paul's Cathedral.'

Middlesbrough and District Tradesmen's Emergency Training Corps

Commenced drill on 30 September 1914, the membership consisting of men engaged in retail shop work. The corps began with sixty members, some 200 being on the roll by the end of 1914. A shilling entrance fee was charged, and a minimum of 3d weekly subscription went towards paying for the hire of a drill hall and instructor.

Middlesbrough Volunteer Force

There exists an oval enamelled lapel badge with this title together with the date 1914. In the centre of the badge, a soldier with rifle standing at ease.

Middlesex Volunteer Regiment

A shield charged with the arms of the county featured in the regiment's cap badge.

Mill Hill Volunteer Training Corps

This north-west London corps attended a church parade held by the Rev St John Corbett at St Paul's Church, Mill Hill on Sunday 6 December 1914.

Milton and District Volunteer Training Corps

At a meeting held in the Church School, Milton, Staffordshire on 30 November 1914, Colonel AH Heath and Dr RH Read reported on the progress that had been made. A committee had been formed and an application had been put in for membership of the Central Association of Volunteer Training Corps. Also present were Mr Albert Moss (chairman) and the vicar of St Phillip and St James's Church, the Rev J Carnegie.

Mitcham Town Guard

An enamelled lapel badge to this corps has the date 1914 and the Union flag.

Mobile Volunteer Corps

Daniel Brinson in his book on Gloucestershire insignia mentions this unit as having been formed in July 1915.

Mortlake, East Sheen & Barnes Volunteer Training Corps

The *Volunteer Training Corps Gazette* for 12 December 1914 reported the existence of this corps under the title of Mortlake and East Sheen Rifle Club Defence Corps. Started at the outbreak of war, its original membership had been provided from within the Rifle Club but was later drawn from the district as a whole. There exists a gilt and blue enamel oval lapel badge bearing the title Mortlake, East Sheen & Barnes Volunteer Training Corps. All three of the areas are to the north of Richmond Park: Mortlake (SW14) and Barnes (SW13), both skirting the Thames, East Sheen (SW14), the park itself.

Mount's Bay Volunteer Training Corps

A circular black and gilt enamel lapel badge exists to this corps which has the title around the edge and the shield from the Cornwall county arms in the centre.

Music Trade Volunteer Training Corps

The *Volunteer Training Corps Gazette* for 26 December 1914 noted that at a meeting held on the previous 15 December it had been decided to form a corps for the Music Trade. A large number of men joined at once, reports the *Gazette,* temporary headquarters being set up at the Allison Piano Factory, Leighton Road, Kentish Town, NW. Mr JA Murdoch was appointed as acting secretary.

Muswell Hill, East Finchley and District Training Corps

This North London corps was mentioned in the *Volunteer Training Corps Gazette* for 5 December 1914 which informed that applicants wishing to join should apply to Headquarters at The Athenaeum, Muswell Hill, the Hon Secretary being Mr Frederick H Stafford of 25 Lynmouth Road, East Finchley. The Athenaeum, a kind of meeting place where literature was taught and discussed, was in Fortis Green Road. In the issue for 9 January 1915, it was reported that the corps had been involved in a sham fight on Boxing Day, some 300 turning out. The operations were under the command of Mr RT Lawlor and the company then included a motor cycle section, signallers, an ambulance corps and transport wagons. The corps later marched from High Barnet to Arkley. The Athenaeum was a public hall built in Fortis Green Road, Muswell Hill by James Edmondson and is now a branch of Sainsbury's. There exists a circular, enamelled, lapel badge to this corps which has Muswell Hill East Finchley & District on a blue outer band, and Training Corps on a red centre. Muswell Hill and East Finchley are both North London suburbs.

Nantwich Cadet Corps

Recognised 23 November 1917 (Army Order 51 of 1918) and affiliated to the 4th Battalion Cheshire Volunteer Regiment.

National Motor Volunteers

The *Volunteer Training Corps Gazette* for 22 January 1916 reported that the motor ambulance recently purchased by the No1 (London) Battalion was inspected on Thursday 13 January by Lord Desborough. The ambulance, a Vulcan, was the very latest model, noted the *Gazette*. The issue for 11 March 1916 noted that the 1st London Battalion was over 100 strong and had covered 5,000 miles in their duties, which included taking hospital patients in London to convalescent homes and hospitals outside the capital. Wounded troops were also taken on pleasure rides to the country and on visits to theatres and other entertainments. Headquarters were at the Connaught Rooms in Great Queen Street, WC. The cap badge of the unit featured the figure of Mercury in the centre of a wheel and the motto *Pro patria*.

Naval Home Defence Corps

The *Volunteer Training Corps Gazette* for 30 January 1915 reported that a Naval Home Service Defence Corps has been formed at Greenwich for the purpose of training men along naval lines for home defence.

New Barnet and District Volunteer Training Corps

The *Volunteer Training Corps Gazette* for 8 May 1915 reported that this corps had been inspected by Major Winton Seton, Chief Recruiting Officer for Watford, on Thursday 8 April.

New Forest Coast Volunteers

This corps had a bronze cap badge comprising a crowned bugle horn in the centre of which was a stag and the date 1915.

New Mosten Civic Guard

A crowned oval enamel lapel badge exists which has the Union flag in the centre and crossed rifles behind. New Mosten, a district within the City of Manchester.

Newbury Volunteer Training Corps

Newbury Castle, which once stood a siege during the reign of Stephen and figures in the town's seal, featured in the badges of this Berkshire corps.

Newcastle-upon-Tyne Volunteer Training Corps

The *Bulletin of the Military Historical Society* for February 1983 includes a fine photograph of Alderman John Fitzgerald, Lord Mayor of Newcastle, as regimental commander. Supplied by Mr Andrew Gavaghan, the image was taken on the occasion of a visit to Tyneside by HM King George V in June 1915 and shows the colonel wearing the GR armband and cap and collar badges of the city arms. Irish-born John Fitzgerald was a brewer and wine merchant who was knighted in 1920. The Sir John Fitzgerald pub chain bears his name.

Newport Rifle Club

On 12 December 1914 Mr F J Webb, from the club's headquarters at the Cattle Market, Newport, Monmouthshire wrote how the Newport Rifle Club had been inaugurated by a meeting of about fifty persons called together on the previous 14 September. The purpose of the club, notes Mr Webb, was 'to give the opportunity to those who are not eligible to join any of the military forces of the Crown of becoming proficient in rifle shooting and elementary drill in case their services should at any time be required by the county.' A committee was elected, who drew up rules and regulations, and a public meeting was called at

the Town Hall in Commercial Street on the 30 September at which about 160 joined as members. Over 600 had enrolled by the end of 1914. Drills were held on two afternoons and two evenings each week, an indoor range being open for use by members every day.

Newton Abbot Volunteer Defence Force

The decision to form a corps at Newton Abbot in Devon was taken at a meeting held in the Town Hall on 29 October 1914. Over 100 men enrolled, some 123 being present at the first parade held on 13 November. The Town Council gave its permission to use the Butter Market (illustrated) for indoor drill, Newton College allowing use of its football field for outdoor parades. In charge of recruiting was Mr EB Wylie, the secretary, a Mr James R Cull, Jun.

Newtown County School Cadet Unit

Recognised 11 December 1917 (Army Order 111 of 1918) and affiliated to the 1st Battalion Montgomeryshire Volunteer Regiment.

Norfolk Volunteer Cadet Corps, 1st

Recognised 27 March 1918 (Army Order 173) and affiliated to the 1st Volunteer Battalion Norfolk Regiment.

North City (Dublin) Volunteer Training Corps

Mr Steven Hurst writes in *The Bulletin of the Military Historical Society* (No 250, November 2012) that the strength of this corps stood at 64 in November 1915.

North Down Volunteer Training Corps

Mentioned by Mr Steven Hurst in his article on Irish Volunteers (*The Bulletin of the Military Historical Society*, No 250, November 2012).

North East Lancashire Volunteer Regiment

The regiment wore the same badge as the 1st Battalion Lancashire Volunteers but with the bottom scroll reading N.E. Lanc Vol Regt.

North London Battalion National Volunteer Reserve

It was reported that 150 men under their Commanding Officer, F. Crisp had recently attended camp at Foxbarrow Farm, Hainault Forest. The *Volunteer Training Corps Gazette* noted that this battalion was from Norwood, Streatham and Clapham,

North London Volunteer Regiment

The *Volunteer Training Corps Gazette* for 22 May 1915 reported that the regiment had held its first Regimental parade at Tufnell Park Athletic Ground on Saturday 15 May. The issue for 21 August 1915 also noted that the Kilburn Volunteer Reserve is part of the regiment. The issue for 25 March 1916 gave the regiment's organisation as: 1st Battalion (Hampstead), 2nd (St Pancras), 3rd (Islington), 4th (Stoke Newington), 5th (Hackney). The Hampstead Volunteer Reserve forms part of the 1st Battalion. The issue also notes that the regiment is made up almost entirely of 'hard working businessmen'.

North London Unit (Hackney) Athletes' Volunteer Force

The *Volunteer Training Corps Gazette* for 6 March 1915 reported that this unit is making steady progress and that drills were being held at headquarters at the Orion Gymnasium in Casterton Street, to the rear of the Hackney Empire. Commanding Officer is given as Captain GT Lewis of the Honourable Artillery Company. The issue for 24 April noted headquarters as the National Reserve Club, 92 Stamford Hill.

North London Volunteer Regiment

The Hackney Athletes' Volunteer Force formed part of the 5th Battalion of this regiment. The 2nd Battalion was at St Pancras, Stoke Newington forming the 4th.

North Riding Volunteer Regiment, 2/1st Battalion Cadet Company

Recognised 1 January 1918 (Army Order 149).

North Riding Volunteer Regiment, 2nd Battalion Cadet Company

Recognised 13 December 1917 (Army Order 111 of 1918).

North Riding Volunteer Regiment, 1/3rd Battalion Cadet Company

Recognised 22 May 1918 (Army Order 209).

North Riding Volunteer Regiment, 2/3rd Battalion Cadet Company

Recognised 25 February 1918 (Army Order 149).

North Riding Volunteer Regiment, 4th Battalion Cadet Company

Recognised 24 November 1917 (Army Order 149 of 1918).

North Staffordshire Regiment, 1st Cadet Battalion 1st Volunteer Battalion

Recognised 4 May 1918 (Army Order 373).

Northallerton Volunteer Training Corps

The decision to form a VTC unit at Northallerton in Yorkshire was taken at a meeting held in the town on Tuesday 1 December 1914. Mr J Hutton, Chairman of the North Riding of Yorkshire County Council, took charge of the proceedings and in a stirring address encouraged many from Northallerton and the surrounding area to enrol. For help and guidance in military matters, two former Volunteers of the Victorian period, and in 1914 both members of the local Territorial Force (4th Battalion, Yorkshire Regiment), Colonel AF Godman, CB, VD and Captain GJE Gardner were appointed as military advisors. Sir Hugh Bell was elected as president, Mr EEL Ringrose, treasurer and Mr AW Berry, secretary.

Northampton Citizen Corps

A bronze cap badge exists to this corps which features the arms and motto of Northampton.

Northbourne Volunteer Training Corps

The idea of Mr Aubrey Waterfield, the Northbourne in Kent VTC was formed as a result of a meeting held at a local school on 28 January 1915. Forming a platoon of 'A' Company of the Cinque Ports Battalion, regular parades were carried out, the *Deal, Walmer and Sandwich Mercury* for 28 August 1915 reporting the corps at Eastry where they were drilling on Cooper's Meadow. Mr Frederick LH Morrice was appointed as platoon commander, Walter Henry James (Lord Northbourne) replacing him after his death in 1915. Other members included Quartermaster William R Burgess, Ernest Mackney, who was a miller, William Moat, landlord of the Hare and Hounds, and the headmaster of Northbourne School, Frederick E Green who acted as bandmaster.

Northern Polytechnic Institute Volunteer Training Corps

Situated in Holloway Road, London, the Northern Polytechnic Institute suspended its gymnastic class within days of war being declared and instead formed an infantry company providing military training to those unable to join the Regular or Territorial Forces. The Commanding Officer, David M Nelson, reported in December 1914 that drills were taking place each Monday, Wednesday and Thursday evening at the institute, weekends at Tufnell Park north-east of Kentish Town. A silver band from that area was used as a regimental band. The bronze cap badge included crossed rifles and the date 1914.

Northampton Citizen Corps

There exists an enamelled lapel badge with this title, the centre of which displays the arms of Northampton.

Northumberland Volunteer Cadet Brigade

Recognised 3 May 1918 (Army Order 240) and affiliated to the Northumberland Volunteer Regiment.

Norwich Volunteer Training Corps

The *Volunteer Training Corps Gazette* for 26 December 1914 reported that a meeting to discuss the formation of a corps had been held on 4 December at the Agricultural Hall, Norwich. Leader of the Conservative party, Mr Edmund Reeve, moved the motion which was carried unanimously. Mr WE Keefe seconded.

Norwood Company National Volunteer Reserve

The *Volunteer Training Corps Gazette* for 8 May 1915 reported that the Norwood Company is very strong on musketry and that there is a large attendance at the range in the crypt of St Luke's Church three nights a week. The company is part of the South London Battalion, NVR.

Nottingham

The *Volunteer Training Corps Gazette* for 5 December 1914 reported that a most successful meeting had recently been held at Nottingham to form a local corps of volunteers. The idea had been proposed by the City Council, several of whom were elected as committee members.

Nottingham and Nottinghamshire Volunteer Citizen Army

There exists a circular badge inscribed with the words Nottm & Notts Volunteer Citizen Army.

Nottinghamshire Volunteer Regiment

The arms of the county and crossed rifles featured in the regiment's cap badge.

Nunhead Defence League

Mentioned in the *Volunteer Training Corps Gazette* for 20 March 1915.

Oban High School Cadet Corps

Recognised 17 April 1918 (Army Order 173) and affiliated to the 1st Battalion Argyllshire Volunteer Regiment.

Old Boys' Corps

Membership of this corps was strictly confined to old Public School and University men and their friends. No unmarried man under thirty-eight was to be admitted, except those that are ineligible for Regular or Territorial service. The corps is featured in the *Volunteer Training Corps Gazette* for 2 January 1915, the article pointing out that inauguration had taken place at a meeting held at the Hotel Cecil in London on 17 August 1914 and that some 1,800 men had joined from the capital alone. Branches were also formed in Bristol and Chelmsford. Corps headquarters were at 6 Upper Baker Street, NW, administrative offices at 25 Victoria Street, SW, drill and camping facilities at Wembley Park. The first Commandant was Brigadier-General Sir Eric Swayne but having been obliged to resign for War Office work, he was replaced by Colonel SG Grant, lately commanding officer of the Cameronians (Scottish Rifles). Chairman and founder of the corps was HE West Taylor.

The *Gazette* noted that a number of well-known literary men and artists were members: Mr Oliver Onions, the novelist is the camp Quartermaster, and several of the staff of *Punch* are included in the ranks. Also noted was that the Old Boys' Corps had become a sort of Officer Training Corps, it having already sent over 200 men to be commissioned, and that a magazine, the *Old Boys' Magazine*, was available. The *Gazette* for 6 March 1915 reported that a meeting held the previous week at the United Arts Force headquarters, Burlington House had decided to merge the following corps under the title of Central London Regiment: United Arts, Optimists, Architects, Old Boys and Inns of Court OTC. They became 3rd Battalion. There exists two different circular gilt lapel badges, each with the initials 'OBC' in old English lettering, and the motto *Pro Patria*. The bronze cap badge comprised the intertwined letters OBC with crown above and scroll inscribed with the motto below.

Old Dunstonians Volunteer Corps

It was reported in the *Volunteer Training Corps Gazette* for 5 December 1914 that the Old Dunstonians Volunteers were to have been inspected by General Sir O'Moore Creagh, VC and Colonel Ridgeway on the previous Saturday at their grounds at Forest Hill. The event, however, was postponed owing to rain. St Dunstan's College, in Stanstead Road, London SE6, dates from 1446 and was the parish school of the City church of St Dunstan in the East.

Old Tollingtonians Defence Corps

Ernest J Martin illustrates a circular lapel badge to this corps in his 1938 article for the Society of Army Historical Research. The name of the unit is inscribed upon a strap, the centre of the badge having a shield charged with two crossed rifles. Tollington School in Muswell Hill North London was founded in 1879 by William Brown.

Oldbury Volunteer Training Corps

A Staffordshire corps reported in the *Volunteer Training Corps Gazette*.

Oldham Rifle Volunteer League

Hon Secretary Mr Thomas Hayes of 5 Clegg Street, Oldham, reported in the *Volunteer Training Corps Gazette* for 12 December 1914 how the Oldham Rifle Volunteer League, being the Oldham branch of the Athletes' Volunteer Force, had been formed on 8 September 1914, the membership being then nineteen. Some 550 had joined by the end of 1914. The Mayor of Oldham was appointed as president and leading corporation officials—the Borough Treasurer acted as Treasurer—became officers. Commandant of the league was Colonel Harries-Jones, late of the 6th Volunteer Battalion Manchester Regiment, and the officers and instructors were appointed by the commandant. Members had the free use of the Armoury for about an hour and a half every night except Saturday, and for a small fee the corporation allowed the league the use of a well-equipped gymnasium at a local council school. Recruits went first to the gymnasium, where they put in ten drills, and had to be passed as reasonably efficient before they can go forward to the Armoury to join one of the companies. Each company had two specified drill nights per week, and on Friday the whole battalion drilled together exclusive of raw recruits. Members who qualified themselves were taken forward for musketry drill. Service rifles were lent by the Oldham Comrades Battalion. Mr Hayes pointed out that the league had no uniform and that amongst its members were representatives of all grades of social life in the district.

Optimists' National Corps

The *Volunteer Training Corps Gazette* for 12 December 1914 featured the corps in an article based on an interview held at the Kingsway office of its founder, London businessman Mr CF Higham. Regarding the title of the corps, Mr Higham pointed out that the Optimists' Club, from which the corps was started, is an organisation which exists for the purpose of creating a better spirit in business. The Optimists' National Corps was formed about the middle of August 1914 and by December totalled 1,500 members—all business and professional men. Headquarters were at 26 Pancras Road, King's Cross—the premises formally known as the German Gymnasium (illustrated) and closed by the War Office at the beginning of the war.

Drills took place here on most days, outdoor parades being at the Botanical Gardens on Parliament Hill and on ground at Ealing. Musketry was under the instruction of acting Lieutenant Jack Manley. Members paid an entrance fee of ten shillings and sixpence. Built in 1864-65, the German Gymnasium was the first purpose-built gymnasium in England. It is now a restaurant.

Mr Higham noted that as the men were in uniform—a khaki fatigue suit with brown buttons and O.N.C. on the shoulder—they were able to give valuable assistance to the Chief Recruiting Officer by transporting recruits from one point in London to another. For this purpose, members providing their own vehicles had been formed into a transport section. A guard of honour was also provided on the occasion of the opening by Mrs Winston Churchill of St Martha's Hall in Cirencester Street, Paddington, where many of the Westlake family were born and brought up.

Of the several sections that had been formed by the Optimists, Mr Higham pointed out that the engineering section was made up of London's leading electrical and general engineers, at least nine well known physicians were members of the ambulance group. General Sir O'Moore Creagh, VC was colonel-in-chief.

There exists a brass badge consisting of the letters ONC above a large letter V. Ernest J Martin states in his 1938 article for the Society of Army Historical Research that the item was used as a cap badge for all ranks, and as a shoulder title by other ranks.

Orpington, Crays and District Rifle Club

Hon Secretary Mr G Livermore wrote in the *Volunteer Training Corps Gazette* for 12 December 1914 that the formation of a Home Defence League under the title Orpington, Crays and District Rifle Club was the outcome of a public meeting held at Orpington in the middle of the previous August. A provisional committee was appointed, and the club was placed under the command of Dr A Tennyson Smith, late Officer Commanding 'K' Company 4th Battalion Royal West Kent Regiment. Enough drill instructors were forthcoming from among the members who, after being brought up-to-date under the OC's guidance, were placed in charge of recruit drills. Members were divided into squads according to locality, and drilling under the instructors began on 1 September. An indoor miniature range in the Village Hall, Orpington was made available, but the hall was later taken over by the British Red Cross Society as a military hospital (Dr A Tennyson Smith being its commandant).

A range of twenty-five yards was opened formally on 14 November by Colonel Schletter, CB, and regular shooting took place two days each week and on Sundays. Dr Tennyson Smith was joined by Mr J Hayter Crickmay, late of the London Rifle Brigade, as second in command. Membership of the club stood at more than 100 by the end of 1914. 'Crays' in the title of the unit is presumably the area of the Cray Valley, or perhaps a reference to one or all of the five towns or villages bearing the name of the river: St Mary Cray, St Paul's Cray, Foots Cray, North Cray and Crayford. Hon Secretary Livingstone's reference to Dr Tennyson Smith having previously been in command on 'K' Company 4th Royal West Kent Regiment is inaccurate in as much as there was no such company in that battalion. Possibly he means 'F' Company, the headquarters of which were at Orpington.

Ossett and Horbury Volunteer Training Corps

Volunteers from these wool-producing West Yorkshire towns were required to be between the ages of thirty-eight and fifty. The men drilled in Ossett Town Hall and at various Council Schools and carried out musketry on land belonging to Mr Robert Reid of Horbury.

Oswestry Volunteer Training Corps

The *Volunteer Training Corps Gazette* for 26 December 1914 reported that Lord Harlech was to be commandant of the corps and is placing a miniature rifle range at its disposal.

Oxfordshire Volunteer Regiment

The cap badge of the regiment featured the ox crossing a ford from the Oxford arms.

Oxford Volunteer Training Corps

Member, Mr AD Godley of 27 Norham Road, Oxford, wrote on 12 December 1914 how the Oxford Volunteer Training Corps had first developed in the previous August. Much help and guidance, he noted, had been forthcoming from former Regular and Territorial Army NCOs and members of the Oxford University OTC. At the time of Mr Godley's letter, some 400 had enrolled, the corps being incorporated as one company with the Central Association in September 1914. A second was begun before the end of the year. The *Volunteer Training Corps Gazette* for 26 December 1914 noted that distinguished member of the university, Mr AD Godley, was commanding officer. In the ranks were Poet Laureate Robert Bridges and Professor Sir Gilbert Murray. The corps was known as 'Godley's Own', and sometimes among the undergraduates as the 'Ungodly'.

Paddington Volunteer Training Corps

The *Volunteer Training Corps Gazette* for 5 December 1914 reported that the Borough of Paddington was one of the first in London to recognise the importance of local volunteer defence. The first public meeting to be held with a view to forming a corps was convened by the Mayor, Alderman HG Handover, JP. Also present was the Duke of Devonshire. The same issue records an enrolled strength of 500, all of them undertaking regular drills and musketry practice—the corps had use of the Wedlake Public Baths in Kensal Road (illustrated) which had been opened in 1898. The use of fifty dummy rifles, on loan from the North Paddington Boys' Club, was reported (*Gazette,* 6 March 1915) as being in use for drills. Headquarters were at the 3rd London Regiment's Paddington Detachment Drill Hall at 207 Harrow Road—a property that had been taken over by the Victorian Volunteer Force in 1895. Commanding the corps was Colonel HS Sankey, VD, formally of the Inns of Court OTC.

A further report on the Paddington VTC appears in the *Gazette* for 30 January 1915 and this notes that a recent Saturday route march did not confine itself to the streets of the borough, marching as it did from Edgware Road via St John's Wood Road and Finchley Road to Hampstead Heath and returning through Kilburn. In the same evening, a recruiting concert had taken place at headquarters. Next day, a church parade was held at St Stephen's, Westbourne Park Road during which the vicar mentioned, with regard to the corps, that good progress was being made and that fifty rifles of 'an obsolete pattern' had been obtained.

There exists an oval enamel lapel badge showing the arms of Paddington and the title of the corps which became part of the West London Volunteer Regiment. For this author, fond memories of Wedlake Baths where I did not learn to swim but took regulars baths on Sunday mornings, the North Paddington Boys' Club, where I regularly played in a band on its stage and once found one of the dummy rifles mentioned, and the drill hall at 207 Harrow Road where, as a cadet, much was learnt about army life.

Palmers Green Civic Guard

See Southgate Training Corps.

Peckham Defence League

Mentioned in the *Volunteer Training Corps Gazette* for 20 March 1915.

Penrith Cadet Company

Recognised 23 September 1917 (Army Order 360) and affiliated to the 1/1st Cumberland Volunteer Regiment.

Pershore and Cropthorne Cadet Company

Recognised 20 October 1917 (Army Order 51 of 1918) and affiliated to the 2nd Battalion Worcestershire Volunteer Regiment.

Perthshire Volunteers

The badge worn was a five-pointed star within a circle inscribed with the title of the unit and the date 1916.

Peterborough Volunteer Training Corps

The *Volunteer Training Corps Gazette* for 5 December 1914 reported that a corps was in the process of formation at Peterborough and that those interested should contact a Mr RF Sergeant.

Pharmacist Volunteer Training Corps

At first the pharmacist, who naturally wished to serve in a capacity most allied to his craft, joined the various ambulance sections then being formed throughout the VTC. On 18 July, 1915, however, a meeting was called by the London Pharmaceutical Association to discuss the possibilities of forming a unit made up entirely of pharmacists. At this gathering, which met at 17 Bloomsbury Square, London, almost all of the eighty men present signed the roll and were to become the first members of the Pharmacists Volunteer Training Corps (PVTC), their intentions being to provide a company trained in sanitation, ambulance work, chemistry and analysis. It was unanimously agreed to form a company that could be placed at the disposal of whatever army medical unit required its services. Shortly after formation, the PVTC was attached to the Central London Volunteer Regiment which contained the 1st to 4th Battalions of the County of London VTC, London being quick off the mark in organising its many thousands of volunteers into large, well trained, and efficient regiments. This, however, and according to the PVTC's first commanding officer, Captain E A Atkins was 'the initial mistake of the Volunteer Association.'

Captain Atkins felt that the fullest benefit from the PVTC would have been derived had it been enrolled as the Sanitary Company for the whole of the County of London. 'As part of one regiment', he wrote, 'its scope for work was limited and this prevented both the development of the Corps, and probably a bigger recognition to pharmaceutical services in the British Army.'

Soon in uniform, the PVTC was to adopt its own special cap badge, this being designed jointly by the CO and paymaster and comprising two retorts surmounted by a mortar and pestle. Below this, and on a scroll, the motto adopted by the corps: Scientia Vincit (Knowledge Wins). There was also a brass shoulder title worn on the green-grey uniform made up of the curved word Pharmacists over the letters VTC.

Headquarters of the PVTC were set up at 17 Bloomsbury Square and its first drills held in the quadrangle belonging to the Prudential Assurance Company building in High Holborn, the services of Quartermaster Sergeant Luke of the 2nd London Sanitary Company (Territorial Force) as drill instructor and lecturer on sanitation having been obtained.

Drills and lectures were held on Sundays and the following extract from the *Pharmaceutical Journal* dated 8 July, 1916 gives indication of the type of training given: 'The company orders for Sunday, July 9, indicate a busy day for the members at their usual rendezvous at Millbank Schools. To start with, all NCOs are required to attend the staff parade at 9.30am. At 10am there is a sergeant-major's parade for squad drill and an officers' meeting in the orderly room. 11am senior sections clean rifles, while recruits receive squad drill.' The item goes on to say that a 'sanitation lecture for recruits' would be held at 12.15pm.

Before moving to Millbank, the PVTC had found a home at the Wesleyan Training College, the premises at the Prudential having proved to be too small. In August, 1916, however, Millbank Schools were taken over by the Australian Army authorities and as a result the PVTC were once again on the move, this time, but only after several weeks without a home, to the Duke of York's Headquarters in King's Road, Chelsea. Here rooms and the use of the parade ground were found.

Although there were few restrictions as to who or what organisation could form a Volunteer Corps, there were, however, many requirements that had to be met if official War Office recognition was to be obtained. At the beginning of 1917, and despite the fact that the PVTC was increasing in numbers and efficiency, recognition by the Government had not been forthcoming. Almost all members were by this time proficient and had actually received the Central Association proficiency badge. The Pharmacists were, to quote Quartermaster H A Mills '...fed up with the Government's constant refusal to recognise the PVTC as part of His Majesty's Forces.'

As a desperate attempt to prove themselves to the authorities, the PVTC planned an exhibition of their skills and sanitary appliances. An appeal to members to take part in the show, which was to be held at Brockwell Park on Sunday, 15 October, 1916, was published in the *Pharmaceutical Journal*. It pointed out that a great deal depended on this inspection, which was to be made by General the Hon Francis Bridgman, and that it was hoped that the past fifteen months' work would be fully rewarded by official War Office recognition, not merely as a Volunteer Corps, but as the Pharmacist Sanitary Company for London.

A great success, reports of the exhibition appeared in several London newspapers. A film was even made by Messrs Path Frères which was shown in cinemas throughout the British Isles. Christening the Pharmacists as the 'Anti-Microbe Corps', the *Daily Express* published the following account of their show on 30 October, 1916:

'The Anti-Microbe Corps is encamped in Brockwell Park. It is a fine exhibition of volunteer enthusiasm and scientific knowledge in the work of keeping our great camps of troops free from bacteria, polluted water, fevers and ill health generally.

'It is the Pharmacists' Volunteer Corps, and every man in its ranks is a qualified chemist. The object of the Corps is to train pharmacists to be of the greatest service in the defence of their country in those matters for which their training as pharmacists best adapts them.

'The camp, which has been inspected on behalf of the War Office and the Army Medical Service, is a wonderful example of thrift. Incinerators, microbe-killing apparatus of various kinds, cooking and heating ovens and boilers, refuse destructors, special sanitation trenches, and other instruments of health for great camps of men have been constructed by druggists in their brief Sunday or weekly afternoon leisure from shops, and the materials have been obtained by little more than a search in the scrap-heap.

'Old glycerine tins embedded in earth, and broken bricks, have been cunningly fashioned into large up-to-date health ovens. Old iron bars, worn-out dustbins, old bits of brick and other apparently worthless things have been utilised in the construction of the camp.'

Despite the great success of the exhibition and the general praise of the inspecting officers, the desired recognition did not come. After several months of negotiations it was subsequently decided by the War Office that recognition could not be given to any non-combatant unit. Other Volunteer units were, albeit that their duties lay in home defence, considered as combatant. Training in their case was based on weapon skills and the ability to engage the enemy if required. True, there were certain units within the VTC performing non infantry roles—motor, ambulance, engineer—but these were all to take their place in the field in the event of invasion.

It was then put to the corps that if they were dissatisfied with existing conditions they should either disband or convert to combatant training. If the latter option was chosen, the PVTC would then be required to become absorbed into one of the London battalions of Volunteers.

Though bitterly disappointed that their efforts had been in vain, a unanimous decision was taken by members to continue service. A General Meeting was held on 4 February, 1917, and the decision arrived at by those present was to amalgamate into the 1st Battalion of London Engineers. Both the CO and Adjutant of the Engineers were present and expressed to the PVTC a hearty welcome.

After many weeks of negotiations between the Pharmacists and the Engineers, the final details were eventually settled and the PVTC were to become No 4 Company London Engineers VTC. However, the proposed merger did not to take place as its sanction was not agreed to by the Volunteer Association Headquarters Staff. Instead an offer, which was later agreed to by the War Office, to join the United Arts Rifles, was accepted and in May, 1917 the PVTC joined as 'D' Company.

Upon joining the United Arts Rifles, who formed the 1st County of London Volunteer Regiment, a khaki uniform was adopted. The Pharmacists' unique cap badge and shoulder title, however, was discarded and replaced by those worn by the United Arts.

So ends the story of a unique, efficient and very necessary unit. As part of the United Arts Rifles, the old PVTC would survive in the role of infantry soldiers, efficient in the skills of company and battalion drill, bayonet fighting, bombing, machine gun work, signalling, musketry and rifle drill, until the end of the war.

Plymouth Volunteer Training Corps

Cap badge, the letters VTC and date 1915 superimposed upon crossed rifles. Beneath this, a scroll inscribed Plymouth.

Polytechnic Volunteer Training Corps

The *Volunteer Training Corps Gazette* for 17 July 1915 mentions this corps at the Polytechnic Institute, 309 Regent Street, London. A letter in the issue for 19 February also tells how a cadet corps had been formed, the boys training alongside of the men. Two versions of an oval lapel badge featuring a Maltese Cross with St George in the centre have been noted. One has Polytechnic 1914 on a circle, the other, Volunteer Training Corps London.

Poplar Volunteer Training Corps

The *Volunteer Training Corps Gazette* for 3 April 1915 noted that this corps numbered some 300 members and that drill centres were at: 'A' (Poplar) Company, Cubitt Town LCC School playground, Wharf Road, 'B' (Poplar) Company, Ricardo Street LCC School playground, 'C (Bromley-by-Bow) Company, St Leonard's Road LCC School playground and 'D' (Bow) Company at the Bow Baths in Roman Road. Combined drills were held at Grove Hall Park in Fairfield Road, Bow on Saturday afternoons. The description of the unit's cap badge is given by Kipling and King as: 'A pear-shaped oval inscribed *Poplar Battalion VTC* surmounted by an Imperial crown. In the centre three shields representing the three parishes from the Borough Council's Seal. Below, a scroll inscribed *East London Regt*.'

Portsmouth Volunteer Training Corps

Began with about two dozen members early in September 1914 and by the following December numbered almost 700. Drills were carried out at the Connaught Drill Hall (headquarters of the 6th Hampshire Regiment), and those occupied by the 1st Wessex Brigade Royal Field Artillery and No 4 Company Hampshire Royal Garrison Artillery in St Paul's Road. Secretary of the corps was Mr Reginald L Blake of 20 Palmerston Road in Southsea. The cap badge of this corps featured the Hampshire Rose surmounted by a sailing ship. The latter is said to be a representation of HMS *Victory*. The name of the corps appears on a scroll below. There is also a cloth shoulder title which has red letters on black, V above 1st P.T.C. The Connaught Drill Hall in Stanhope Road, Portsmouth was badly damaged by a bomb in 1941, the scene later put on canvas (illustrated) by Edward Robert King. (Courtesy of the Portsmouth Museums and Visitor Service).

Post Office Engineering Volunteer Training Corps

The *Volunteer Training Corps Gazette* for 20 February 1915 noted that the commandant of this corps was Mr HC Gunton, and that its members were almost all qualified technical or mechanical engineers. The *Gazette* for 6 March 1915 reported on an inspection of the corps by General Sir O'Moore Creagh, VC, which took place on Saturday 27 February at Hyde Park. Various demonstrations in signalling were carried out, one air-line being taken over the Serpentine and around the Round Pond to the front of Kensington Palace. The article also noted that the members, being all civil servants, are exempt from military service and that the area around the General Post Office had been used by the corps for trench digging. There exists a circular enamelled lapel badge with crossed rifles, a target, and the words 'Rifle Club' in the centre. The outer circle is inscribed 'London Postal Service'. The cap badge comprised crossed rifles, the letters VTC and the date 1915 within a crowned wreath. P.O. Engineers is inscribed on a scroll below.

Putney Volunteer Training Corps

Formed 1 December 1914, headquarters were first situated at a garage in Chelverton Road, Putney where drills took place on Tuesdays, Wednesdays, Thursdays and Saturdays. There was also a rifle range opposite St Mary's Church. By December, however, a move had been made to 162 High Street opposite the London and South Western Railway Station. Drill nights remained at the garage. Commandant of the corps was Mr WFR Avery of 7 Carmalt Gardens, Putney, Mr Alfred E Nightingale acting as secretary. A subscription of two shillings and sixpence was paid and a badge bearing the borough arms with the words 'We Serve', was available to members at one shilling. Possibly the Putney VTC became part of the 1st VB Wandsworth Volunteer Regiment. The motto We Serve is from the arms of that borough. By June 1915 headquarters had moved yet again, this time to the White Lion Hotel in Putney High Street.

Queen Elizabeth Grammar School Cadet Corps

Recognised 11 March 1918 (Army Order 173) and affiliated to the 2nd Cumberland and Westmoreland Volunteer Battalion Border Regiment.

Queen Elizabeth's Ashbourne Cadet Corps

Recognised 4 February 1918 (Army Order 149) and affiliated to the 5th Derbyshire Volunteer Regiment.

Queenborough Glass Works Sports Club

Two miles south of Sheerness on the Isle of Sheppey in Kent, the Queenborough Glass Works Corps was holding drills by November 1914. Mr W Casey was secretary.

Queen's University Belfast Veterans Corps

Some 253 members are on record as having joined this corps by October 1915. The cap badge displays the arms of the university inside a crowned wreath, below this a two-piece scroll inscribed Queen's over Veterans Corps 1914. Examples of the badge so far noted bear the manufacturer's name of SD Neill, Donegall Place, Belfast.

Ramsgate Volunteer Training Corps

Hon Secretary of the corps, Mr G Searle of The Cottage, Ramsgate, pointed out how residents in his area were conscious of the fact that Ramsgate may well be open to raids by the enemy, and this led to the problem of spies. 'This neighbourhood', he noted, 'is well known to thousands of Germans who were wont to spend their holidays in our midst. With all this in mind, it would take little effort to form the residence of Ramsgate into a home defence corps'. Some 300 had enrolled by November 1914. An oval lapel badge exists which has the name of the corps and the date 1914 on a blue ground and gilt crossed rifle in the centre.

Rathmines Volunteer Training Corps

Mr Steven Hurst writes in *The Bulletin of the Military Historical Society* (No 250, November 2012) that the strength of this Irish corps stood at 50 in November 1915.

Rayleigh And District Volunteer Corps

Formed at a meeting held at the Rayleigh Rifle Club on 2 December 1914. Mr Acker took the chair. Appointed to the committee were Messrs Burroughs, Francis, Ackers, Johnson, Phillips and Sparrow. Some thirty-three members enrolled. Featured on the cap badge was the arms of Rayleigh: a seax with rising sun above and castle situated on a mount below.

Raunds

It would seem that, despite several attempts to raise a volunteer corps in this east Northamptonshire shoe and boot making village of Raunds by the commandant of nearby Wellingborough and District VTC, Herbert Dudley, nothing was forthcoming. Details of meetings were notified in the *Northamptonshire Evening Telegraph*, the *Rushden Echo* telling of one last attempt made at the end of October 1916.

Reddish Volunteer Defence Corps

Formed in 1914, the badge of the corps featured the Union Flag with crossed rifles behind. Reddish is now an area of the Metropolitan Borough of Stockport.

Redditch Cadet Company

Recognised 20 July 1918 (Army Order 342) and affiliated to the 3rd Volunteer Battalion Worcestershire Regiment.

Reigate and Redhill Volunteer Training Corps

Member Mr AJ Knight of 74 Station Road, Redhill wrote in the *Volunteer Training Corps Gazette* on 19 December 1914 that he would like to see the VTC in a tweed headdress with a triangular cloth badge bearing the unit designation.

Rhymney Valley Volunteer Training Corps

The Rev Thomas H Pountney, who was appointed as secretary of the corps, noted in December 1914 that under this title three companies existed: Bargoed, Caerphilly and Hengoed. These had been formed early in the war and subsequently merged. Some 150 had enrolled by December 1914.

Renfrewshire Volunteer Regiment, 1st Cadet Company 1/1st Battalion

Recognised 15 February 1918 (Army Order 209).

Richmond and District Volunteer Training Corps

At the Drill Hall of 'B' and 'C' Companies of the 6th Battalion East Surrey Regiment (Territorial Force) in Richmond on Monday 23 November 1914, it was decided to form a VTC unit for Richmond and the surrounding area. The same meeting formed a provisional committee comprising members of the Kew Rifle Club: Mr ER Lascelles, a Mr Clode and one other gentleman who were both members of the Richmond Rifle Club, Special Constables EJ Fisher and R Hutchinson, a Doctor Blair, Mr AA Boddy, Major James and Lieutenant Hayton.

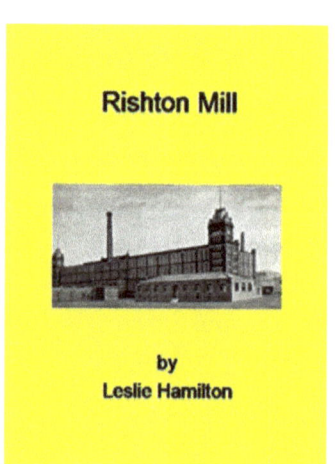

Rishton Mill by Leslie Hamilton

Correspondence with the corps could be made via either Secretary Martin Jarry, who could be contacted at the Richmond Hippodrome, or Mr P Lampson of 34 Sydney Road, Richmond. Corps finances were dealt with by Treasurer, Walker Marsden, at the Richmond branch of Farrow's Bank. Members paid an entrance fee of one shilling, with a maximum annual subscription of four shillings.

Rishton Volunteer Training Corps

The *Volunteer Training Corps Gazette* for 26 December 1914 reported that this corps had just completed formation (with some 100 enrolled) and that its committee was composed of members of the Rishton Urban District Council: Captain John Barr, MB, JP, who was a member of the 5th East Lancashire

Regiment National Reserve battalion (chairman and president), Councillor Bernard Smith (vice chairman), Mr R Gilroy (treasurer) and Mr WP Hutchinson (secretary). Messrs Chadwick, Greenwood, Harrison and Irvin were appointed as drill instructors. The corps was given the use of an empty spinning shed by Miss and Mr Hanson, owners of the Rishton Mill (illustrated) and drills were held there on Mondays, Wednesdays, Fridays and Saturdays. The Rishton Mill photograph is from the cover of a book by Leslie Hamilton.

Rocester and Denstone Home Guards

This Staffordshire corps is known to have existed.

Rochester Volunteer Training Corps

Later incorporated into the Kent Volunteer Fencibles, the corps wore a cap badge featuring the arms of Rochester: a cross marked with the lower case letter r and with a lion above.

Ross Volunteer Training Corps

Major James Kelly wrote in December 1914 that the Herefordshire town of Ross-on-Wye had always responded to the call for volunteers, forty-two from the town having served in South Africa during the Boer War. One hundred and twenty had joined the VTC.

Rotherhithe Volunteer Training Corps

The *Volunteer Training Corps Gazette* for 9 January 1915 reported how Mr E Challis of 420 Rotherhithe Street, SE, could not find a corps in his area so started one. A committee was formed and by 22 October, 1914 'we had obtained an instructor and drill hall, and on that date we had our first open drill and commenced enrolling recruits…our numbers at present are 220'. A brass band was formed and membership, notes Mr Challis, is 'practically all men of the artisan and labouring classes.' The *Gazette* for 16 January 1915 reported that the corps had changed its name to the Borough of Bermondsey Volunteer Training Corps so as to encourage men from all over the borough to enrol. The *Volunteer Gazette* for 27 March 1915 noted that headquarters were at Silwood Street near South Bermondsey Railway Station.

Rotten Park Rifle Corps

The enamel lapel badge worn by this unit consisted of a crowned circular strap inscribed with the title. In the centre, the Union flag. Rotton Park, Birmingham.

Royal Courts of Justice Volunteer Training Corps

The *Volunteer Training Corps Gazette* for 20 February 1915 reported that this is one of the special corps where membership is confined to a profession. It consists entirely of those employed in government departments, namely the Courts of Justice, Public Records Office, Public Trustee Office, Land Registry, Bankruptcy and Companies Winding-up Office, the Valuation Office of the Inland Revenue and the Bank of England (Law Courts Branch). A recent decision, however, had been made to invite other government departments to join. The Lord Chancellor was President, the commanding officer Master Bonner, one of the Masters of the Supreme Court. Drills took place in the Law Courts.

Royston and District Volunteer Training Corps

Formed before the end of 1914, this Hertfordshire corps had Lord Robert Cecil as president, and Lords Braybrook and Knutsford as vice-presidents. The hon secretary was Mr R Douglas Willan of 'Oakdene', Royston.

St Andrew's, Stockwell Volunteer Training Corps

Illustrated is a photograph which shows both the corps and its cadet section.

St Andrew's Volunteer Training Corps (1)

An oval badge was worn which featured in the centre, St Andrew standing behind his cross. The name of the corps appears around the outer edge. Later became the 9th Volunteer Battalion Black Watch.

St Andrew's Volunteer Training Corps (2)

Mr Steven Hurst writes in *The Bulletin of the Military Historical Society* (No 250, November 2012) mentioning a corps by this name having been raised in Ireland. He gives a strength of 54 in November 1915.

St Annes-on-the-Sea Training Corps

The *Volunteer Training Corps Gazette* for 26 December 1914 reported that this corps had been formed under the auspices of the chairman of the local council by Messes Gibbs and Sharett, both old Volunteers of the Victorian period, early in September. Membership in December was 208. Headquarters were at St George's Hall, St Annes.

St Barnabas, Hove Home Defence Corps

The flint and red brick St Barnabas's Church in Sackville Road, Hove in Sussex was less than twenty years old when the corps was formed on 23 September 1914. A company of the Church Lads' Brigade existed there and it would be its commanding officer, Major HD Smythe, that became secretary to the St Barnabas Volunteers. The Rev Smythe had been vicar at St Barnabas's Church since its opening.

St Botolph Bishopsgate Rifle Club

Illustrated in *The Bulletin* of the Military Historical Society (No 248, May 2012) is a circular enamel lapel badge bearing this title. In the centre is a Bishop's mitre above crossed rifles. The item appears on a page carrying the wording 'A selection of Volunteer Corps badges'. St Botolph-without-Bishopsgate is a c1212 church in the City of London.

St Marylebone Volunteer Training Corps

The *Volunteer Training Corps Gazette* for 13 March 1915 reported that this corps had held a recruiting concert in the Portman Rooms, Baker Street on Wednesday 3 March. The *Gazette* for 10 April 1915 noted that the corps had recently been inspected at their drill hall, the Royal West End Riding School in Seymour Place. Total strength, 350, commanding officer, Lieutenant-Colonel Newnham Davis. The corps recruiting office is at 60 Paddington Street. There exists a gilt and enamel lapel badge comprising a crowned circle, crossed rifles and the words 'S. Marylebone' in the centre, 'Volunteer Training Corps' around the edge. Later became a battalion of the West London Volunteer Regiment with the metal shoulder title West London Regt. over V.T.C. over St. Marylebone.

St Neots and District Drill Club

This corps, reported Hon Secretary Percy Tomson in the *Volunteer Training Corps Gazette* on 5 December 1914, was formed on the previous 12 November and held its drills at the St Neots Corn Exchange (illustrated). He names Messrs SG Wilkinson, J Mead, A Hayter and JJ Barry as 'four very competent drill instructors'. A miniature rifle range at the St Neots Rifle Club was put at the disposal of the corps. With some ninety members, former officer of the Victorian Volunteer Movement, Mr JW Addington, was appointed as president. Mr Tomson also noted that ambulance and signalling classes were taking place and that his corps was the first to be formed in Huntingdonshire. The St Neots Corn Exchange, on the corner of High Street and South Street, was destroyed by fire in 1929.

St Pancras Cadet Corps

Recognised 17 December 1917 (Army Order 111 of 1918) and affiliated to the 1/8th Battalion London Volunteer Regiment.

St Pancras Volunteer Training Corps

The *Volunteer Training Corps Gazette* for 24 April 1915 reported that this corps had started last Autumn and that the commanding officer was the Mayor of St Pancras, Alderman J May, JP. Headquarters were at the Drill Hall in High Street, Camden Town. Later became the 2nd (St Pancras) Battalion North London Volunteer Regiment.

St Paul's (Cheltenham) Cadet Corps

Recognised 18 December 1917 (Army Order 149 of 1918) and affiliated to the 3rd Battalion Gloucestershire Volunteer Regiment.

St Paul's Company Volunteer Training Corps

A report concerning the company's first dinner, which took place at its Camperdown House headquarters on Friday 27 November 1914, noted that Mr P Jolowicz took the Chair. Others present included Mr HJ Beesley, who had organised the event, Mr EW Hind, Mr G Rowland Smith and a Mr Egglestone. On the day after, despite a heavy rain storm, the company took part in its first route march and was complimented on its smart turnout. Camperdown House, London E1 (Stepney), situated in Half Moon Passage after Nos 20-24, was built in 1913 and was premises occupied by the Jewish Lads' Brigade.

St Thomas's Drill Corps, Stockport

Secretary of the corps, Mr JC Bowles, wrote in December 1914 that this corps had been formed in August by forty-two gentlemen and that it was the first to be raised in Stockport. Membership, at time of writing, stood at 200.

Sale and Ashton Civilian Corps

Both Sale and, to give it its full name, Ashton-upon-Mersey, lie about five miles south-west of Manchester and provided residences for a number of city merchants and businessmen. Formation of the corps began after a crowded meeting held in the Brooklands Parish Room on 1 September 1914 at which Mr EF Stockton and Mr EW Wingate-Saul gave patriotic speeches. Some 200 men enrolled on the day and were soon seen drilling during weekday evenings in a number of schools provided by local churches and chapels. On Saturdays, the Sale Football Club put their field at the disposal of the corps. A committee was formed which included Mr EF Stockton as chairman, Mr EW Wingate-Saul, treasurer and Mr HD Parmiter who was elected as secretary. The corps was divided into five companies, each being drilled by one Sergeant Jepson. Regular route marches took place, brass bands from both Sale and Ashton helping the men on their way. On the invitation of Captain A Dean-Willcocks, the District Recruiting Officer, the corps took part in a drum-head service held in the Market Place at Altrincham on 15 November 1914 and on the following day attended a memorial service for Lord Roberts at St Mary's, Ashton-under-Mersey. Brooklands Parish Room was associated with the Church of St John the Devine at Sale in Cheshire.

Salford Voluntary Defence Corps

Comprising some 400 members, about 100 of which were Special Constables, by November 1914 this corps was drilling at the Corporation playing fields and at Manchester race course. President was Mr Humphrey Roberts, Hon Secretary, Mr A Popperwell.

Sandbach School Cadet Corps

Recognised 3 January 1918 (Army Order 149) and affiliated to the 4th Battalion Cheshire Volunteer Regiment.

Saxmundham and District Volunteer Training Corps

This corps was formed as a result of a meeting held at Saxmundham on Saturday 21 November 1914 and presided over by Major General Sir Ronald Lane, KCB. Twenty-five men enrolled on the day, this number having doubled by the end of the month. Colonel H Abdy Collins, who has served with the old 1st Suffolk Rifle Volunteer Corps and held the Volunteer Decoration, was appointed as commanding officer. Mr J Forsdike of Saxmundham became secretary.

Seaton Volunteer Training Corps

A meeting to discuss the formation of a Volunteer Corps in Seaton, Devon was held in the Royal Clarence Hotel during the second week of December 1914. It was decided to proceed at once, Mr JH Alabaster being appointed as secretary.

Selby Cadet Company

Recognised 20 September 1918 (Army Order 342) and affiliated to the 2nd Volunteer Battalion King's Own Yorkshire Light Infantry.

Sevenoaks Cadet Company

Recognised 18 June 1918 (Army Order 307) and affiliated to the 1st Volunteer Battalion Queen's Own Royal West Kent Regiment.

Shanklin Volunteer Training Corps

Formed as the result of a meeting held on 30 November 1914 which had been arranged by Mr E Moorman, Secretary of the Shanklin Rifle Club. Fifty enrolled.

Shepton Mallet Cadet Corps

Recognised 19 December 1917 (Army Order 111 of 1918) and affiliated to the 3rd Battalion Somerset Volunteer Regiment.

Shepton Mallet Civilian Corps

The *Volunteer Training Corps Gazette* for 26 December 1914 reported that this corps numbered 100, the town surveyor and former member of the Dorset Yeomanry, Mr Daniel Hinchcliffe, being appointed as drill instructor and secretary. The headmaster of Shepton Mallet Grammar School, Mr Aldridge, had placed his miniature range at the disposal of the corps.

Shepton Mallet Grammar School Cadet Corps

Recognised 7 October 1917 (Army Order 360) and affiliated to the 3rd Battalion Somerset Volunteer Regiment.

Shere Volunteer Training Corps

A Volunteer Corps, noted the *Volunteer Training Corps Gazette*, had been formed at Shere, six miles west of Dorking in Surrey by November 1914.

Sheringham Miniature Rifle Club and Drill Association

Mr F Hall, secretary of the corps, wrote in December 1914 how a meeting had been held on 3 September requesting the formation of a corps of 'Norfolk veterans'. Forty men enrolled. Membership by December had risen to ninety. Parades were held at the local drill hall and headquarters were established in the Council's offices.

Shrewsbury Athletes' Volunteer Force

Secretary of the corps, Mr TH Bullimore, wrote in December 1914 that the corps had been formed some weeks ago after a public meeting in the town. Now almost 500 strong, the membership was made up, he noted, of all classes of society. Four drills each week were taking place.

Shropshire Volunteer Corps

An oval blue and gold enamel lapel badge exists with this title on a strap around the edge. In the centre, the arms of the county.

Shropshire Volunteer Regiment

The arms of the county on a shield within a crowned circle and wreath formed the regiment's cap badge.

Sidmouth Volunteer Corps

Mr FC Purcell, secretary of the corps, wrote in December 1914 that the Sidmouth Volunteers had just formed, holding its first parade, at which sixty-four enrolled, on 1 December. Major-General Gwynne had been appointed as commanding officer. Drills were carried out in a local garage and headquarters were at a hall belonging to the Boy Scouts.

Smethwick Volunteer Training Corps

Officially commenced on 1 January, headquarters being at the Drill Hall, Bloomfield. Membership, 150.

Somerset County Volunteer Regiment

The cap badge featured the dragon rampant from the county arms.

Somerset Light Infantry, 1st Cadet Corps 1st Volunteer Battalion

Recognised 10 June 1918 (Army Order 240).

Somerset Light Infantry, 2nd Cadet Corps 1st Volunteer Battalion

Recognised 14 August 1918 (Army Order 307).

South City Dublin Volunteer Training Corps

Mr Steven Hurst writes in *The Bulletin of the Military Historical Society* (No 250, November 2012) that the strength of this corps stood at 50 in November 1915.

South East London Regiment National Volunteer Reserve

The *Volunteer Training Corps Gazette* for 26 June 1915 reported that the Lewisham Volunteer Training Corps, together with the Blackheath, Forest Hill Company, had now become a unit of the National Volunteer Reserve and was now part of the National Volunteer Reserve Battalion of the South-East London Regiment.

South London Battalion National Volunteer Reserve

The *Volunteer Training Corps Gazette* for 8 May 1915 reported that the battalion would rendezvous at the bottom of Stratham Common on Sunday 10 May for a route march to Warlington.

South London Volunteer Training Corps

A cap badge has been noted which includes crossed rifles and the date 1915.

South London Volunteer Regiment

The *Volunteer Training Corps Gazette* for 27 March 1915 reported that Major-General Sir Desmond O'Callaghan, KCVO had recently been appointed as commandant of the newly-formed South London Regiment. The *Gazette* for 17 April 1915 also noted that a regimental headquarters had been set up at 59 Fleet Street. Another issue mentions 1st (Lewisham) Battalion and another, a Camberwell and Peckham Battalion. The *Gazette* for 2 October 1915 reported that in future headquarters will be at 3 Brick Court, Temple. The issue for 18 December, however, records a function at which all eight battalions were represented: 1st (Lambeth), 2nd (Southwark and Bermondsey), 3rd (Dulwich, Camberwell and Norwood), 4th (Southfields), 5th (Wandsworth), 6th (Streatham), 7th (Deptford), 8th (Lewisham). The issue for 29 January 1916 tells that the regiment now comprised 7,500 men and that the eight battalions were made up of twenty-four individual corps. There exists two patterns of cap badge with the title South London VTC: one has crossed rifles and the date 1915 within a crowned wreath, the other, the shield of the City of London with crown above. A bronze shoulder title has the letters SLRV in a straight line.

South Norwood Volunteer Company

Sir Henry Craik, MP addressed a meeting at headquarters on 10 December 1914.

South Staffordshire Regiment, 1st Cadet Battalion 2nd Volunteer Battalion

Recognised 13 April 1918 (Army Order 173).

South Tottenham and Harringay Volunteer Training Corps

A St Ann's Section of this corps is mentioned in the *Volunteer Training Corps Gazette* for 5 February 1916.

South West Lancashire Volunteer Regiment

The regiment wore an oval bronze badge featuring the arms of England.

South West London Division Home Defence League

The *Volunteer Training Corps Gazette* for 26 December 1914 reported that this corps had held a concert at the Balham Hippodrome on the previous Saturday in which bioscope views of the men in training were shown. Proceeds for the event were to be devoted to the equipment fund.

Southend National Guard

Mentioned in *Volunteer Training Corps Gazette* for 26 December 1914. A cap badge was worn featuring the arms of this Essex seaside resort.

Southfields Defence Force

There exists a silver and blue enamel lapel badge bearing the title Southfields Defence Force. It has crossed rifles in the centre and the date 1914 below. Southfields, SW18 and SW19, is part of Wandsworth, close to Wimbledon Park.

Southgate Training Corps

Within a week of the declaration of war, this North London corps had been formed under the name of the Palmer's Green Civic Guard—over 1,000 enquiries regarding membership being received by Hon Secretary Mr V Shillingford at No 5 The Market, Palmer's Green during the first few days alone. Drills were carried out at a private park in Arnos Grove, Cannons Hill, Southgate—much of the area until 1918 was owned by the Walker brewing family—and also at the London General Omnibus Company's garage in Green Lanes, Palmers Green. Signal, ambulance and engineering sections had been formed, along with a drum and fife band. In another issue of the *Volunteer Training Corps Gazette*, that for 19 December 1914, it was noted that a section of the Southgate Training Corps had been formed at Harringay. Drills were held in Harringay on Tuesday evenings at Allison Hall, and on Thursdays at Beresford Hall. A circular enamelled lapel badge made up of crossed rifles and a crown was worn.

Southampton Civil Volunteer Corps

The *Volunteer Training Corps Gazette* for 2 January 1915 reported that this corps, together with the Southampton Civil Volunteer Training Association, had taken part in a long route march on Saturday 26 December. The march was led by the band of the 5th Hampshire Regiment. Cap badge: A rifle with bayonet fixed and a sling inscribed with the name of the corps. Between the rifle and sling, the date 1914.

Southampton United Professions Training Corps

The *Volunteer Training Corps Gazette* for 26 December 1914 reported that this company was started on 13

November 1914 with a view to the incorporation of a number of professional men, the number being limited to 240. The first drill was held at the RGA Drill Hall in St Mary's Road, Southampton. Headquarters were at the Union Bank Chambers, Hon Secretary, Mr PW Beverley.

Southampton Volunteer Training Corps

Comprised some 400 members by November 1914, 'some of the leading men of the town being among its ranks' noted the *Volunteer Training Corps Gazette*.

Southport Volunteers

The arms of Southport and the motto *Salus populi* featured on the unit's bronze badges.

Southwark Volunteer Training Corps

The *Volunteer Training Corps Gazette* for 11 March 1916 reported that this corps had united with Bermondsey as 2nd Battalion South London Volunteer Regiment. The unit later became known as the Southwark Volunteer Battalion and as such wore a bronze badge featuring the Borough Council's arms within a crowned circle.

Spilsby and District Volunteer Training Corps

Formed after a public meeting held at Spilsby in Lincolnshire on 24 November 1914. A Colonel Swan was appointed president, Dr R Slocock the treasurer, Mr B Robinson, secretary and Mr John F Rawnsley, chairman.

Sportsmen's Volunteer Corps

An exact title was not included, but a report in the 5 December 1914 edition of the *Volunteer Training Corps Gazette* noted that a committee had been formed for the purpose of forming a company of Volunteers to consist of 120 men drawn from the ranks of old rugby football men and cricketers, etc. Those interested in joining were invited to contact Mr GH Harnett (acting Hon Secretary) at 3 Brick Court, Temple in the City.

Spring Grove Volunteers

A corps at Spring Grove in Middlesex was noted in the *Volunteer Training Corps Gazette* as having been formed by December 1914.

Stafford Volunteer Training Corps

A meeting was called with a view to raising a corps by the Earl of Dartmouth at the County Buildings in Stafford on 3 December.

Stepney Volunteer Training Corps

The *Volunteer Training Corps Gazette* for 13 March 1915 reported that this corps was making good progress and that membership then stood at 150. Application for membership should be made at No 2 Church Lane, Whitechapel, or at the Davenant Schools on Mondays or Thursdays. Later became 3rd Battalion East London Volunteer Regiment.

Stewarty Volunteer Training Corps

The cap badge of this Dumfriesshire corps featured a lion rampant crowned.

Stirling Cadet Companies, 1st, 2nd, 3rd

Recognised 4 September 1917 (Army Order 360) and affiliated to the 1st Stirlingshire Volunteer Regiment.

Stoke Newington Volunteer Training Corps

The *Volunteer Training Corps Gazette* for 12 May 1915 reported that this corps had been involved in quelling the recent anti-German riots. *The War Budget* for 17 February 1916 also mentions the corps and tells how it had formed a guard of honour recently when the Bishop of London dedicated motor ambulances presented by Stoke Newington subscribers to the British Ambulance Committee and the British Red Cross Society. The corps later became 4th Battalion North London Volunteer Regiment.

Stourbridge Volunteer Training Corps

Mentioned as being in existence in the *Volunteer Training Corps Gazette* for 26 December 1914.

Stourport Cadet Company

Recognised 20 October 1917 (Army Order 51 of 1918) and affiliated to the 1st Battalion Worcestershire Volunteer Regiment.

Stratford-upon-Avon General Duty Reserves

Formed on 4 August 1914 by William Jaggard (Navy and Army Recruiting Officer for the Stratford area) and at first known as the Stratford-upon-Avon Riflemen, this formation comprised about 200 men by the end of 1914. As well as Stratford, there were also detachments at Alverston, Binton, Ettington, Goldicote, Grafton, Tiddington and Wilmcote. The General Duty Reserves enrolled men who for various reasons considered that they would be unable to join the Regular forces, but were prepared, nevertheless, to drill for home defence duties. However, it was recorded in the *Volunteer Training Corps Gazette* for 12 December 1914 that when Lord Kitchener called for recruits for his New Army, some fifty-per-cent of the enrolled strength had already enlisted. Drills took place at Yeomanry Hall Stratford (headquarters of 'D' Squadron, Warwickshire Yeomanry)—broomsticks being used as a substitute for rifles. The Commanding Officer was Major TH Bairnsfather, father of artist and writer Bruce.

Streatham Rifle Club

Mr EJ Martin illustrates a lapel badge to this corps in his 1938 VTC Uniform article (*Journal of the Society for Army Historical Research*, Vol 17). Upon a shield, a crown over crossed rifle with below, the letters SRC.

Streatham Volunteer Training Corps

The *Volunteer Training Corps Gazette* for 1 May 1915 reported that during the week commencing 3 May, there would be a special performance at the Brixton Theatre of 'Waterloo' and the 'Speckled Band', the whole of the proceeds going to the Equipment Fund. Written by Sir Arthur Conan Doyle as a Sherlock Holmes short story, 'The Speckled Band' was first published under the title of 'The Spotted Band' in the *Strand Magazine* for February 1892.

Street Volunteer Training Corps

Formed in Somerset by December 1914.

Stroud Cadet Corps

Recognised 17 June 1918 (Army Order 240) and affiliated to the 4th Battalion Gloucestershire Volunteer Regiment.

Suffolk Volunteer Training Corps

A gilding metal cap badge to this corps includes crossed rifles, the date 1915 and the word Suffolk on a scroll below.

Surrey Volunteer Regiment, 1st Cadet Battalion 2nd Battalion

Recognised 12 November 1917 by Army Order 51 of 1918.

Surrey Volunteer Training Corps

A gilding metal cap badge to this corps includes crossed rifles, the date 1915 and the word Surrey on a scroll below.

Surrey Volunteer Training Corps, 6th (Guildford) Battalion

The cap badge featured the arms of Guildford.

Sussex Home Protection Brigade

The enamel lapel badge worn by this corps had the Union flag in its centre.

Sussex Volunteer Regiment, No 1 Cadet Company 3rd Battalion

Recognised 31 December 1917 (Army Order 111 of 1918).

Sussex Volunteer Regiment, No 2 Company 3rd Battalion

Recognised 4 January 1918 (Army Order 173).

Sussex Volunteer Regiment, 4th Battalion Cadet Company

Recognised 4 February 1918 (Army Order 173).

Sussex Volunteer Regiment, No Cadet Company 6th Battalion

Recognised 5 April 1918 (Army Order 173).

Sussex Volunteer Regiment, No 1 Cadet Company 9th Battalion

Recognised 3 April 1918 (Army Order 173).

Sussex Volunteer Training Corps

The six martlets from the county arms featured in the unit's cap badge. Also noted is a solid metal shoulder title made up of the intertwined letters VTC above Sussex. The photograph is a father and son from Brighton, JH

and DJ Geall, the son being a member of the Sussex Yeomanry Cadets, the father one of the Sussex Volunteer Training Corps.

Swansea Rugby Football and Cricket Training Corps

This corps was started soon after war was declared and was under the command of former captain of the Swansea Rugby Reserves, Major AA Perkins. He was also a former member of the Victorian Volunteers and, after 1908, an officer with the 7th (Cyclist) Battalion of the Welsh Regiment. Second-in-command was Mr J Aubrey Smith who was a member of the rugby team. From the 700 or more that had joined since formation, noted the *Gazette*, some 300 had passed on to HM Forces. For rifle practice, a miniature range was built below the grandstand at the Rugby Club ground.

Swindon and District Volunteer Training Corps

A bronze cap badge to this corps has been noted which featured the arms of Swindon.

Sydenham and Forest Hill Volunteer Training Corps

The *Volunteer Training Corps Gazette* for 7 August 1915 refers to this corps as being part of the 4th West Kent Volunteer Fencibles.

Sydenham Defence League

Mentioned in the *Volunteer Training Corps Gazette* for 20 March 1915.

Tamworth Grammar School Cadet Corps

Recognised 17 July 1915 (Army Order 302) and affiliated to the 6th Battalion North Staffordshire Regiment. Transfer to the Staffordshire Volunteer Regiment was notified in Army Order 51 of 1918.

Tamworth Volunteer Cadet Corps

Recognised 15 November 1917 (Army Order 51 of 1918) and affiliated to the 2nd Battalion Staffordshire Volunteer Regiment.

Taplow Volunteer Training Corps

Member of the committee, Mr E Ion Pool, wrote to the *Volunteer Training Corps Gazette* in December 1914 regarding uniform.

Teddington Volunteer Training Corps

In existence by December 1914.

Teignmouth Volunteer Corps

A corps at Teignmouth in Devon was noted as having been formed and drilling by the end of 1914. A number of retired military officers were helping with training, the Hon Secretary of the corps being Mr CG Sparrow of St Michael's Lodge, Teignmouth.

Tetbury Detachment

The *Gloucestershire Journal* for 17 July 1915 reported formation.

Tewkesbury and District Volunteer Training Corps

The strength of this corps by November 1914 had reached 100, the adjacent villages to Tewkesbury recruiting on a steady basis. Major Gresham Moore of the 5th Battalion Gloucestershire Regiment (Territorial Force) gave regular lectures at the Saturday afternoon parades. Hon Secretary of the corps, Mr Nevill J Moore, could be contacted at the Public Officers in Tewkesbury.

Thornhill Volunteer Training Corps

A corps was formed at Thornhill in Dumfriesshire just before the end of November 1914. The Duke of Buccleuch was elected as president, Dr Bryson, commandant, Mr John McKenzie, secretary.

Tideswell Grammar School Cadet Corps

Recognised 5 November 1918 (Army Order 31 of 1919) and affiliated to the 5th Volunteer Battalion Notts and Derby Regiment.

Tipton Volunteer Training Corps

A Staffordshire corps known to have existed.

Todmorden Volunteer Training Corps

The badge of this Yorkshire unit featured the arms of the town.

Tonbridge Rifle and Drill Club

Formed in the early weeks of the war by secretary of the corps Mr MI Christie of Castle Hill, Tonbridge, and comprised some 300 members by November. Training was provided by Captain D Laing.

Tonbridge Veterans Volunteer Training Corps

The *Volunteer Training Corps Gazette* for 26 December 1914 reported that newly formed sections from surrounding villages had joined bringing the overall strength of the corps up to twenty-nine members. Some of the new men, under the command of SG Hallam and MS David met on 20 December on Leigh Green where they were inspected by Colonel Rattray.

Tottenham Athletes' Volunteer Force

Formed in November from 100 members of the Tottenham Rifle Club. Drills took place on Tuesday and Thursday evenings, and on Sunday mornings.

Tottenham Polytechnic Company Athletes' Volunteer Force

Formed at the Polytechnic in High Road, Tottenham by the end of August 1914 and by November had a membership of 300 men. Military drills were under the direction of Sergeant Major Bullock and physical exercise classes were taken by Mr George Mason. Commandant of the company was Mr JW Tomlinson, its secretary, Mr Frederick H Ogg. Drills were held at headquarters on Mondays and Fridays, route marches taking place on Sundays.

Tottenham and Edmonton Volunteer Training Corps

The *Volunteer Training Corps Gazette* for 27 May 1916 reported that this corps had amalgamated with the Tottenham and Harringay VTC to form a single unit of the Middlesex Volunteer Regiment.

Tottenham and Harringay Volunteer Training Corps

The *Volunteer Training Corps Gazette* for 27 May 1916 reported that this corps had amalgamated with the Tottenham and Edmonton VTC to form a single unit of the Middlesex Volunteer Regiment.

Tottenham Volunteer Training Corps

The *Volunteer Training Corps Gazette* for 17 April 1915 reported that this corps had recently gained permission to use the Risley Avenue School playground for drill purposes, members marching there from headquarters (Tottenham Hotspur Football Ground) for the first time on 30 March.

Troon Citizen Training Corps

The *Volunteer Training Corps Gazette* for 2 February 1915 reported that it had been decided to form a corps at a meeting held the previous week. Over 100 men joined on the day.

Trumpington Volunteer Training Corps

The Trumpington Local History Group website recalls the first newspaper report (*Cambridge Chronicle,* 27 November 1914) to mention the corps: 'We hear it is possible that a company of "old crocks"…will be organised in the near future on lines similar to the Cambridge Civilian Corps.' Much information is given on the website, including that the corps was established on 3 December 1914 after a meeting was held at the village hall. The gathering was presided over by the Rev RG Bury. Members were to pay one shilling on enrolment, with the exception of agricultural labourers who would be admitted for sixpence. A route march to Shelford took place on 17 December 1914 and a rifle range opened on the 22nd by Mrs G Foster of Anstey Hall.

Tunstall Volunteer Training Corps

Hon Secretary Mr G Price Edwards wrote to the editor thanking him for the *Gazette's* first Issue. A later issue noted that parades were taking place at Tunstall Drill Hall. 'D' Company, 5th Battalion North Staffordshire Regiment occupied the drill hall. An enamelled lapel badge exists comprising a crowned shield bearing the name of the corps placed above and below a Union flag.

Twickenham Volunteer Training Corps

In existence by December 1914.

United Arts Rifles

The *Volunteer Training Corps Gazette* for 13 March 1915 noted that this volunteer regiment was recruited for home defence from the artistic professions. Many prominent artists, actors, singers and musicians were members. Lord Desborough was president and the chairman was the famous playwright, Sir Arthur Pinero. The *Gazette* also records that the corps has just moved into new headquarters at the Imperial College Union, Prince Consort Road, behind the Royal Albert Hall.

United Arts Volunteers

Mr Raymond Rose is credited with being the founder of the United Arts Volunteers and on 5 December 1914, as Hon Secretary, he reported that its membership then stood at more than 1,200. The enrolled strength had previously been in excess of 1,500, he commented, but commissions and enlistments into the Regular Army had caused the reduction.

United Arts Volunteer Force

The *Volunteer Training Corps Gazette* for 16 January 1915 noted that steps were being taken to form a light car section under the command of Mr AJ Dreydel. Motor car owners interested should communicate with headquarters at Burlington House, Piccadilly. The *Gazette* for 6 March 1915 reported that a meeting held the previous week at the United Arts Force headquarters, Burlington House, decided to merge the following corps under the title of Central London Regiment: United Arts, Optimists, Architects, Old Boys and Inns of Court OTC. The United Arts became 1st Battalion. The Pharmacists Corps became 'D' Company of United Arts. The United Arts VTF was affectionately known as the 'Unshrinkables' due to the white sweaters worn by the men while drilling. An eagle grasping a sword in its beak featured in the unit's cap badge.

Upper Norwood Defence League

Mentioned in the *Volunteer Training Corps Gazette* for 20 March 1915.

Uttoxeter Volunteer Training Corps

A report at the end of 1914 noted that this corps was nearly 100 strong and had made its first public appearance at a recent route march. Inspected on 19 August, the men first marched through High Street and Smithfield Road. This would also be the first formal appearance of the corps in uniform.

Uxbridge Volunteer Training Corps

In existence by December 1914.

Veteran Athletes' Volunteer Force

The *Volunteer Training Corps Gazette* for 6 March 1915 reported that this corps was inspected by Staff Captain EC Baker on Friday 26 February at the City of London School. The hon commandant is Mr PM Thornton, late MP for Clapham.

Volunteer Civil Force

The Volunteer Civil Force (VCF), or as it was known locally in London, the 'Westminster Guard', was in active existence before the war broke out, having been formed in 1912 through the energy and persistence of Mr WM Power who had joined the 22nd Middlesex Rifle Volunteers Corps (renumbered 13th in 1880) and accompanied it to America in 1906 where it shot against a team provided by the 7th National Guard. The VCF had arisen really as a volunteer police force with the object of assisting the police with fully trained men in times of stress. It continued in that form until the declaration of war when the body was re-organised as a Home Defence Force aiming to provide training for men unable to join the Army and to render them proficient in drill and shooting.

By the end of 1914 the VCF had grown to a large body of some two thousand enrolled members in London alone, some five hundred or more of that number joining either the Regular or Territorial Forces. In addition to this, over a thousand members were also enrolled as Special Constables and, in that capacity, rendered valuable assistance to the authorities throughout the war. The VCF had branches established in various towns throughout the country, but owing to the war and the consequent loss of many of its members to active service, some of these were closed down. Those members remaining were advised to join local VTC units where they could.

There was a Plymouth Division known as the Plymouth Guard formed in June 1914. The VCF had a special light and dark-blue uniform of its own and its membership was open to all. A subscription of ten shillings per year was payable for which members were allowed the use of several facilities at headquarters—social club, game rooms, billiard tables, etc. Headquarters were at Ruskin House, Rochester Row, Westminster, a very large concrete building which included extensive accommodation, an armoury and officers' and sergeants' messes.

Regular classes in Ju-Jitsu, boxing, fencing and ambulance work were provided daily. Across the street from headquarters were secured some large empty stables which were turned into four rifle firing ranges and another for service revolvers. There was also what was described as: 'a cinema or animated target range, on which moving pictures, of men running, hydroplanes moving in the water, or airships moving in the air, are projected on to the screen, and the men fire at these with an explosive bullet, enabling them to see exactly where they hit.' One of the pictures used showed the Kaiser receiving his troops which 'came in for a good peppering from those who were fortunate enough to be holding guns at the time.' There was a Ladies' Branch of the VCF which carried with it some 150 members. They were taught to shoot, as well as signalling and ambulance work. A Miss F Wearing is on record as winning, in November 1914, a silver challenge cup.

Volunteer Horse, 1st

The *Volunteer Training Corps Gazette* for 18 September 1915 reported that this corps had just held its fourth mounted Sunday parade, the men assembling at the new headquarters, the Royal Hyde Park Riding School, Gloucester Terrace, Hyde Park, Paddington and marching to Wormwood Scrubs. The *Gazette* comments that this was the only mounted volunteer corps in

London. The issue for 2 October 1915 noted that the corps was now under the command of Major Dudley B Gurowski (late High Sheriff of Berkshire). The *Gazette* for 6 November 1915 noted that the corps had been attached to the West London Regiment, VTC was now to be known as the West London Mounted Rifles. An oval bronze shoulder tiles exists with the wording 'West London' over 'VTC' over 'Mounted Rifles'. The issue for 15 April 1916 noted that a cyclist section had been formed and that applicants should apply to the Cyclist Officer, Mr Dixon, at 54 Maddox Street, Bond Street. The same issue gives headquarters as Orsett Mews, 215 Gloucester Terrace, Bishop's Road, Paddington.

Waggon Works Cadet Corps

Recognised 17 June 1918 (Army Order 240) and affiliated to the 3rd Battalion Gloucestershire Volunteer Regiment.

Wakefield

Under this heading, Kipling and King include the bronze badge of a fleur-de-lys with the title scroll Wakefield. The authors also point out that the town's volunteers later became 1st Volunteer Battalion King's Own Yorkshire Light Infantry.

Walsall Volunteer Training Corps

An item published in the *Volunteer Training Corps Gazette* on 12 December 1914 noted that a Volunteer Corps was particularly valuable in Walsall on account of the great number of military workers resident at the time, these having been denied by the government membership of the Regular forces. Chairman of the corps was Mr EN Marshall, MA and vice chairman, Mr AC Fraser Wood. Mr HN Grove of 19 Lichfield Street, Walsall was acting as organising secretary. The corps was formed in October 1914 and by the end of the following month numbered some 400 members. Public halls and parks were used for parades and training. The Drill Hall belonging to the 5th Battalion South Staffordshire Regiment was also used.

Waltham Abbey Cadet Corps

Recognised 13 November 1918 (Army Order 69 of 1919) and affiliated to the 2nd Volunteer Battalion Essex Regiment.

Waltham Abbey Volunteer Training Corps

A photograph of the corps shows the VTC uniform and GR arm band.

Walthamstow Athletes' Volunteer Force

The *Volunteer Training Corps Gazette* for 2 January 1915 reported that members of this corps were meeting every Tuesday at Markhouse Road Schools, Thursdays at the Elms, Coppermill Lane and Sundays at the Mann, Crossman and Paulin, Ltd athletic ground in Blackhorse Lane. Membership stood at eighty and the entrance fee was one shilling and sixpence, which included an AVF badge. Headquarters were at the Elms. The issue for 8 May 1915 reported that the corps has its own magazine with a circulation of 10,000. Later became the Athletes' Company 8th (Wandsworth) Battalion Essex Volunteer Regiment.

Walthamstow Ensign Volunteer Training Corps

Mentioned in the *Volunteer Training Corps Gazette* for 6 November 1915. The issue for 20 May 1916 noted that the corps had been formed on 19 September 1914 by attachment to the Ensign Rifle Club. Became 'A' (Walthamstow Ensign) Company 8th (Walthamstow) Battalion, Essex Volunteer Regiment.

Walthamstow Volunteer Training Corps

The *Volunteer Training Corps Gazette* for 20 May 1916 reported that a rifle club had been formed by the Hoe Street Company at its Church Hill headquarters. The issue also states that the company is of the 8th Battalion Essex Volunteer Regiment.

Wandsworth and Earlesfield Athletes' Volunteer Force

The *Volunteer Training Corps Gazette* for 10 April 1915 noted that this corps was the first to be formed in Wandsworth after war had been declared, and that the commandant was Lieutenant-Colonel W Haskett-Smith.

Wandsworth Regiment Volunteer Training Corps

The *Volunteer Training Corps Gazette* for 24 April 1915 noted a Battersea Battalion of this regiment and also made reference to a 1st and 2nd VB Wandsworth Regiment VTC. There exists a lapel badge and a cloth shoulder title with the title 1st VB Wandsworth V.T.C. The badges have the arms of Wandsworth (illustrated) on a star with the borough's motto We Serve on a scroll below.

Wandsworth Battalion Volunteer Defence Force, 1st

The *Volunteer Training Corps Gazette* for 19 December 1914 included an article by its commander, FAM Webster, who recalls how on 12 September 1914 he arrived at the Heathfield Cricket Field, hereafter to be known as the Parade Ground, and found sixteen men of various ages. Soon there would be 100 members who had paid an entrance fee of two shillings and sixpence and, when the corps was 1,000, it went for its first route march. As of December 1914, he notes, the strength was 2,000 all ranks. Drills were also carried out on the London Welsh Rugby Club grounds, and on those belonging to Messrs Holloway Bros. Mr Webster, who had served with the old 2nd (Hertfordshire) Volunteer Battalion of the Bedfordshire Regiment, noted in his article the good work carried out on behalf of the battalion by Sergeant Bugby, another old Volunteer and Bisley marksman, Orderly Room Clerk Sidney Butler and Councillor Russell J Pickering. The battalion was divided into four companies: 'A' under the command of Mr PS Doherty, 'B' commanded by a former 25th London Regiment quartermaster, HF Joyce, 'C', Lieutenant JAE Etherington, late of the 2nd Volunteer Battalion Royal Fusiliers, and 'D' by JH Anderson. Headquarters were at 123 Trinity Road.

Wanstead Volunteer Reserve

The *Volunteer Training Corps Gazette* for 17 April 1915 reported that 150 men under their commanding officer, F Guy, had recently attended camp at Hainault Forest.

Warwickshire Horse

Noted as drilling with sword, lance and carbine, by the end of 1914, the Warwickshire Horse numbered forty, each Volunteer supplying his own uniform and paying for the hire of his horse. Headquarters were at Lime Grove, Moseley Road, Birmingham.

Warwickshire Volunteer Regiment

A recruiting poster to this regiment is illustrated.

Waterloo Civilian Association

At Waterloo near Liverpool, the commanding officer Mr WH Richards wrote in December 1914 how his corps had started with thirteen men and was now 113 strong.

Watford and District Volunteer Training Corps

Hon Secretary CH Peacock of 101 High Street, Watford reported in the *Volunteer Training Corps Gazette* for 26 December 1914 that this corps had been started as the result of articles in the *Watford Observer* which he had followed up by calling a meeting on 19 November. Lord Essex was appointed as president, some 250 having enrolled.

Wednesbury Volunteer Training Corps

There is a brief mention of this corps in the *Volunteer Training Corps Gazette* for 9 December 1916. Mr J Robert Williams, however, provides a detailed history of the Wednesbury VTC in his article for the Military Historical Society (*The Bulletin,* August 1978). He tells how it was probably organised towards the end of 1914. He also states that the corps became a unit of the Mid-Staffordshire Battalion of the Staffordshire Volunteer Regiment in 1915, 'C' Company of the 3rd Battalion Staffordshire Volunteer Regiment in December 1916 and a company of the 1st Volunteer Battalion South Staffordshire Regiment, July 1918. Mr Williams's article includes a clear photograph of the bronze cap badge (illustrated, courtesy of Gary Gibbs) worn which has a fighting cock above a Stafford Knot. Below this, a scroll inscribed Wednesbury V.T.C. The Stafford Knot, of course, requires no explanation. The Fighting Cock, however, can be explained in the fact that for many years Wednesbury had been famous for its cock fighting and is on record as having trained birds for the King. Run by the Spittle family, the 'Cockfighting Arms' was a prominent venue for the 'sport', the cock pit in Potters Lane also attracting the nobility and sporting fraternity from all over the country. Should you visit Wednesbury's St Bartholomew's Church, which stands on the site of a Saxon castle, you will see a fine lectern of gilded plaster on an oak pedestal. No eagle with outstretched wings this time, but a fighting cock.

Wellingborough Volunteer Training Corps

By the end of 1914 membership of the Wellingborough VTC in Northamptonshire stood at over 400, 100 of whom were recruited from Finedon three miles to the north-east.

Wells Boys Blue School Cadet Company

Recognised 1 June 1918 (Army Order 240) and affiliated to the 3rd Battalion Somerset Volunteer Regiment.

Wembley Defence Corps

'A' company of the Wembley Defence Corps was formed as a result of a meeting held at Alperton by the

Alperton and Wembley Rifle Club on 14 August 1914—some 100 men enrolled that night. 'B' Company was soon to follow at Wembley Hill, 'C' at Wembley Central and 'D' in Sudbury. With permission of the local authority, council schools were placed at the disposal of the corps for drill purposes. General Sir O'Moore Creagh, VC made an inspection, the corps then almost 600 strong, on 14 November. Photographs exist of the corps drilling on ground that in 1923 would become Wembley Stadium.

West Bromwich Volunteer Rifle Corps

The *Volunteer Training Corps Gazette* for 26 December 1914 reported that this corps, which was initiated by Mr Fred W Hartland, had held its first drill on Tuesday 1 December 1914 at the drill hall which was used as headquarters. One hundred men paraded, many of them former members of the forces. Drills were being held on Tuesdays, Thursdays and Saturdays. Members paid an annual subscription of five shillings. Colonel G Walton Walker was commandant, Mr W Lawley, Jun was appointed as secretary, Sergeant Beale, instructor. Details of the uniform and badges worn by the corps appeared in *The Bulletin* of the Military Historical Society for February 1978. By Mr J Robert Williams, it tells how green-grey uniforms with bronze general service buttons were worn with no collar badges or shoulder titles. The grey-green cap had a dark band upon which was mounted a crowned Stafford knot in white metal. Mr Williams shows in his detailed article a c1915 photograph of Platoon Commander FWT Hartland in full uniform and complete with sword. All ranks, he notes, wore breeches and puttees, the other ranks having brown leather waistbelts. Weapons are mentioned too: Martini Henri rifles with bayonets for the men, pistols and swords for officers. The article is well illustrated, one photograph showing FWT Hartland's platoon on parade at Handsworth Carriage Works in May 1916. Mr Williams follows up his article in the May issue of *The Bulletin* with information concerning the inclusion of the West Bromwich Volunteer Rifle Corps with the South Staffordshire Battalion Staffordshire Volunteer Regiment in 1915. Illustrations include fine studies of Private Johnson in October 1916, Quartermaster Sergeant Dudley Lay, 1917, the Bugle Band on 2 July 1916 and the officers at Rawnsley Camp near Hednesford, August 1917.

West Didsbury Volunteer Defence Corps

There exists a gilt and coloured enamel badge to this corps which comprises a crowned oval superimposed upon crossed rifles. The union flag appears in the centre of a circle, the latter having the name of the corps, together with the date 1914.

West Ham Cadet Corps

Recognised 9 May 1918 (Army Order 240) and affiliated to the 1st Battalion Essex Volunteer Regiment.

West Ham Volunteer Training Corps

The decision to form this corps was taken at a meeting held at the Town Hall, Stratford, on 5 November 1914. Colonel J Brooker Ward, late of the 6th Essex Regiment (Territorial Force) consented to take command. Some 200 had enrolled, each member paying a subscription of one shilling. Ambulance, signalling and cycling sections were later established. Mr SF Mann was appointed secretary. Headquarters were at the town hall and drills were carried out in several council schools.

West Hertfordshire Volunteer Training Corps

The cap badge comprised the large letters VTC upon which was superimposed a stag's head. Below this, a scroll inscribed West Herts.

West Kent Volunteer Fencibles

The *Volunteer Training Corps Gazette* for 7 August 1915 reported that the Sydenham and Forest Hill VTC was now part of the 4th West Kent Volunteer Fencibles. Worn by the 3rd Battalion was a metal shoulder title made up of a separate number 3 above a curved WKVF.

West London Mounted Rifles

See 1st Volunteer Horse.

West London Regiment Volunteer Training Corps

The *Volunteer Training Corps Gazette* for 21 August 1915 noted that this regiment comprised nine battalions of which eight are mentioned: Kensington, Chelsea, Fulham, Hammersmith, Holborn, Paddington, Polytechnic, St Marylebone. The 1st Volunteer Horse (renamed West London Mounted Rifles) was attached by November 1915. The *Gazette* for 8 January 1916 featured the regiment and states that the battalions are made up from eight London boroughs: Westminster, Kensington, Holborn, Paddington, St Marylebone, Hammersmith, Chelsea, Fulham. Westminster provides two battalions, Marylebone also providing the Polytechnic Battalion. Total, ten infantry battalions. The West London Mounted Rifles, it is noted, had its headquarters in Paddington. Seven individual metal shoulder titles have been noted—Chelsea, Fulham, Hammersmith, Kensington, Paddington, Westminster, St Marylebone—which have the wording West London Regt over V.T.C. over the name of the battalion. The Mounted Rifles had West London over V.T.C. over Mounted Rifles.

West London Volunteers

The *Volunteer Training Corps Gazette* for 16 January 1915 noted that this corps was based on the physical standard required by the 'Victorian volunteer system'—its recruits being medically examined before allowed to enrol. There are four companies: Hammersmith, Fulham, Ealing and North Kensington. Hammersmith had some 200 members, the others, 100 each.

West London Volunteers

No 1 Company of this corps held a smoking concert at the Coronation Hall, Hammersmith Broadway on 19 December 1914.

West Riding Volunteers

A rose above a three-part scroll inscribed with the tile was the unit's cap badge. Also noted is a bronze shoulder tile for the 8th Battalion which has the number 8 over a curved WRV.

Westbury-on-Trim Drill Club

Formed in April 1915 and later became part of the 2nd (Coliseum) Battalion Bristol Volunteer Regiment.

Wigan Corps Lancashire Volunteers

The unit wore a bronze badge which Kipling and King describe as 'A heart-shaped plate surmounted by a coronet. Below this a shield bearing the Arms of England with a label of three points. Either side a Talbot holding an ostrich feather. Below the shield the Red Rose of Lancaster. Scrolls on either side of the Rose inscribed *Lancashire Volunteers*. A further scroll at the base of the design inscribed *Wigan Corps*. Sprigs of laurel at both ends of the scroll.'

Willaston School (Nantwich) Cadet Corps

Recognised 7 September 1915 (Army Order 430) and affiliated to the 4th Battalion Cheshire Volunteer Regiment.

Willenhall Volunteer Training Corps

Mentioned in the *Volunteer Training Corps Gazette* as guarding railways, bridges and canals.

Willesden and District Defence League

The *Volunteer Training Corps Gazette* for 26 December 1914 recorded that this corps was formed as a direct result of a meeting held at Willesden Green on 1 October at which the Rev EA Morgan took the chair. Sixty enrolled that same evening and by the end of the month the roll stood at 300. At present, notes the *Gazette*, there are three drill centres: Leopold Road School (illustrated) in Harlesden; Salisbury Road School in Kilburn, and St Andrew's School which is in St Andrew's Road, High Road, Willesden Green. Another at Dudden Hill School was to be added after Christmas. There are four companies: Harlesden ('A') under Mr Brockwell, Willesden Green and Cricklewood companies under Mr Sulman and the Kilburn Company which was commanded by Lieutenant Groom. Signalling and ambulance detachments were formed. The *Gazette* for 10 April 1915 reported that in future the corps would be known as the Willesden Battalion Middlesex Volunteer Regiment.

Williton Volunteer Training Corps

On the road from Taunton to Minehead, the small town of Williton in Somerset raised its Volunteer Corps after a meeting held at the Reading Room of Tuesday 24 November 1914, reported the *VTCG*. Mr T Hosegood took the chair and among others present were Mr T Evered, Mr CW Frowde, Mr TC Gooding, Dr S Graham, Mr F Risdon, Mr SL Rogers and Mr G Wilson. A committee was soon formed and this, in addition to some of those mentioned, would also include Lord St Audries. Two drills each week were held (Wednesdays and Saturdays), a room belonging to St Peter's Church (illustrated) being used, and for shooting, the Cleve Rifle Club gave assistance in musketry. The Local Territorial Force ('B' Company 5th Battalion Somerset Light Infantry) were also helpful in allowing the VTC the use of its miniature rifle range.

Wiltshire Regiment, 1st Volunteer Battalion Cadet Corps

Recognised 10 April 1918 (Army Order 173).

Wimbledon Athletes' Volunteer Force

The *Volunteer Training Corps Gazette* for 5 December 1914 reported that this corps had been in existence six weeks and had already enrolled almost 400 men. Colonel EA Neville, VD was in command. Drills were taken at Haydon's Road Recreation Ground, at the rear of the Fire Station in Queen's Road and at the Council Depot and school, also in Queen's Road. Hon secretary was Mr A Bellman of 78 Griffiths Road, Wimbledon. An ambulance section was run by Medical Officer of Health for Wimbledon, Mr EHT Nash. Formed into two companies, a third ('C') was proposed at a meeting held at the Masonic Committee Room, Merton on 15 January 1915. This was to be made up from Merton and district. All existing Merton volunteers then serving with 'A' or 'B' Companies were to transfer. Rutlish School (illustrated) in Rutlish Road was provided for drill purposes.

Windlesham Volunteer Training Corps

At Windlesham in north-west Surrey on the border with Berkshire, Lord Erskine presided over a meeting to form a village corps on Tuesday 8 December 1914.

Wisbech Grammar School Cadet Corps

Recognised 2 February 1918 (Army Order 149) and affiliated to the 3rd Battalion Cambridgeshire Volunteer Regiment.

Wisbech Volunteer Training Corps

The *Volunteer Training Corps Gazette* for 26 December 1914 reported that a corps had been formed at Wisbech by Messrs HL Grimwade and IDM English. Drills were taking place at the Corn Exchange on Mondays and Thursdays. About 100 had enrolled. On the committee were the Mayor of Wisbech, Messrs TR Dawbarn, HH English and WW West. Both HL Grimwade (lieutenant, 6th Norfolks) and IDM English (lieutenant in the old Wisbech Volunteers) were former army officers and were appointed as instructors.

Wolverhampton Rifle Corps

This corps by the end of 1914 had a membership of 150, all fully armed with .303 pattern rifles and side arms and under the instruction of two Bisley marksmen. It was noted by the *Volunteer Training Corps Gazette* for 6 February 1914 as one of the best organised and equipped in the country. A photograph of the corps taken at St Peter's Collegiate Church, Wolverhampton preparing for a route march to Himley shows the men without uniforms.

Wolverhampton Volunteer Defence Force

Inaugurated on 9 November 1914 and now, reported the *Volunteer Training Corps Gazette,* had over 400 members. There exists a bronze cap badge which features the arms of Wolverhampton (illustrated) on an eight-pointed star and a shoulder title consisting of the letters WVDF in a straight line.

Wood Green Volunteer Training Corps

The *Volunteer Training Corps Gazette* for 23 January 1915 noted that at a meeting held at the Wood Green Town Hall (illustrated) it was announced that some sixty had already applied for membership. Mr William P Harding was appointed commanding officer, Mr GT Graham the hon secretary, Mr EB Ridgway of the London & Provincial Bank, the treasurer. Mr Harding had for many years served with the 1st Volunteer Battalion Welsh Regiment, 2nd Volunteer Battalion Hampshire Regiment and the Honourable Artillery Company. Members were to pay a subscription of one shilling per quarter, officers to pay two shillings and sixpence. The *Gazette* for 13 February 1915 reported that the corps now had an ambulance section which consisted of all the ministers of religion in the district. They met twice a week for instruction in first aid etc. The corps provided a guard of honour for HM Queen Mary when she opened the Tipperary Club for wives of soldiers and sailors at Noel Park, Wood Green on Thursday 11 March 1915. There exists a small, circular, enamelled lapel badge which has crossed rifles and the title Wood Green Volunteer Training Corps.

Woodford Volunteer Training Corps

Headquarters of this Essex corps were at Churchfields Council Schools (illustrated), and its secretary, MGE Watts of 'St Denys', Fuller's Road, South Woodford. The corps had been started at the end of October 1914. Elected president was Mr A Lister Harrison, JP who put two fields at the disposal of the corps for drill purposes. Other training was undertaken at Epping Forest. Part of the land owned by Mr A Lister Harrison was acquired by Woodford Urban District Council in 1921 and later developed into Woodford Recreational Ground.

Wookey Hole Volunteer Training Corps

Formed by December 1914.

Woolwich Defence League

Formed 15 March 1915.

Wordsley Home Defence Corps

A meeting to discuss formation was held at Church Schools, Wordsley on 30 November 1914. A Mr Cochrane explained the working of the Stourbridge VTC and went on to say that he 'did not think the Germans would ever set foot in England, but should the unexpected happen, their villages, wives and children would share a similar fate to that of the Belgians.'

Wordsley Volunteer Training Corps

It was decided to form a corps at a public meeting held in the Church Schools, Wordsley on Monday 30 November 1914, reported the *Volunteer Training Corps Gazette*. Mr Stuart took the chair and Mr Collett was elected as secretary. Possibly the same corps as above.

Worcester Cadet Battalion

'A' Company recognised 13 April 1918 (Army Order 173) and 'B' Company recognised 25 May 1918 (Army Order 209). Both were affiliated to the 2nd Volunteer Battalion Worcestershire Regiment.

CHAPTER 4
HIGHER ORGANISATION

Artillery

First called Volunteer Artillery, designated as Royal Garrison Artillery (Volunteers) in 1918. The several units raised were:

Argyllshire Royal Garrison Artillery (Volunteers)
One company at Hanover Street, Dunoon.

City of Aberdeen Royal Garrison Artillery (Volunteers)
One company at Fonthill Barracks, Aberdeen.

City of Dundee Royal Garrison Artillery (Volunteers)
One company at Dundee.

City of Edinburgh Royal Garrison Artillery (Volunteers)
One company at Edinburgh.

Durham Royal Garrison Artillery (Volunteers)
Headquarters in Hartlepool and with three companies: Nos 1 and 2 at Hartlepool, No 3 at Sunderland.

East Yorkshire Royal Garrison Artillery (Volunteers)
Two companies, both located at the RAMC Barracks in Walton Street, Hull.

Hampshire Royal Garrison Artillery (Volunteers)
One company with headquarters at the Wessex Drill Hall in Portsmouth.

Northumberland Royal Garrison Artillery (Volunteers)
One company at Newcastle-upon-Tyne.

Engineers

First called Volunteer Engineers, designated Royal Engineers (Volunteers) in 1918

City of Dundee Royal Engineers (Volunteers)
One fortress (electric lights) company at Broughty Ferry.

City of Edinburgh Royal Engineers (Volunteers)
Headquarters at 8 Wemyss Place in Edinburgh with one signal company and one electric lights company.

City of Glasgow Royal Engineers (Volunteers)
One signal company and two motor airline sections at Jardine Street, Glasgow.

County of London Royal Engineers (Volunteers)

Headquarters at 43 Newgate Street, EC1 with one corps signal company, two motor airline sections and three army troops companies under the heading Post Office Companies (GPO South) at Carter Lane, EC4. Another section was titled London Army Troops Companies with headquarters at Balderton Street, Oxford Street, W1.

Durham Royal Engineers (Volunteers)
One signal and one electric lights company at West Hartlepool, one electric lights company and one works company in Stockton.

East Yorkshire Royal Engineer (Volunteers)
Headquarters at the Royal Engineers Barracks in Colonial Street, Hull with one signal company, one fortress (works) company and one electric lights company.

Lincolnshire Royal Engineers (Volunteers)
One signal company at the Old Barracks, Lincoln.

North Riding Royal Engineers (Volunteers)
One signal company, one fortress (works) company and one electric lights company, all at the Royal Exchange in Middlesbrough.

Northumberland Royal Engineers (Volunteers)
Headquarters at the Northumbrian Divisional Royal Engineers Drill Hall in Barras Bridge, Newcastle-upon-Tyne with one fortress (works) company and one signal company at Newcastle-upon-Tyne, and one electric lights company in Tynemouth.

Renfrewshire Royal Engineers (Volunteers)
One fortress (electric lights) company at 13 St James Place, Paisley.

Warwickshire Royal Engineers (Volunteers)
Headquarters as The Drill Hall, Thorpe Street, Birmingham with one corps signal company and one motor airline section.

Volunteer Regiments and Volunteer Battalions

Anglesey Volunteer Regiment
1st Battalion at Shire Hall, Llangefni, later moving to Church Street. Became 1st Volunteer Battalion Royal Welsh Fusiliers.

Argyllshire Volunteer Regiment
1st Battalion at The Drill Hall in Queen Street, Dunoon.

Ayrshire Volunteer Regiment
1/1st Battalion at South Harbour Street, Ayr.
2/1st Battalion at The RFA Drill Hall in John Finnie Street, Kilmarnock, later moving to the 4th Battalion Royal Scots Fusiliers Drill Hall in Titchfield Street.

Banffshire Volunteer Regiment
1st Battalion at The Drill Hall, Keith.

Bedfordshire Regiment
1st and 2nd Volunteer Battalions, see 1st and 2nd Battalions Bedfordshire Volunteer Regiment.

Bedfordshire Volunteer Regiment
1st Battalion at TF Headquarters in Ashburnham Road, Bedford. Became 1st Volunteer Battalion Bedfordshire Regiment.

2nd Battalion at Bank Chambers, Luton, later to The Armoury in Park Street. Became 2nd Volunteer Battalion, Bedfordshire Regiment.

Berkshire Volunteer Regiment

1st Battalion at The Drill Hall, St Mary's Butts, Reading. Became 1st Volunteer Battalion Royal Berkshire Regiment.

2nd Battalion at The Market Place, Wallingford, later to 12 St Mary's Street, Wallingford. The regiment disappeared from the Volunteer List during 1918. A possible amalgamation as the officers were now listed with those of the 1st Battalion.

Berwickshire Volunteer Regiment

1st Battalion at the Drill Hall, Duns. Became 2nd Volunteer Battalion King's Own Scottish Borderers.

Black Watch

1st Volunteer Battalion, see 1/1st Battalion City of Dundee Volunteer Regiment.
2nd Volunteer Battalion, see 2/1st Battalion City of Dundee Volunteer Regiment.
3rd Volunteer Battalion, see 1/1st Battalion Forfarshire Volunteer Regiment.
4th Volunteer Battalion, see 2/1st Battalion Forfarshire Volunteer Regiment.
5th Volunteer Battalion, see 1st Battalion Perthshire Volunteer Regiment.
6th Volunteer Battalion, see 2nd Battalion Perthshire Volunteer Regiment.
7th Volunteer Battalion, see 1/1st Battalion Fifeshire Volunteer Regiment.
8th Volunteer Battalion, see 2/1st Battalion Fifeshire Volunteer Regiment.
9th Volunteer Battalion, see 2nd Battalion Fifeshire Volunteer Regiment.

Border Regiment

1st Volunteer Battalion, see 1st Battalion Cumberland Volunteer Regiment.
2nd (Cumberland and Westmorland) Volunteer Battalion, see 1st Battalion Westmorland Volunteer Regiment.

Border Rifles Volunteer Battalion

Shown in the Volunteer List for October 1917 as an administrative unit for the Roxburghshire Volunteer Regiment and Selkirk Volunteer Regiment. The battalion later appeared in that for August 1918 as the Roxburghshire and Selkirk Volunteer Regiment, the Roxburghshire and Selkirkshire battalions now amalgamated under the title 1st Volunteer Battalion King's Own Scottish Borderers with headquarters at Island House, Galashiels.

Buckinghamshire Volunteer Regiment

Major-General JC Swain in his book, *The Citizen Soldiers of Buckinghamshire 1795-1926*, records how the regiment was formed on 7 December 1914 as the Buckingham Volunteer Defence Corps with three companies and a fourth soon added. The Volunteer Force List for July 1917 shows:

1st Battalion at The Drill Hall, Slough. Major-General Swain notes that the 4th Battalion was absorbed in 1918, providing the left half of the 1st Battalion at Wycombe. Became 3rd Volunteer Battalion Oxfordshire and Buckinghamshire Light Infantry in 1918.

2nd Battalion at 31 Market Square, Aylesbury. Became 4th Volunteer Battalion Oxfordshire and Buckinghamshire Light Infantry in 1918.

3rd Battalion at Lathbury Park, Newport Pagnell. Became 5th Volunteer Battalion Oxfordshire and Buckinghamshire Light Infantry in 1918.

4th Battalion at 12 Easton Street, High Wycombe. Amalgamated with 1st Battalion and disappeared from the Volunteer List in 1918.

Buffs (East Kent Regiment)
1st Volunteer Battalion, see 1st Kent Battalion Kent Volunteer Regiment.
2nd Volunteer Battalion, see 2nd Kent Battalion Kent Volunteer Regiment.
3rd Volunteer Battalion, see 4th Kent Battalion Kent Volunteer Regiment.
4th Volunteer Battalion, see 8th Kent Battalion Kent Volunteer Regiment.

Caithness and Sutherland Highland Volunteer Regiment
1st Battalion at the Drill Hall, Golspie, Sutherland.

Cambridgeshire Regiment
1st Volunteer Battalion, see 1st Battalion Cambridgeshire Volunteer Regiment.
2nd Volunteer Battalion, see 2nd Battalion Cambridgeshire Volunteer Regiment.
3rd Volunteer Battalion, see 3rd Battalion Cambridgeshire Volunteer Regiment.

Cambridgeshire Volunteer Regiment
1st Battalion at the Territorial Drill Hall in East Road, Cambridge. Became 1st Volunteer Battalion Cambridgeshire Regiment.
2nd Battalion at County Hall, Hobson Street, Cambridge, later to the Territorial Old Headquarters at 14 Corn Exchange Street. Became 2nd Volunteer Battalion Cambridgeshire Regiment in 1918.
3rd Battalion at The Barracks, Silver Street, Ely. Became 3rd Volunteer Battalion Cambridgeshire Regiment in 1918.

Carmarthenshire Volunteer Regiment
1st Battalion at the Drill Hall, Llanelli. Amalgamated with Pembrokeshire Volunteer Regiment to form Pembrokeshire and Carmarthenshire Volunteer Regiment in 1918.

Carnarvonshire Volunteer Regiment
The bronze cap badges of this regiment featured the arms of Caernarvon Borough Council: the three lions of England and the eagle of Owen Gwynedd, Prince of North Wales.
1st Battalion (Northern) at Mostyn Street, Llandudno. Became 3rd Volunteer Battalion Royal Welsh Fusiliers in 1918.
2nd Battalion (Southern) at Tower Buildings, Carnarvon. Disappeared from the Volunteer List in 1918, the officers afterwards listed with those of the 1st Battalion.

Cheshire Regiment
1st Volunteer Battalion, see 1st Battalion Cheshire Volunteer Regiment.
2nd Volunteer Battalion, see 2nd Battalion Cheshire Volunteer Regiment.
3rd Volunteer Battalion, see 3rd Battalion Cheshire Volunteer Regiment.
4th Volunteer Battalion, see 4th Battalion Cheshire Volunteer Regiment.
5th Volunteer Battalion, see 5th Battalion Cheshire Volunteer Regiment.
6th Volunteer Battalion, see 6th Battalion Cheshire Volunteer Regiment.
7th Volunteer Battalion, see 7th Battalion Cheshire Volunteer Regiment.
8th Volunteer Battalion, see 9th Battalion Cheshire Volunteer Regiment.
9th Volunteer Battalion, see 10th Battalion Cheshire Volunteer Regiment.
10th Volunteer Battalion, see 11th Battalion Cheshire Volunteer Regiment.

Cheshire Volunteer Regiment
The regiment was divided into two groups: Group A with the 1st, 4th 5th, 6th, 7th and 9th Battalions, Group B with the 2nd, 3rd, 8th, 10th and 11th.
1st Battalion (Altrincham) at the Drill Hall, Hale. Became 1st Volunteer Battalion Cheshire Regiment.

2nd Battalion (Birkenhead) at Grange Road West, Birkenhead. Became 2nd Volunteer Battalion Cheshire Regiment.

3rd Battalion (Chester & Eddisbury) at the Drill Hall, Chester. Became 3rd Volunteer Battalion Cheshire Regiment.

4th Battalion (Crewe) at 7 Market Street, Crewe. Became 4th Volunteer Battalion Cheshire Regiment.

5th Battalion (East Cheshire) at the Drill Hall, Stalybridge. Became 5th Volunteer Battalion Cheshire Regiment.

6th Battalion (Knutsford) at the Drill Hall, Wilmslow. Became 6th Volunteer Battalion Cheshire Regiment.

7th Battalion (Macclesfield) at the Drill Hall, Macclesfield. Designated 7th Volunteer Battalion Cheshire Regiment.

8th Battalion (Northwich) at the Drill Hall, Darwin Street, Northwich. Disappeared from the Volunteer List during 1918, the officers now listed with those of the 4th Battalion.

9th Battalion (Stockport) at the Armoury, Stockport. Became 8th Volunteer Battalion Cheshire Regiment.

10th Battalion (Wirral) at Beechfield, Heswall. Became 9th Volunteer Battalion Cheshire Regiment.

11th Battalion (Wallasey) at the Old Fire Station in Manor Road, Wallasey. Became 10th Volunteer Battalion Cheshire Regiment.

City of Aberdeen Volunteer Regiment

1st Battalion at 80 Hardgate, Aberdeen.

City of Bristol Volunteer Regiment

1st Battalion (University) at University Road, Bristol, later to SMRE, 32 Park Road, Bristol. Became 2nd (Bristol) Volunteer Battalion Gloucestershire Regiment.

2nd Battalion (Coliseum) at 9 Cave Street, Portland Square, Bristol, later to St Michael's Hill, Bristol. Became 4th (Bristol) Volunteer Battalion Gloucestershire Regiment.

3rd Battalion (Athletes) at 36 Queen Square, Bristol, moving to Old Market Street, Bristol. Became 6th (Bristol) Volunteer Battalion Gloucestershire Regiment.

City of Dundee Volunteer Regiment

1/1st Battalion at the Douglas Street Drill Hall in Dundee. Designated 1st Volunteer Battalion Black Watch in 1918.

2/1st Battalion at Douglas Street Drill Hall, Dundee, moving later to Bell Street, Dundee. Designated 2nd Volunteer Battalion Black Watch in 1918.

City of Edinburgh Volunteer Regiment:

1/1st Battalion at Forest Hill, Edinburgh. Designated 1st Volunteer Battalion Royal Scots (Lothian Regiment) in 1918.

2/1st Battalion at Forest Hill Edinburgh. Designated 2nd Volunteer Battalion Royal Scots (Lothian Regiment) in 1918.

City of Glasgow Volunteer Regiment

1st Battalion, 24 Hill Street, Garnethill, Glasgow.

2nd Battalion, Coplaw Street, Victoria Road, Glasgow

3rd Battalion, 19 Taylor Street, Glasgow

4th Battalion, Yorkhill Parade, Glasgow.

City of London Volunteer Regiment

The regiment was divided into two groups: Group A, containing 1/1st, 2/1st and 2nd Battalions, Group B with the 4th, 5th and 6th.

1/1st Battalion at 57/58 Leadenhall Street, EC3, later moving to 57a Farringdon Road, EC1.

2/1st Battalion, Pitfield Street Baths, Hoxton, N1, later moving to 112 Shaftesbury Street, N.

2nd Battalion, Guildhall, EC2, later moving to the Drill Hall, Handel Street, Bloomsbury, WC1.

3rd Battalion. Not shown in Volunteer List for October 1917.

4th Battalion (National Guard) at 9 Throgmorton Avenue, EC2, later moving to 130 Bunhill Row, EC2.

5th Battalion (National Guard) at 51 Calthorpe Street, WC1.

6th Battalion (National Guard) at London House, 3 New London Street, EC3, later moving to 85 Minories, EC1. The history of the City of London National Guard records how in July 1916 the Baltic, Mincing, and Mark Lane Volunteers were absorbed as companies.

Clackmannanshire Volunteer Regiment

1st Battalion at the Drill Hall, Alloa.

Cornwall Volunteer Regiment

1st Battalion (Western) at The Drill Hall in Pydar Street, Truro. Became 1st Volunteer Battalion Duke of Cornwall's Light Infantry.

2nd Battalion (Eastern) at Cross Street, Padstow. Became 2nd Volunteer Battalion Duke of Cornwall's Light Infantry.

County of Aberdeen Volunteer Regiment

1/1st Battalion at 52 Guild Street, Aberdeen.

2/1st Battalion at 52 Guild Street, Aberdeen, later to 156 Union Street.

County of London Volunteer Regiment

The regiment is divided into six groups: Central Group containing 1st, 2nd, 3rd and 4th Battalions; Eastern Group with 5th, 1/6th and 2/6th Battalions; Northern Group, 7th, 8th, 1/9th and 2/9th Battalions; South-Eastern Group, 1/11th, 2/11th, 16th and 17th Battalions; South-Western Group, 19th. 1/12th, 2/12th, 13th, 14th and 15th Battalions and Western Group, 18th, 19th, 20th and 21st Battalions.

1st Battalion at Imperial College, Union Street, Kensington, SW7.

2nd Battalion at 1 Paper Buildings, Temple, EC4, later to Elverton Street, Westminster.

3rd Battalion at Lord's Cricket Ground, St John's Wood, NW8. The battalion was not shown in the Volunteer List for August 1918.

4th Battalion at 26 Pancras Road, NW1.

5th Battalion (Bethnal Green) at 33a Bonner Road, Bethnal Green, SE, later to Victoria Park Square, Bethnal Green.

1/6th Battalion (Poplar and Holborn) at 5 Verulam Buildings, Gray's Inn, WC1.

2/6th Battalion (Finsbury) at Finsbury Town Hall, Rosebery Avenue, EC1.

3/6th Battalion (Stepney) at the Foundation Schools, 179 Whitechapel Road, E1.

7th Battalion (Hampstead) at Holly Bush Vale, Hampstead, NW3, later to 90 Henry Street, St John's Wood, NW8 and afterwards 76 High Street, Camden Town, NW1.

1/8th Battalion (St Pancras) at 105 Charlotte Street, Fitzroy Square, W1, later to 76 High Street, Camden Town, NW1. The battalion was not shown in the August 1918 Volunteer List, its officers now included with those of the 7th Battalion.

2/8th Battalion (Islington) at the Central Library, Holloway Road, N, later to the RGA Depot, Offord Road, N1. The August 1918 Volunteer List shows the battalion now designated as 1st.

1/9th Battalion (Stoke Newington) at 92 Stamford Hill, N16, later to 7 Albion Grove, Albion Road, Stoke Newington, N16. The battalion is not shown in the Volunteer List for August 1918, its officers now with those of the 2/9th which has been designated as 9th.

2/9th Battalion (Hackney) at 92 Stamford Hill, N6. Title changed to 9th Battalion.

10th Battalion (Lambeth) at 5 Electric Lane, Brixton, SW2

1/11th Battalion (Southwark) at the Town Hall, Walworth Road, SE17, later to St John's Institute, Larcom Road, Walworth Road, SE17.

2/11th Battalion (Bermondsey) at the Volunteer Drill Hall, Yalding Road, Bermondsey, later to 67 Southwark Park Road.

1/12th Battalion (Dulwich) at 533 Lordship Lane, Dulwich, SE22, later to Grove House, Dulwich Common, SE.

2/12th Battalion (Camberwell) at 6 Peckham Road, SE5

13th Battalion (Southfields and Putney) at London County and Westminster Bank, Southfields, SW19

14th Battalion (Wandsworth), 123 Trinity Road, Upper Tooting, SW17, later to 27 St John's Hill, Clapham Junction, SW11.

15th Battalion (Streatham) at 10 Mitcham Lane, Streatham, SW16, later to 344 Streatham High Road, SW16.

16th Battalion (Deptford) at 221 New Cross Road, SE14.

17th Battalion (Lewisham) at 272 High Street, Lewisham, SE13.

18th Battalion (Westminster) at City Hall, Charing Cross Road, WC2. Not shown in Volunteer List for August 1918.

19th Battalion (Kensington and Paddington) at 8 Bayswater Hill, W2. The battalion was later divided as 1/19th Battalion at 8 Bayswater Road, W2 and 2/19th Battalion. No location for the latter appeared and it was not shown in August 1918 Volunteer List.

20th Battalion (Hammersmith) at 10 Ravenscourt Park, Hammersmith, W6, later to the Drill Hall, Wood Lane, Shepherd's Bush, W12.

21st Battalion (St. Marylebone) at The Polytechnic, Regent Street, W1.

Cumberland and Westmoreland Volunteer Regiment

See Cumberland Volunteer Regiment.

Cumberland Volunteer Regiment

Cap badge, a circle inscribed Cumberland Volunteer Regiment surmounted by an Imperial crown. In the centre, the shield from the arms of Carlisle: a cross with a rose in each corner and another in the centre of the cross.

1/1st Battalion at Albert House, Albert Street, Carlisle. Became 1st Volunteer Battalion Border Regiment.

2/1st Battalion at the Drill Hall, Edrin Street, Workington. Disappeared from the Volunteer List between February and August 1918.

Sometime between February and August 1918, the regiment was designated, after amalgamation, as the Cumberland and Westmoreland Volunteer Regiment and went on to provide two volunteer battalions: 1st Volunteer Battalion Border Regiment at Albert House, Albert Street, Carlisle. (the former 1/1st Battalion) and 2nd (Cumberland and Westmoreland) Volunteer Battalion Border

Regiment, at the Drill Hall, Edrin Street, Workington (the former 1st Battalion, Westmoreland Volunteer Regiment).

Denbighshire Volunteer Regiment

A cap badge was worn which featured in the centre of an eight-pointed star, a shield bearing the lion rampant from the arms of Denbigh Borough Council.

1st Battalion at the Drill Hall, Colwyn Bay. In 1918 the regiment amalgamated with the Flintshire Volunteer Regiment under the title Flintshire and Denbighshire Volunteer Regiment. Later, the 2nd Volunteer Battalion Royal Welsh Fusiliers. See Flintshire Volunteer Regiment.

Derbyshire Volunteer Regiment

The regiment was divided into two groups: Group A with the 2nd, 3rd, 4th and 8th Battalions, Group B with 1st, 5th, 6th and 7th.

1st Battalion at 25 The Wardwick, Derby, later to 87 Siddals Road, Derby. Became 1st Volunteer Battalion Sherwood Foresters (Nottinghamshire and Derbyshire Regiment).

2nd Battalion at 4 Iron Gate, Chesterfield, later to The Drill Hall, Chesterfield. Became 2nd Volunteer Battalion Sherwood Foresters (Nottinghamshire and Derbyshire Regiment).

3rd Battalion at Stanton Street, Ilkeston. Became 3rd Volunteer Battalion Sherwood Foresters (Nottinghamshire and Derbyshire Regiment).

4th Battalion at Staveley Iron Works, Chesterfield, later to The Drill Hall, Staveley. Became 4th Volunteer Battalion Sherwood Foresters (Nottinghamshire and Derbyshire Regiment).

5th Battalion at Foston Hall, Derby. Became 5th Volunteer Battalion Sherwood Foresters (Nottinghamshire and Derbyshire Regiment).

6th Battalion at The Gardens, Buxton. Became 6th Volunteer Battalion, Sherwood Foresters (Nottinghamshire and Derbyshire Regiment).

7th Battalion. The following locations are given in the Volunteer List: Aston Hall, Derby, later to Alderslade, Aston-on-Trent and afterwards to Ashton-on-Trent, Derby. Became 7th Volunteer Battalion Sherwood Foresters (Nottinghamshire and Derbyshire Regiment).

8th Battalion at Belper. Became 8th Volunteer Battalion Sherwood Foresters (Nottinghamshire and Derbyshire Regiment).

Devonshire Regiment

1st Volunteer Battalion, see 1st Battalion Devonshire Volunteer Regiment.

2nd Volunteer Battalion, see 2nd Battalion Devonshire Volunteer Regiment.

3rd Volunteer Battalion, see 4th Battalion Devonshire Volunteer Regiment.

Devonshire Volunteer Regiment

1st Battalion (Exeter) at St James's Park, Exeter, later to 12 Longbrook Street, then back to St James Street. Became 1st Volunteer Battalion Devonshire Regiment, headquarters again sown as 12 Longbrook Street by December 1918.

2nd Battalion (Plymouth) at The Orderly Room, The Guildhall, Plymouth, later to 23 Ford Park Road, Plymouth Became 2nd Volunteer Battalion Devonshire Regiment.

3rd Battalion (North Devon) at The Drill Hall, Torridge Hill, Bideford, later to Crelake Hall, Tavistock. Disappears from Volunteer List between February and August 1918.

4th Battalion (South Devon) at Albert Road, Torquay. Became 3rd Volunteer Battalion Devonshire Regiment.

5th Battalion (East Devon) at Avishayes, Sidmouth, later to Market Place, Sidmouth. Disappears from Volunteer List between February and August 1918.

Dorsetshire Regiment

1st Volunteer Battalion, see 1st Battalion Dorsetshire Volunteer Regiment.

Dorsetshire Volunteer Regiment

The cap badge featured the three lions from the seal of Dorset County Council.

1st Battalion at 2 West Walks, Dorchester. Became 1st Volunteer Battalion Dorsetshire Regiment.

Duke of Cornwall's Light Infantry

1st Volunteer Battalion, see 1st Battalion Cornwall Volunteer Regiment.

2nd Volunteer Battalion, see 2nd Battalion Cornwall Volunteer Regiment.

Duke of Wellington's Regiment

1st Volunteer Battalion, see 2nd Battalion West Riding Volunteer Regiment.

2nd Volunteer Battalion, see 9th Battalion West Riding Volunteer Regiment.

3rd Volunteer Battalion, see 8th Battalion West Riding Volunteer Regiment.

4th Volunteer Battalion, see 20th Battalion West Riding Volunteer Regiment.

5th Volunteer Battalion, see 6th Battalion West Riding Volunteer Regiment.

Dumbartonshire Volunteer Regiment

1st Battalion at Artillery Drill Hall, Helensburgh.

2nd Battalion at The Drill Hall, Kirkintilloch, later to 194 Bath Street, Glasgow, then to 44 West George Street, Glasgow.

Dumfriesshire Volunteer Regiment

The cap badge featured the winged figure of Victory standing on a dragon and with a sword in her right hand and a shield on the left arm.

1st Battalion (Dumfries). Became 3rd Volunteer Battalion King's Own Scottish Borderers.

Durham Light Infantry

1st Volunteer Battalion, see 1st Battalion Durham Volunteer Regiment.

2nd Volunteer Battalion, see 2nd Battalion Durham Volunteer Regiment.

3rd Volunteer Battalion, see 3rd Battalion Durham Volunteer Regiment.

4th Volunteer Battalion, see 4th Battalion Durham Volunteer Regiment.

5th Volunteer Battalion, see 5th Battalion Durham Volunteer Regiment.

6th Volunteer Battalion, see 6th Battalion Durham Volunteer Regiment.

7th Volunteer Battalion, see 7th Battalion Durham Volunteer Regiment.

8th Volunteer Battalion, see 12th Battalion Durham Volunteer Regiment.

9th Volunteer Battalion, see 9th Battalion Durham Volunteer Regiment.

10th Volunteer Battalion, see 10th Battalion Durham Volunteer Regiment.

11th Volunteer Battalion, see 11th Battalion Durham Volunteer Regiment.

Durham Volunteer Regiment

The regiment was divided into two groups: Group A with 1st, 3rd, 4th and 9th Battalions, Group B with the 2nd 5th, 6th, 7th, 8th. 10th and 11th Battalions. In the Volunteer List for October 1917 three groups are shown: Group A with the 5th, 6th and 10th Battalions, Group B with the 2nd, 7th, 8th, 11th and 12th, Group C, the 1st, 3rd, 4th and 9th.

1st Battalion at Elm Terrace Drill Hall, Gateshead. Became 1st Volunteer Battalion Durham Light Infantry.

2nd Battalion at Sunderland. Became 2nd Volunteer Battalion Durham Light Infantry.

3rd Battalion at Bishop Auckland. Became 3rd Volunteer Battalion Durham Light Infantry.

4th Battalion at Darlington, the Volunteer List for October 1917 giving the location as Stockton, but that for August 1918 gives Drill Hall, Darlington. Became 4th Volunteer Battalion Durham Light Infantry.

5th Battalion at Stockton-on-Tees. Became 5th Volunteer Battalion Durham Light Infantry.

6th Battalion at West Hartlepool. Became 6th Volunteer Battalion Durham Light Infantry.

7th Battalion at Pallion Yard, Sunderland. Became 7th Volunteer Battalion Durham Light Infantry.

8th Battalion at Pallion Yard, Sunderland. Disappeared from the Volunteer List between February and August 1918, the officers now with 7th Battalion which has been designated 7th Volunteer Battalion Durham Light Infantry.

9th Battalion at Birtley. Became 9th Volunteer Battalion Durham Light Infantry.

10th Battalion at The Dockyard, West Hartlepool. Became 10th Volunteer Battalion Durham Light Infantry.

11th Battalion at Sunderland. Became 11th Volunteer Battalion Durham Light Infantry.

12th Battalion at Houghton-le-Spring. Became 8th Volunteer Battalion Durham Light Infantry.

East Lancashire Regiment

1st Volunteer Battalion, see 10th Battalion Lancashire Volunteer Regiment.
2nd Volunteer Battalion, see 1/11th Battalion Lancashire Volunteer Regiment.
3rd Volunteer Battalion, see 2/11th Battalion Lancashire Volunteer Regiment.
4th Volunteer Battalion, see 3/11th Battalion Lancashire Volunteer Regiment.

East Surrey Regiment

1st Volunteer Battalion, see 2nd Battalion Surrey Volunteer Regiment.
2nd Volunteer Battalion, see 5th Battalion Surrey Volunteer Regiment.
3rd Volunteer Battalion, see 9th Battalion Surrey Volunteer Regiment.

East Yorkshire Regiment

1st Volunteer Battalion, see 1st Battalion East Yorkshire Volunteer Regiment.
2nd Volunteer Battalion, see 2nd Battalion East Yorkshire Volunteer Regiment.
3rd Volunteer Battalion, see 1/3rd Battalion East Yorkshire Volunteer Regiment.
4th Volunteer Battalion, see 2/3rd Battalion East Yorkshire Volunteer Regiment.

East Yorkshire Volunteer Regiment

1st Battalion at Artillery Barracks, Park Street, Hull. Became 1st Volunteer Battalion East Yorkshire Regiment.

2nd Battalion at the Cyclist Barracks, Park Street, Hull. Became 2nd Volunteer Battalion East Yorkshire Regiment.

1/3rd Battalion at The Drill Hall, Grayburn. Became 3rd Volunteer Battalion East Yorkshire Regiment in 1918 with headquarters at 4 Railway Street, Beverley.

2/3rd Battalion at 4 Railway Street, Beverly. Became 4th Volunteer Battalion East Yorkshire Regiment with headquarters at The Drill Hall, Greyburn Lane, Beverley.

Essex Regiment

1st Volunteer Battalion, see 1st Battalion Essex Volunteer Regiment.
2nd Volunteer Battalion, see 1/2nd Battalion Essex Volunteer Regiment.
3rd Volunteer Battalion, see 3rd Battalion Essex Volunteer Regiment.
4th Volunteer Battalion, see 4th Battalion Essex Volunteer Regiment.
5th Volunteer Battalion, see 5th Battalion Essex Volunteer Regiment.
6th Volunteer Battalion, see 2/2nd Battalion Essex Volunteer Regiment.

7th Volunteer Battalion, see 3/2nd Battalion Essex Volunteer Regiment.

Essex Volunteer Regiment

The arms of Essex, three seaxes, featured on the cap badges.

1st Battalion at the Town Hall, West Ham, later The Cedars, West Ham, E15. Became 1st Volunteer Battalion Essex Regiment in 1918.

1/2nd Battalion at Woodredon, Waltham Abbey, later to Warlies, Waltham Abbey. Became 2nd Volunteer Battalion Essex Regiment with headquarters at The Drill Hall, Market Road, Chelmsford.

2/2nd Battalion at 17 Sir Isaac's Walk, Colchester. Became 6th Volunteer Battalion Essex Regiment.

3/2nd Battalion at Braxted Park, Witham, later to High Street, Witham. Became 7th Volunteer Battalion Essex Regiment, headquarters moving to Madina Villa, Witham between September and December 1918.

3rd Battalion at 23 Fillebrook Road, Leytonstone, later to 536 High Road, Leytonstone. Became 3rd Volunteer Battalion Essex Regiment.

4th Battalion at The Drill Hall, East Street, Prittlewell. Became 4th Volunteer Battalion Essex Regiment in 1918.

5th Battalion at 3 Hermon Hill, Wanstead. *The War Budget* for 17 February 1916 refers to the battalion as 5th (Epping Forest) Battalion and mentions that the Hale End Company was a present helping forwarding the work on the new Red Cross Hospital which their President, Mr T Armstrong, is building for the district. Became 5th Volunteer Battalion Essex Regiment with headquarters at Tylney House, Eagle Lane, Snaresbrook.

Fifeshire Volunteer Regiment

1st Battalion (Western) at Kirkcaldy. The Volunteer List for October 1917 shows the battalion divided as: 1/1st Battalion at The Drill Hall, Hunter Street, Kirkcaldy. Became 7th Volunteer Battalion Black Watch. 2/1st Battalion at Municipal Buildings, Dunfermline. Became 8th Volunteer Battalion, Black Watch.

2nd Battalion (Eastern), St Andrew's, later to The Drill Hall, City Road, St Andrew's. Became 9th Volunteer Battalion Black Watch.

Flintshire Volunteer Regiment

1st Battalion at The Drill Hall, Mold. The regiment amalgamated with Denbighshire in 1918 to form the Flintshire and Denbighshire Volunteer Regiment containing 2nd Volunteer Battalion Royal Welsh Fusiliers at The Drill Hall, Rhyl.

Flintshire and Denbighshire Volunteer Regiment

See Flintshire Volunteer Regiment.

Forfarshire Volunteer Regiment

1/1st Battalion at The Drill Hall, Forfar. Became 3rd Volunteer Battalion Black Watch.

2/1st Battalion at 61 High Street, Arbroath. Became 4th Volunteer Battalion Black Watch.

Glamorganshire Volunteer Regiment

The Volunteer List for October 1917 shows the regiment organised into two groups: Western Group with the 3rd and 4th Battalions, Eastern Group with 1st, 2nd and 5th.

1st Battalion at The Drill Hall, Dumfries Place, Cardiff. Became 2nd Volunteer Battalion Welsh Regiment.

2nd Battalion at The Drill Hall, Merthyr. Became 3rd Volunteer Battalion Welsh Regiment.

3rd Battalion at The Drill Hall, Swansea. Became 4th Volunteer Battalion Welsh Regiment.

4th Battalion at The Drill Hall, Neath. Became 5th Volunteer Battalion Welsh Regiment.

5th Battalion at 31 Gelliwasted Road, Pontypridd. Became 6th Volunteer Battalion Welsh Regiment.

Gloucestershire Regiment

1st Volunteer Battalion, see 1st Battalion Gloucestershire Volunteer Regiment.

2nd (Bristol) Volunteer Battalion, see 1st Battalion City of Bristol Volunteer Regiment.

3rd Volunteer Battalion, see 3rd Battalion Gloucestershire Volunteer Regiment.

4th (Bristol) Volunteer Battalion, see 2nd Battalion City of Bristol Volunteer Regiment.

5th Volunteer Battalion, see 4th Battalion Gloucestershire Volunteer Regiment.

6th (Bristol) Volunteer Battalion, see 3rd Battalion City of Bristol Volunteer Regiment.

Gloucestershire Volunteer Regiment

1st Battalion (Berkeley Vale) at Dursley. Became 1st Volunteer Battalion Gloucestershire Regiment.

2nd Battalion. Not shown in Volunteer List for October 1917.

3rd Battalion (Gloucester and Cheltenham) at Gloucester. Became 3rd Volunteer Battalion Gloucestershire Regiment.

4th Battalion (Stroud and Cirencester) at Stroud. Became 5th Volunteer Battalion Gloucestershire Regiment.

Haddingtonshire Volunteer Regiment

1st Battalion at Haddington. Became 5th Volunteer Battalion Royal Scots (Lothian Regiment).

Hampshire Regiment

1st Volunteer Battalion, see 1st Battalion Hampshire Volunteer Regiment.

2nd Volunteer Battalion, see 2nd Battalion Hampshire Volunteer Regiment.

3rd Volunteer Battalion, see 3rd Battalion Hampshire Volunteer Regiment.

4th Volunteer Battalion, see 4th Battalion Hampshire Volunteer Regiment.

Hampshire Volunteer Regiment

1st Battalion at Hyde Close, Winchester. Became 1st Volunteer Battalion Hampshire Regiment.

2nd Battalion at Hamilton House, Commercial Road, Southampton. Became 2nd Volunteer Battalion Hampshire Regiment.

3rd Battalion at Portsmouth. Became 3rd Volunteer Battalion Hampshire Regiment.

4th Battalion at The Drill Hall, Lansdowne, Bournemouth. Became 4th Volunteer Battalion Hampshire Regiment.

Herefordshire Regiment

1st Volunteer Battalion, see 1st Battalion Herefordshire Volunteer Regiment.

Herefordshire Volunteer Regiment

1st Battalion at The Drill Hall, Friar Street, Hereford. Became 1st Volunteer Battalion Herefordshire Regiment.

Hertfordshire Regiment

1st Volunteer Battalion, see 1st Battalion Hertfordshire Volunteer Regiment.

2nd Volunteer Battalion, see 2nd Battalion Hertfordshire Volunteer Regiment.

3rd Volunteer Battalion, see 3rd Battalion Hertfordshire Volunteer Regiment.

Hertfordshire Volunteer Regiment

Cap badge, the Hart lodged from the county arms.

1st Battalion at 103 Walworth Road, Hitchin, later to 28 St Andrew's Street, Hereford. Became 1st Volunteer Battalion Hertfordshire Regiment.

2nd Battalion at Clarendon Hall, Watford. Became 2nd Volunteer Battalion Hertfordshire Regiment.

3rd Battalion at The Drill Hall, Hatfield Road, St Albans. Became 3rd Volunteer Battalion Hertfordshire Regiment.

Huntingdonshire Volunteer Regiment

1st Battalion at Huntingdon.

Isle of Wight Volunteer Regiment

1st Battalion at 32 Holyrood Street, Newport, later to the RFA Drill Hall, Newport.

Kent Volunteer Regiment

The regiment is divided into three groups: East Kent Group with 1st, 2nd and 4th Battalions, Mid-Kent Group with 3rd, 5th, 6th and 8th Battalions, West Kent Group, 7th, 9th, 10th, 11th and 12th.

1st Battalion (Cinque Ports) at 114 High Street, Hythe, later to Conduit Street, then to 70 Marine Parade. Became 1st Volunteer Battalion Buffs (East Kent Regiment).

2nd Battalion (St Augustine's) at The Drill Hall, St Peter's Lane, Canterbury. Became 2nd Volunteer Battalion Buffs (East Kent Regiment) in 1918.

3rd Battalion (Tonbridge) at The Drill Hall, Tonbridge. Became 1st Volunteer Battalion Queen's Own (Royal West Kent Regiment).

4th Battalion (Thanet) at The Banks, Broadstairs. Became 3rd Volunteer Battalion Buffs (East Kent Regiment).

5th Battalion (Maidstone) at Old Palace, Maidstone. Became 2nd Volunteer Battalion Queen's Own (Royal West Kent Regiment).

6th Battalion (Thames and Medway) at The Drill Hall, New Road, Chatham. Not shown in the Volunteer List for August 1918.

7th Battalion at 12 Bromley Road, Beckenham, later to The Drill Hall, Parish Lane, Penge. Became 3rd Volunteer Battalion Queen's Own (Royal West Kent Regiment).

8th Battalion (Weald) at Chantry, Headcorn, later to The Drill Hall, Ashford. Became 4th Volunteer Battalion Buffs (East Kent Regiment).

9th Battalion at the Council Offices, Bexley Heath, later to 'Trevethan', Bexley Road, Erith. Became 4th Volunteer Battalion Queen's Own (Royal West Kent Regiment).

10th Battalion at 31 Silverdale, London, SE16. Not in the Volunteer List for August 1918, the officers now with the 7th Battalion which has been designated 3rd Volunteer Battalion Queen's Own (Royal West Kent Regiment).

11th Battalion at Court Road, Eltham, later to The Drill Hall, Southend Road, Eltham, SE9. Not in Volunteer List for August 1917.

12th Battalion at Argyle House, Sevenoaks. Not shown in the Volunteer List for August 1918, the officers now with the 3rd Battalion which has been designated 1st Volunteer Battalion Queen's Own (Royal West Kent Regiment).

The regiment is divided into three groups

Kincardineshire Volunteer Regiment

1st Battalion at 28 Guild Street, Aberdeen, later to 5 Union Terrace, Aberdeen.

King's (Liverpool Regiment)

1st Volunteer Battalion, see 5th Battalion Lancashire Volunteer Regiment.

2nd Volunteer Battalion, see 6th Battalion Lancashire Volunteer Regiment.

3rd Volunteer Battalion, see 8th Battalion Lancashire Volunteer Regiment.

King's Own (Royal Lancaster Regiment)
1st Volunteer Battalion, see 13th Battalion Lancashire Volunteer Regiment.
2nd Volunteer Battalion, see 14th Battalion Lancashire Volunteer Regiment.

King's Own Scottish Borderers
1st Volunteer Battalion, see Border Rifles Volunteer Battalion.
2nd Volunteer Battalion, see 1st Battalion Berwickshire Volunteer Regiment.
3rd Volunteer Battalion, see 1st Battalion Dumfriesshire Volunteer Regiment.
4th Volunteer Battalion, see 1st Battalion Kirkcudbrightshire Volunteer Regiment.

King's Own Yorkshire Light Infantry
1st Volunteer Battalion, see 10th Battalion West Riding Volunteer Regiment.
2nd Volunteer Battalion, see 7th Battalion West Riding Volunteer Regiment.
3rd Volunteer Battalion, see 19th Battalion West Riding Volunteer Regiment.

King's (Shropshire Light Infantry)
1st Volunteer Battalion, see 1st Battalion Shropshire Volunteer Regiment.
2nd Volunteer Battalion, see 2nd Battalion Shropshire Volunteer Regiment.

Kinross-shire Volunteer Regiment
1st Battalion at Kinross.

Kirkcudbrightshire Volunteer Regiment
1st Battalion at Castle Douglas. Became 4th Volunteer Battalion King's Own Scottish Borderers.

Lanarkshire Volunteer Regiment
1/1st Battalion at Coatbridge
2/1st Battalion at The Drill Hall, Motherwell
3/1st Battalion at The Drill Hall, Lanark.

Lancashire Fusiliers
1st Volunteer Battalion, see 3rd Battalion Lancashire Volunteer Regiment.
2nd Volunteer Battalion, see 4th Battalion Lancashire Volunteer Regiment.
3rd Volunteer Battalion, see 9th Battalion Lancashire Volunteer Regiment.
4th Volunteer Battalion, see 16th Battalion Lancashire Volunteer Regiment.

Lancashire Volunteer Regiment
The regiment was divided into four groups: Manchester Group with the 1st, 2nd, 3rd, 9th, 1/15th, 2/15th, 16th and 17th Battalions, Liverpool Group with the 5th, 6th, 7th and 8th Battalions, North-Eastern Group with the 10th, 1/11th, 2/11th and 3/11th, North-Western Group with the 12th, 13th and 14th.
1st Battalion at Temple Street, Manchester. Became 1st Volunteer Battalion Manchester Regiment.
2nd Battalion at 73 Seymour Grove, Old Trafford, Manchester. Became 2nd Volunteer Battalion Manchester Regiment.
3rd Battalion at Great Clowes Street, Manchester, later to 94 Market Street, Manchester, but moved to Great Clowes Street again by January 1918. Became 1st Volunteer Battalion Lancashire Fusiliers.
4th Battalion at The Drill Hall, Cross Lane, Salford. Became 2nd Volunteer Battalion Lancashire Fusiliers.
5th Battalion at 65 St Ann Street, Liverpool. Became 1st Volunteer Battalion King's (Liverpool Regiment).
6th Battalion at 44 Church Street, Liverpool. Became 2nd Volunteer Battalion King's (Liverpool

Regiment) in 1918.

7th Battalion at Princes Park Barracks, Upper Warwick Street, Liverpool. Became 1st Volunteer Battalion South Lancashire Regiment.

8th Battalion at The Drill Hall, Manchester Road, Southport. Became 3rd Volunteer Battalion King's (Liverpool Regiment).

9th Battalion at Central Chambers, Fleece Street, Rochdale, later to The Drill Hall, 6th Battalion, Lancashire Fusiliers, Rochdale. Became 3rd Volunteer Battalion Lancashire Fusiliers.

10th Battalion at The Drill Hall, Witton, Blackburn, later to The Sessions House, Blackburn. Became 1st Volunteer Battalion East Lancashire Regiment.

11th Battalion at The Drill Hall, Keighley Green, Burnley. The Volunteer List for October 1917 now shows the battalion divided into three, 1/11th, 2/11t and 3/11th.

1/11th Battalion at The Drill Hall, Keighley Green, Burnley. Became 2nd Volunteer Battalion East Lancashire Regiment.

2/11th Battalion at The Drill Hall, Cloughfold, Rawtenstall. Became 3rd Volunteer Battalion East Lancashire Regiment.

3/11th Battalion at 91 Carr Road, Nelson. Became 4th Volunteer Battalion East Lancashire Regiment.

12th Battalion at The Drill Hall, Stanley Street, Preston. Became 1st Volunteer Battalion Loyal North Lancashire Regiment.

13th Battalion at 2 Chapel Street, Preston, later to The Drill Hall, Dallas Road, Lancaster. Became 1st Volunteer Battalion King's Own (Royal Lancaster Regiment).

14th Battalion at The Drill Hall, Barrow-in-Furness. Became 2nd Volunteer Battalion King's Own (Royal Lancaster Regiment).

1/15th Battalion at The Drill Hall, Rifle Street, Oldham. Became 3rd Volunteer Battalion Manchester Regiment.

2/15th Battalion at The Drill Hall, Rifle Street, Oldham. Became 4th Volunteer Battalion Manchester Regiment.

16th Battalion at 10 Union Street, Bury, later to the Territorial Depot, Castle Armoury, Bury. Became 4th Volunteer Battalion, Lancashire Fusiliers.

17th Battalion at the 3rd East Lancashire Brigade, RFA, Drill Hall in Silverwell Street, Bolton. Became 2nd Volunteer Battalion Loyal North Lancashire Regiment.

Leicestershire Regiment

1st Volunteer Battalion, see 1/1st Battalion Leicestershire Volunteer Regiment.

2nd Volunteer Battalion, see 2nd Battalion Leicestershire Volunteer Regiment.

3rd Volunteer Battalion, see 3rd Battalion Leicestershire Volunteer Regiment.

4th Volunteer Battalion, see 2/1st Battalion Leicestershire Volunteer Regiment.

Leicestershire Volunteer Regiment

1st Battalion (Leicester) at The Empress Rink, Leicester. The Volunteer List for October 1917 shows the battalion divided as 1/1st and 2/1st.

1/1st Battalion at The Empress Rink, Leicester. Became 1st Volunteer Battalion Leicestershire Regiment.

2/1st Battalion. The Junior Training Hall, Leicester. Became 4th Volunteer Battalion, Leicestershire Regiment.

2nd Battalion (Loughborough) at The Shrubbery, Ashby-de-la-Zouch, later to The Drill Hall, Loughborough. Became 2nd Volunteer Battalion Leicestershire Regiment.

3rd Battalion (Market Harborough and Melton Mowbray) at The Magazine, Leicester. Became 3rd Volunteer Battalion Leicestershire Regiment.

Lincolnshire Regiment

1st Volunteer Battalion, see 1st Battalion Lincolnshire Volunteer Regiment.

2nd Volunteer Battalion, see 2nd Battalion Lincolnshire Volunteer Regiment.

3rd Volunteer Battalion, see 3rd Battalion Lincolnshire Volunteer Regiment.

4th Volunteer Battalion, see 4th Battalion Lincolnshire Volunteer Regiment.

Lincolnshire Volunteer Regiment

1st Battalion at The Drill Hall, Broadgate, Lincoln, later to The Orderly Room, Spilsby. Became 1st Volunteer Battalion Lincolnshire Regiment.

2nd Battalion at The Drill Hall, Sleaford, the Volunteer List for January 1918 giving location as Market Street, Sleaford. Became 2nd Volunteer Battalion Lincolnshire Regiment.

3rd Battalion at The Orderly Room, Spilsby, later to The Drill Hall, Doughty Road, Grimsby. Became 3rd Volunteer Battalion Lincolnshire Regiment.

4th Battalion, Earlsfields, Grantham, later to The Drill Hall, Broadgate, Lincoln. Became 4th Volunteer Battalion Lincolnshire Regiment.

Linlithgowshire Volunteer Regiment

1st Battalion at Linlithgow. Became 6th Volunteer Battalion Royal Scots (Lothian Regiment).

Loyal North Lancashire Regiment

1st Volunteer Battalion, see 12th Battalion Lancashire Volunteer Regiment.

2nd Volunteer Battalion, see 17th Battalion Lancashire Volunteer Regiment.

Manchester Regiment

1st Volunteer Battalion, see 1st Battalion Lancashire Volunteer Regiment.

2nd Volunteer Battalion, see 2nd Battalion Lancashire Volunteer Regiment.

3rd Volunteer Battalion, see 1/15th Battalion Lancashire Volunteer Regiment.

4th Volunteer Battalion, see 2/15 Battalion Lancashire Volunteer Regiment.

Merionethshire Volunteer Regiment

1st Battalion at The Drill Hall, Dolgelly. Became 4th Volunteer Battalion Royal Welsh Fusiliers in 1918.

Middlesex Regiment

1st Volunteer Battalion, see 1st Battalion Middlesex Volunteer Regiment.

2nd Volunteer Battalion, see 2nd Battalion Middlesex Volunteer Regiment.

3rd Volunteer Battalion, see 3rd Battalion Middlesex Volunteer Regiment.

4th Volunteer Battalion, see 4th Battalion Middlesex Volunteer Regiment.

5th Volunteer Battalion, see 5th Battalion Middlesex Volunteer Regiment.

6th Volunteer Battalion, see 6th Battalion Middlesex Volunteer Regiment.

7th Volunteer Battalion, see 7th Battalion Middlesex Volunteer Regiment.

Middlesex Volunteer Regiment

Included a battalion formed from the Willesden and District Defence League early in 1915. Also included a Hendon Battalion, which had a Golders Green Detachment, one formed from the Finchley, Friern Barnet and New Southgate VTC, and an Ealing Battalion. The *Volunteer Training Corps Gazette* for 2 October 1915 reported that the Hornsey VTC and Muswell Hill, East Finchley and District VTC is to form a battalion of the Middlesex Volunteer Regiment. The new battalion to be known as Hornsey. The issue for 9 October 1915 refers to a Crouch End Detachment of the Middlesex Volunteer

Regiment. There was also battalions in Ealing and Harrow. Two bronze cap badges have been notes, each bearing the county arms and the title Middlesex Volunteer Regiment. The regiment was divided into two groups: Northern Group with the 1st, 3rd, 5th and 7th Battalions, Southern Group, 2nd, 4th and 6th Battalions.

1st Battalion at The Council Offices, Palmers Green, later to 51 Bowes Road, Palmers Green. Became 1st Volunteer Battalion Middlesex Regiment.

2nd Battalion at The Drill Hall, Twickenham. Became 2nd Volunteer Battalion Middlesex Regiment.

3rd Battalion at 16 Peterborough Road, Harrow. Became 3rd Volunteer Battalion Middlesex Regiment.

4th Battalion at 287 High Road, Chiswick, later to 211 High Road, Chiswick. Became 4th Volunteer Battalion Middlesex Regiment.

5th Battalion at Devonshire Lodge, Colney Hatch Lane, Muswell Hill, N10. Became 5th Volunteer Battalion, Middlesex Regiment.

6th Battalion at 1 St Mary's Road, Harlesden, NW10, later to The Drill Hall, Pound Lane, Willesden, NW6. Became 6th Volunteer Battalion Middlesex Regiment.

7th Battalion at The Drill Hall, Tottenham, later to The Education Offices, Phillip Lane, Tottenham and then 7 Bruce Grove, Tottenham. Became 7th Volunteer Battalion Middlesex Regiment.

Midlothian Volunteer Regiment

1/1st Battalion at 53 Hanover Street, Edinburgh. Became 3rd Volunteer Battalion Royal Scots (Lothian Regiment).

2/1st Battalion at 24 Constitution Street, Leith. Became 4th Volunteer Battalion Royal Scots (Lothian Regiment).

Monmouthshire Regiment

1st Volunteer Battalion, see 1st Battalion Monmouthshire Volunteer Regiment.

Monmouthshire Volunteer Regiment

1st Battalion at Stow Hill Drill Hall, Newport. Became 1st Volunteer Battalion Monmouthshire Regiment.

Montgomeryshire Volunteer Regiment

1st Battalion at The Armoury, Welshpool. Became 5th Volunteer Battalion Royal Welsh Fusiliers.

Morayshire Volunteer Regiment

1st Battalion at The Drill Hall, Elgin.

Norfolk Regiment

1st Volunteer Battalion, see 1st Battalion Norfolk Volunteer Regiment.

2nd Volunteer Battalion, see 2nd Battalion Norfolk Volunteer Regiment.

3rd Volunteer Battalion, see 4th Battalion Norfolk Volunteer Regiment.

4th Volunteer Battalion, see 6th Battalion Norfolk Volunteer Regiment.

Norfolk Volunteer Regiment

The regiment was divided into two groups: Group A with the 1st, 3rd and 4th Battalions, Group B, 2nd, 5th and 6th Battalions.

1st Battalion (Norwich) at Howard House, King Street, Norwich. Became 1st Volunteer Battalion Norfolk Regiment. *The War Budget* for 17 February 1916 shows a photograph of Lieutenant-Colonel Leathes Prior, VD, Commandant.

2nd Battalion at The Drill Hall, York Road, Great Yarmouth. Became 2nd Volunteer Battalion Norfolk Regiment.

3rd Battalion (Lynn), the Volunteer List for October 1917 giving location as Hunstanton. Not in the August 1918 List, the officers now with 4th Battalion.

4th Battalion (Coast) at Foulsham. Became 3rd Volunteer Battalion Norfolk Regiment.

5th Battalion at Ditchingham. Not in August 1918 Volunteer List.

6th Battalion at Attleborough. Became 4th Volunteer Battalion Norfolk Regiment.

North Riding Volunteer Regiment

The regiment was divided into three groups: Group A with the 1/1st, 2/1st and 5th Battalions, Group B with 2nd and 4th Battalions, Group C, 1/3rd and 2/3rd Battalions.

1st Battalion at Bridge House, Normanby, Eston. The Volunteer List for October 1917 shows the battalion divided as 1/1st and 2/1st.

1/1st Battalion at 23 Wilson Street, Middlesborough. Became 1st Volunteer Battalion Yorkshire Regiment.

2/1st Battalion. Became 6th Volunteer Battalion Yorkshire Regiment.

2nd Battalion at Castlegate, Malton. Became 2nd Volunteer Battalion Yorkshire Regiment in 1918.

1/3rd Battalion at Bedale, later to Church House, Thirsk. Became 3rd Volunteer Battalion Yorkshire Regiment.

2/3rd Battalion at Hartford Grange, Richmond. Became 7th Volunteer Battalion Yorkshire Regiment.

4th Battalion at 81 Newborough, Scarborough, later to Falsgrave Barracks, St John's Road, Scarborough. Became 4th Volunteer Battalion Yorkshire Regiment.

5th Battalion at The Britannia Works, Middlesbrough. Became 5th Volunteer Battalion Yorkshire Regiment.

North Staffordshire Regiment

1st Volunteer Battalion, see 1st Battalion Staffordshire Volunteer Regiment.

2nd Volunteer Battalion, see 2nd Battalion Staffordshire Volunteer Regiment.

Northamptonshire Regiment

1st Volunteer Battalion, see 1st Battalion Northamptonshire Volunteer Regiment.

2nd Volunteer Battalion, see 2nd Battalion Northamptonshire Volunteer Regiment.

Northamptonshire Volunteer Regiment

1st Battalion at Clare Street, Northampton. Became 1st Volunteer Battalion Northamptonshire Regiment.

2nd Battalion at Clare Street, Northampton. Became 2nd Volunteer Battalion Northamptonshire Regiment.

Northern Counties Highland Volunteer Regiment

1/1st Battalion (Inverness and Nairn) at ASC Hall, Inverness.

2/1st Battalion (Ross and Cromarty) at Old Militia Barracks, Dingwell.

Northumberland Fusiliers

1st Volunteer Battalion, see 1st Battalion Northumberland Volunteer Regiment.

2nd Volunteer Battalion, see 2nd Battalion Northumberland Volunteer Regiment.

3rd Volunteer Battalion, see 3rd Battalion Northumberland Volunteer Regiment.

4th Volunteer Battalion, see 5th Battalion Northumberland Volunteer Regiment.

Northumberland Volunteer Regiment

1st Battalion at Royal Grammar School, Eakdale Terrace, Jesmond, Newcastle-upon-Tyne, later to Hutton Terrace Drill Hall, Sandyford Road, Newcastle-upon-Tyne. Became 1st Volunteer Battalion Northumberland Fusiliers.

2nd Battalion at 64 Linkskill Terrace, North Shields, later to 1 Lovaine Place, North Shields. Became 2nd Volunteer Battalion Northumberland Fusiliers

3rd Battalion at 40 Bridge Street, Blyth. Became 3rd Volunteer Battalion Northumberland Fusiliers.

4th Battalion at 5 Eldon Place, Newcastle-upon-Tyne, later to Gibson House, Hexham-on-Tyne. Not shown in the August 1918 Volunteer List, the officers now with the 1st Battalion.

5th Battalion at The Drill Hall, Fenkie Street, Alnwick. Became 4th Volunteer Battalion Northumberland Fusiliers.

Nottinghamshire Volunteer Regiment

1st Battalion at Territorial Headquarters, Derby Road, Nottingham. Became 9th Volunteer Battalion Sherwood Forester (Nottinghamshire and Derbyshire Regiment.

2nd Battalion at Park Court, Park Street, Nottingham. Became 10th Volunteer Battalion Sherwood Forester (Nottinghamshire and Derbyshire Regiment.

3rd Battalion at Territorial Headquarters, Derby Road, Nottingham. Became 11th Volunteer Battalion Sherwood Forester (Nottinghamshire and Derbyshire Regiment.

4th Battalion at Cromwell House, Westgate, Mansfield. Became 12th Volunteer Battalion Sherwood Forester (Nottinghamshire and Derbyshire Regiment.

Oxfordshire Volunteer Regiment

1st Battalion at New College, Oxford. Became 1st Volunteer Battalion Oxfordshire and Buckinghamshire Light Infantry.

2nd Battalion at 60 Woodstock Road, Oxford. Became 2nd Volunteer Battalion Oxfordshire and Buckinghamshire Light Infantry.

Oxfordshire and Buckinghamshire Light Infantry

1st Volunteer Battalion, see 1st Battalion Oxfordshire Volunteer Regiment.
2nd Volunteer Battalion, see 2nd Battalion Oxfordshire Volunteer Regiment.
3rd Volunteer Battalion, see 1st Battalion Buckinghamshire Volunteer Regiment.
4th Volunteer Battalion, see 2nd Battalion Buckinghamshire Volunteer Regiment.
5th Volunteer Battalion, see 3rd Battalion Buckinghamshire Volunteer Regiment.

Peebleshire Volunteer Regiment

1st Battalion at Peebles. Became 7th Volunteer Battalion Royal Scots (Lothian Regiment).

Pembrokeshire Volunteer Regiment

1st Battalion at The Drill Hall, Haverfordwest. The regiment amalgamated with Carmarthenshire Volunteer Regiment to form Pembrokeshire and Carmarthenshire Volunteer Regiment in 1918, then designated 1st Volunteer Battalion Welsh Regiment.

Pembrokeshire and Carmarthenshire Volunteer Regiment

See Pembrokeshire Volunteer Regiment.

Perthshire Volunteer Regiment

1st Battalion at The Drill Hall, Tay Street, Perth. Became 5th Volunteer Battalion Black Watch.
2nd Battalion at The Drill Hall, Crieff. Became 6th Volunteer Battalion Black Watch.

Queen's Own (Royal West Kent Regiment)
1st Volunteer Battalion, see 3rd Battalion Kent Volunteer Regiment.
2nd Volunteer Battalion, see 5th Battalion Kent Volunteer Regiment.
3rd Volunteer Battalion, see 7th Battalion Kent Volunteer Regiment.
4th Volunteer Battalion, see 9th Battalion Kent Volunteer Regiment.

Queen's (Royal West Kent Regiment)
1st Volunteer Battalion, see 1st Battalion Surrey Volunteer Regiment.
2nd Volunteer Battalion, see 4th Battalion Surrey Volunteer Regiment.
3rd Volunteer Battalion, see 6th Battalion Surrey Volunteer Regiment.

Renfrewshire Volunteer Regiment
1/1st Battalion at The Drill Hall, 68 High Street, Paisley.
2/1st Battalion, The Drill Hall, Finnart Street, Greenock.

Royal Berkshire Regiment
1st Volunteer Battalion, see 1st Battalion Berkshire Volunteer Regiment.

Royal Scots (Lothian Regiment)
1st Volunteer Battalion, see 1/1st Battalion City of Edinburgh Volunteer Regiment.
2nd Volunteer Battalion, see 2/1st Battalion City of Edinburgh Volunteer Regiment.
3rd Volunteer Battalion, see 1/1st Battalion Midlothian Volunteer Regiment.
4th Volunteer Battalion, see 2/1st Battalion Midlothian Volunteer Regiment.
5th Volunteer Battalion, see 1st Battalion Haddingtonshire Volunteer Regiment.
6th Volunteer Battalion, see 1st Battalion Linlithgowshire Volunteer Regiment.
7th Volunteer Battalion, see 1st Battalion Peebles-shire Volunteer Regiment.

Royal Sussex Regiment
1st Volunteer Battalion, see 1st Battalion Sussex Volunteer Regiment.
2nd Volunteer Battalion, see 4th Battalion Sussex Volunteer Regiment.
3rd Volunteer Battalion, see 7th Battalion Sussex Volunteer Regiment.
4th Volunteer Battalion, see 3rd Battalion Sussex Volunteer Regiment.
5th Volunteer Battalion, see 6th Battalion Sussex Volunteer Regiment.
6th Volunteer Battalion, see 9th Battalion Sussex Volunteer Regiment.

Royal Warwickshire Regiment
1st Volunteer Battalion, see 1st Battalion Warwickshire Volunteer Regiment.
2nd Volunteer Battalion, see 2nd Battalion Warwickshire Volunteer Regiment.
3rd Volunteer Battalion, see 3rd Battalion Warwickshire Volunteer Regiment.
4th Volunteer Battalion, see 4th Battalion Warwickshire Volunteer Regiment.
5th Volunteer Battalion, see 5th Battalion Warwickshire Volunteer Regiment.

Royal Welsh Fusiliers
1st Volunteer Battalion, see 1st Battalion Anglesey Volunteer Regiment.
2nd Volunteer Battalion, see Flintshire Volunteer Regiment.
3rd Volunteer Battalion, see 1st Battalion Carnarvonshire Volunteer Regiment.
4th Volunteer Battalion, see 1st Battalion Merionethshire Volunteer Regiment.
5th Volunteer Battalion, see 1st Battalion Montgomeryshire Volunteer Regiment.

Roxburghshire Volunteer Regiment
1st Battalion Island House, Galashiels. The Volunteer List for October 1917 shows the regiment as

included in the Border Rifles Volunteer Battalion, an administrative unit which also includes the Selkirk Volunteer Regiment. Sometime in 1918 the two are merged as Roxburghshire and Selkirkshire Volunteer Regiment, then in the same year designated 1st Volunteer Battalion King's Own Scottish Borderers.

Rutlandshire Volunteer Regiment

1st Battalion at The Drill Hall, Penn Street, Oakham.

Selkirk Volunteer Regiment

1st Battalion. The Volunteer List for October 1917 shows the regiment included in the Border Rifles Volunteer Battalion, an administrative unit which also included the Roxburghshire Volunteer Regiment. Headquarters now given as Galashiels. Sometime in 1918 the two are merged as Roxburghshire and Selkirkshire Volunteer Regiment, then in the same year designated 1st Volunteer Battalion King's Own Scottish Borderers.

Sherwood Foresters (Nottinghamshire and Derbyshire Regiment)

1st Volunteer Battalion, see 1st Battalion Derbyshire Volunteer Regiment.
2nd Volunteer Battalion, see 2nd Battalion Derbyshire Volunteer Regiment.
3rd Volunteer Battalion, see 3rd Battalion Derbyshire Volunteer Regiment.
4th Volunteer Battalion, see 4th Battalion Derbyshire Volunteer Regiment.
5th Volunteer Battalion, see 5th Battalion Derbyshire Volunteer Regiment.
6th Volunteer Battalion, see 6th Battalion Derbyshire Volunteer Regiment.
7th Volunteer Battalion, see 7th Battalion Derbyshire Volunteer Regiment.
8th Volunteer Battalion, see 8th Battalion Derbyshire Volunteer Regiment.
9th Volunteer Battalion, see 1st Battalion Nottinghamshire Volunteer Regiment.
10th Volunteer Battalion, see 2nd Battalion Nottinghamshire Volunteer Regiment.
11th Volunteer Battalion, see 3rd Battalion Nottinghamshire Volunteer Regiment.
12th Volunteer Battalion, see 4th Battalion Nottinghamshire Volunteer Regiment.

Shropshire Volunteer Regiment

1st Battalion (Northern) at Wellington. Became 1st Volunteer Battalion King's (Shropshire Light Infantry).
2nd Battalion (Southern) at Kingston House, Shrewsbury, later to 13 Belmont, Shrewsbury. Became 2nd Volunteer Battalion King's (Shropshire Light Infantry).

Somerset Light Infantry

1st Volunteer Battalion, see 1st Battalion Somerset Volunteer Regiment.
2nd Volunteer Battalion, see 2nd Battalion Somerset Light Infantry in 1918.
3rd Volunteer Battalion, see 3rd Battalion Somerset Light Infantry in 1918.

Somerset Volunteer Regiment

1st Battalion at 60 Clare Street, Bridgwater. Became 1st Volunteer Battalion Somerset Light Infantry.
2nd Battalion at 39 Gay Street, Bath, later to The Drill Hall, Lower Bristol Road, Bath. Became 2nd Volunteer Battalion Somerset Light Infantry.
3rd Battalion at The Infantry Drill Hall, Yeovil. Became 3rd Volunteer Battalion Somerset Light Infantry.

South Lancashire Regiment

1st Volunteer Battalion, see 7th Battalion Lancashire Volunteer Regiment.

South Staffordshire Regiment
1st Volunteer Battalion, see 3rd Battalion Staffordshire Volunteer Regiment.
2nd Volunteer Battalion, see 4th Battalion Staffordshire Volunteer Regiment.

Staffordshire Volunteer Regiment
1st Battalion at The Drill Hall, Victoria Street, Hanley. Became 1st Volunteer Battalion North Staffordshire Regiment.
2nd Battalion at 1 Martin Street, Stafford, later to The Drill Hall, Newport Road, Stafford. Became 2nd Volunteer Battalion North Staffordshire Regiment.
3rd Battalion at The Drill Hall, Walsall. Became 1st Volunteer Battalion South Staffordshire Regiment.
4th Battalion at The Drill Hall, Stafford Street, Wolverhampton. Became 2nd Volunteer Battalion South Staffordshire Regiment.

Stirlingshire Volunteer Regiment
1st Battalion at The Drill Hall, Princess Street, Stirling.

Suffolk Regiment
1st Volunteer Battalion, see 1st Battalion Suffolk Volunteer Regiment.
2nd Volunteer Battalion, see 2nd Battalion Suffolk Volunteer Regiment.
3rd Volunteer Battalion, see 3rd Battalion Suffolk Volunteer Regiment.
4th Volunteer Battalion, see 4th Battalion Suffolk Volunteer Regiment.
5th Volunteer Battalion, see 5th Battalion Suffolk Volunteer Regiment.
6th Volunteer Battalion, see 6th Battalion Suffolk Volunteer Regiment.

Suffolk Volunteer Regiment
The regiment was divided into two groups: Group A with the 1st, 2nd and 5th Battalions, Group B, 3rd, 4th and 6th Battalions.
1st Battalion (Ipswich). Became 1st Volunteer Battalion Suffolk Regiment.
2nd Battalion (Bury St Edmunds) at 84 Whiting Street, Bury St Edmund's. Became 2nd Volunteer Battalion Suffolk Regiment.
3rd Battalion (Lowestoft) at Lowestoft, later Peddars Lane Drill Hall, Beccles. Became 3rd Volunteer Battalion Suffolk Regiment.
4th Battalion (Woodbridge). Became 4th Volunteer Battalion Suffolk Regiment.
5th Battalion (Sudbury). Became 5th Volunteer Battalion Suffolk Regiment.
6th Battalion (Saxmundham). Became 6th Volunteer Battalion Suffolk Regiment.

Surrey Volunteer Regiment
The regiment was divided into three groups: Northern Group with the 5th, 8th, 9th and 11th Battalions, Eastern Group with the 1st, 4th, 10th and 12th Battalions, Western Group, 2nd, 3rd, 6th and 7th Battalions.
1st Battalion at 2 Poplar Walk, Croydon. Became 1st Volunteer Battalion Queen's (Royal West Surrey Regiment).
2nd Battalion at 126 Maple Road, Surbiton, later to 62 Claremont Road, Surbiton. Became 1st Volunteer Battalion East Surrey Regiment.
3rd Battalion at Eldridge, Chertsey, later to The Emergency Committee Offices, Guildford Street, Chertsey. Not shown in the August Volunteer List, the officers now with the 2nd Battalion.
4th Battalion at Albion House, Reigate, later to The Armoury, Reigate. Became 2nd Volunteer Battalion Queen's (Royal West Surrey Regiment).
5th Battalion at The Council Officers, New Malden, later to The Drill Hall, St George's Road,

Wimbledon, SW10. Became 2nd Volunteer Battalion East Surrey Regiment.

6th Battalion at 25 High Street, Guildford, later to Sandfield House Drill Hall, Guildford. Became 3rd Volunteer Battalion Queen's (Royal West Surrey Regiment).

7th Battalion at 8 The Broadway, Woking, later to 10 The Broadway and then The Drill Hall, Walton Road, Woking. Not shown in the August 1918 Volunteer List, the officers now with the 6th Battalion.

8th Battalion at The Drill Hall, Richmond. Not shown in the August 1918 Volunteer List, the officers now with the 5th Battalion.

9th Battalion at The Public Hall Chambers, Sutton, later to Bridge House, Mulgrave Road, Sutton. Became 3rd Volunteer Battalion East Surrey Regiment.

10th Battalion at 6 and 7 Great Tower Street, London, EC3, later to The Drill Hall, North Street, Leatherhead. Not shown in the August 1918 Volunteer List. .

11th Battalion at Penhurst, Sheridan Road, Merton Park, later to Coombe Villa, 105 Merton Road, Wimbledon, SW19. Not shown in the August 1918 Volunteer List, the officers now with the 9th Battalion.

12th Battalion at 14 Cherry Orchard Road, Croydon. Not shown in the August 1918 Volunteer List, the officers now with the 1st Battalion.

Sussex Volunteer Regiment

1st Battalion at 170 North Street, Brighton, later to The Drill Hall, Church Street, Brighton. Became 1st Volunteer Battalion Royal Sussex Regiment.

2nd Battalion at 49 Goldstone Villas, Hove. Amalgamated with 4th Battalion in 1918 to form 2nd Volunteer Battalion Royal Sussex Regiment.

3rd Battalion at Selborne Road, Hove. Became 4th Volunteer Battalion Royal Sussex Regiment.

4th Battalion at 26 Robertson Street, Hastings, later to The Drill Hall, The Downs, Bexhill. Became 2nd Volunteer Battalion Royal Sussex Regiment after amalgamation with the 2nd Battalion.

5th Battalion at Leyton, Grassington Road, Eastbourne. Not shown in the Volunteer List for October 1917.

6th Battalion at 23 Eastport Lane, Lewes, later to The Drill Hall, Ham Lane, Lewes. Became 5th Volunteer Battalion Royal Sussex Regiment.

7th Battalion at 3 Queen's Road, East Grinstead, later to Selborne Road, Hove. Became 3rd Volunteer Battalion Royal Sussex Regiment.

8th Battalion at 17 Park Street, Horsham. Not shown in the Volunteer List for August 1918. the officers now with the 7th Battalion.

9th Battalion at Otterham House, Bognor. Became 6th Volunteer Battalion Royal Sussex Regiment.

Warwickshire Volunteer Regiment

1st Battalion at The Drill Hall, Thorp Street, Birmingham, later to The Drill Hall, ASC Headquarters, Witton, Birmingham. Became 1st Volunteer Battalion Royal Warwickshire Regiment.

2nd Battalion at Clarenden Avenue, Leamington Spa, later to 9 Clarenden Place, Leamington Spa. Became 2nd Volunteer Battalion Royal Warwickshire Regiment.

3rd Battalion at The Drill Hall, Thorp Street, Birmingham. Became 3rd Volunteer Battalion Royal Warwickshire Regiment.

4th Battalion at Stoney Lane Barracks, Mosely. Became 4th Volunteer Battalion Royal Warwickshire Regiment.

5th Battalion at Witton Barracks, Birmingham. The Volunteer List for October 1917 gives location as

The Drill Hall, Infantry Headquarters, Witton, Birmingham. Became 5th Volunteer Battalion Royal Warwickshire Regiment.

Welsh Regiment

1st Volunteer Battalion, see 1st Battalion Pembrokeshire Volunteer Regiment.
2nd Volunteer Battalion, see 1st Battalion Glamorganshire Volunteer Regiment.
3rd Volunteer Battalion, see 2nd Battalion Glamorganshire Volunteer Regiment.
4th Volunteer Battalion, see 3rd Battalion Glamorganshire Volunteer Regiment.
5th Volunteer Battalion, see 4th Battalion Glamorganshire Volunteer Regiment.
6th Volunteer Battalion, see 5th Battalion Glamorganshire Volunteer Regiment.

West Riding Volunteer Regiment

The regiment is divided into five groups: Wakefield Group with the 1st, 7th, 10th, 14th and 22nd Battalions, Bradford Group with 2nd, 3rd, 4th, 5th and 21st Battalions, Huddersfield Group with 6th, 8th, 9th and 20th Battalions, Leeds Group with the 11th, 12th, 13th and 15th Battalions, Sheffield Group, 16th, 17th, 18th and 19th Battalions.

1st Battalion at Barnsley. Became 1st Volunteer Battalion York and Lancaster Regiment.
2nd Battalion at Batley, later to The School Buildings, Heckmondwike. Became 1st Volunteer Battalion Duke of Wellington's Regiment.
3rd Battalion (Bradford) at The Coliseum, Toller Lane, Bradford. Became 1st Volunteer Battalion West Yorkshire Regiment.
4th Battalion (1st Bradford City) at Bell Vue Barracks, Bradford. Became 2nd Volunteer Battalion West Yorkshire Regiment.
5th Battalion (2nd Bradford City) at The Drill Hall, Otley Road, Bradford. Became 3rd Volunteer Battalion West Yorkshire Regiment.
6th Battalion (Keighley). Became 5th Volunteer Battalion Duke of Wellington's Regiment.
7th Battalion (Goole and Selby) at Selby. Became 2nd Volunteer Battalion King's Own Yorkshire Light Infantry.
8th Battalion (Halifax). Became 3rd Volunteer Battalion Duke of Wellington's Regiment.
9th Battalion (Huddersfield). Became 2nd Volunteer Battalion Duke of Wellington's Regiment.
10th Battalion (Wakefield) at Bank Street, Wakefield. Became 1st Volunteer Battalion King's Own Yorkshire Light Infantry.
11th Battalion (1st Leeds) at Carlton Barracks, Leeds. Became 5th Volunteer Battalion West Yorkshire Regiment.
12th Battalion (2nd Leeds). Amalgamated with 11th Battalion as 5th Volunteer Battalion West Yorkshire Regiment.
13th Battalion (South Leeds). Became 6th Volunteer Battalion West Yorkshire Regiment.
14th Battalion (Pontefract). Not shown in the August 1918 Volunteer List.
15th Battalion (Ripon) at Harrogate. Became 7th Volunteer Battalion West Yorkshire Regiment.
16th Battalion (Rotherham). Became 2nd Volunteer Battalion York and Lancaster Regiment.
17th Battalion (Sheffield). Became 3rd Volunteer Battalion York and Lancaster Regiment.
18th Battalion (Sheffield). Became 4th Volunteer Battalion York and Lancaster Regiment in 1918.
19th Battalion (Doncaster). Became 3rd Volunteer Battalion King's Own Yorkshire Light Infantry.
20th Battalion (Wharfedale). The Volunteer List for October 1917 gives location as Ilkley and that for January 1918, The Drill Hall, Guiseley. Became 4th Volunteer Battalion Duke of Wellington's Regiment.

21st Battalion at 39 Leeds Road, Bradford, later to Horton Grange Road Council Schools, Bradford. Became 4th Volunteer Battalion West Yorkshire Regiment with headquarters at 11 Stratford Road, Bradford.

22nd Battalion. Became 8th Volunteer Battalion West Yorkshire Regiment with headquarters at The Drill Hall, Colliergate.

West Yorkshire Regiment

1st Volunteer Battalion, see 3rd Battalion West Riding Volunteer Regiment.
2nd Volunteer Battalion, see 4th Battalion West Riding Volunteer Regiment.
3rd Volunteer Battalion, see 5th Battalion West Riding Volunteer Regiment.
4th Volunteer Battalion, see 21st Battalion West Riding Volunteer Regiment.
5th Volunteer Battalion, see 11th Battalion West Riding Volunteer Regiment.
6th Volunteer Battalion, see 13th Battalion West Riding Volunteer Regiment.
7th Volunteer Battalion, see 15th Battalion West Riding Volunteer Regiment.
8th Volunteer Battalion, see 22nd Battalion West Riding Volunteer Regiment.

Westmorland Volunteer Regiment

1st Battalion at The Drill Hall, Queen Katharine Street, Kendal. Disappears from the Volunteer List sometime between February and August 1918, the officers now with 2nd (Cumberland and Westmoreland) Volunteer Battalion Border Regiment and Westmoreland Volunteer Regiment. (See Cumberland Volunteer Regiment).

Wiltshire Regiment

1st Volunteer Battalion, see 1st Battalion Wiltshire Volunteer Regiment.

Wiltshire Volunteer Regiment

1st Battalion at The Drill Hall, Ivy Place, Chippenham. Became 1st Volunteer Battalion Wiltshire Regiment.

Worcestershire Regiment

1st Volunteer Battalion, see 1st Battalion Worcestershire Volunteer Regiment.
2nd Volunteer Battalion, see 2nd Battalion Worcestershire Volunteer Regiment.
3rd Volunteer Battalion, see 3rd Battalion Worcestershire Volunteer Regiment.

Worcestershire Volunteer Regiment

1st Battalion at The Drill Hall, George Street, Kidderminster. Became 1st Volunteer Battalion Worcestershire Regiment.

2nd Battalion at The Guildhall, Worcester, later to 16 Silver Street, Worcester. Became 2nd Volunteer Battalion Worcestershire Regiment.

3rd Battalion at The Drill Hall, Easemore Road, Redditch. Became 3rd Volunteer Battalion Worcestershire Regiment.

York and Lancaster Regiment

1st Volunteer Battalion, see 1st Battalion West Riding Volunteer Regiment.
2nd Volunteer Battalion, see 16th Battalion West Riding Volunteer Regiment.
3rd Volunteer Battalion, see 17th Battalion West Riding Volunteer Regiment.
4th Volunteer Battalion, see 18th Battalion West Riding Volunteer Regiment.

Yorkshire Regiment

1st Volunteer Battalion, see 1/1st Battalion North Riding Volunteer Regiment.
2nd Volunteer Battalion, see 2nd Battalion North Riding Volunteer Regiment.

3rd Volunteer Battalion, see 1/3rd Battalion North Riding Volunteer Regiment.
4th Volunteer Battalion, see 4th Battalion North Riding Volunteer Regiment.
5th Volunteer Battalion, see 5th Battalion North Riding Volunteer Regiment.
6th Volunteer Battalion, see 2/1st Battalion North Riding Volunteer Regiment.
7th Volunteer Battalion, see 2/3rd Battalion North Riding Volunteer Regiment.

Transport and Supply Column Volunteers

Designated Army Service Corps (Volunteers) in 1918

East Yorkshire

The Volunteer Force List for July 1917 shows No 1 Company at The Yeomanry Barracks, Walton Street, Hull.

Motor Volunteer Corps

Designated Army Service Corps Mechanical Transport (Volunteers) in 1918.

Aberdeen, City of

Appears for first time in Volunteer List between January and August 1918 comprising two heavy sections located at Artillery Drill Hall, North Silver Street, Aberdeen. Officer's commission dated 5th May 1918.

Aberdeen, County of

The Volunteer List for July 1917 shows headquarters as 28 Guild Street, Aberdeen. No officers are listed. The List for August 1918 shows one heavy section and officers with commissions dated 8th April 1918.

Ayrshire

Appears for the first time in Volunteer List between August and October 1917. No location or officers are listed. The August List gives three sections at 6 Wellington Square, Ayr.

Banffshire

The Volunteer List for July 1917 shows headquarters as Drill Hall, Keith. No officers are listed. The List for August 1918 lists one heavy section.

Bedfordshire

Appears as a heading only in Volunteer List between November 1917 and January 1918. That for August 1918 gives four heavy sections at Ashburnham Road, Bedford.

Berkshire

The Volunteer List for July 1917 shows headquarters as 15 Friar Street, Reading. No officers are listed. The List for October 1917 shows officers with commissions dated 18th August 1917. The List for August 1918 has three heavy sections and one half light section at The Cedars, Bridge Street, Maidenhead.

Carnarvonshire

Appears as a heading only in Volunteer List between November 1917 and January 1918. The List for August 1918 shows one heavy section at Port Dinorwie, Carnarvon. Officers' commissions are all dated 21st December 1917.

Cheshire

Appears as a heading only in Volunteer List between November 1917 and January 1918. The List for August 1918 has five heavy sections and one light section at Manchester Road, Knutsford.

Clackmannanshire

Appears for first time in Volunteer List between January and August 1918. One heavy section at Conigsby Place, Alloa.

Cumberland

The Volunteer List for July 1917 shows headquarters as Orderly Room, Drill Hall, Strand Road, Carlisle. The List for August 1918 shows three heavy sections and one light section at Orderly Room, Drill Hall, Swiss Lane, Carlisle.

Denbighshire

The Volunteer List for July 1917 shows headquarters as The Premier Garage, Wrexham. The List for August 1918 shows one heavy section.

Derbyshire

The Volunteer List for July 1917 shows headquarters as Walton Lodge, Chesterfield. That for August 1918 shows twelve sections at Electricity Works, Chesterfield.

Devonshire

Appears in the Volunteer List between August and October 1917. That for August 1918 shows three sections at Exeter.

Dorsetshire

Appears for the first time in Volunteer List between February and August 1918. Location given as c/o C.C. Calder, Dorchester.

Dumbartonshire

One heavy section at County Buildings, Dumbarton.

Dundee, City of

Appears for the first time in Volunteer List between February and August 1918. Four heavy sections at Drill Hall, Bell Street, Dundee.

Durham

Twelve heavy sections, five light sections and two field ambulance sections at 54 Old Elvet, Durham.

Edinburgh, City of

The Volunteer List for July 1917 shows heading only, no headquarters or officers are listed. The List for October 1917 shows officers with commissions dated 16th August 1917 and that for January 1918 the location, 8 Wemyss Place, Edinburgh. Ten heavy sections.

Essex

The Volunteer List for July 1917 shows headquarters as 39-41 New Broad Street, London, EC2. No officers are listed. The List for October 1917 gives location as Drill Hall, Chelmsford and a commanding officer with commission dated 31st May 1917. The List for August 1918 shows twenty-five heavy sections and two light sections at Felix Hall, Kelvedon. The unit is shown in the Volunteer List divided into three groups: South Easter, Northern and South Western.

Fifeshire

Three heavy sections at 96 North Street, St Andrew's.

Forfarshire

Two heavy sections at the Drill Hall, Forfar.

Glamorganshire

The Volunteer List for July 1917 shows headquarters as City Hall, Cardiff. First officer commissioned 28th March 1917. Ten heavy sections and one field ambulance section.

Glasgow, City of

The Volunteer List for July 1917 shows headquarters as 98 Hope Street, Glasgow. Eighteen heavy sections.

Gloucestershire

Appears for the first time in the Volunteer List between August and October 1917. Three heavy sections at Chronicle Buildings, Bell Lane, Gloucester.

Haddingtonshire

The Volunteer List for July 1917 shows headquarters as Haddington. Officers' commissions are dated 2nd May 1917. One heavy section.

Hampshire

Four heavy sections and two field ambulance sections at Winchester..

Herefordshire

The Volunteer List for July 1917 shows headquarters as 36 Bridge Street, Hereford. First officer commissioned 20th April 1917.

Hertfordshire

One section at Capital and Counties Bank, St Albans.

Kent

The Volunteer List for July 1917 shows headquarters as Bayham Abbey, Lamberhurst. The List for August 1918 shows thirty-one heavy sections, four light sections and seven field ambulance sections at The Drill Hall, Gravesend. The unit is divided into three numbered groups.

Kinross-shire

Appears for the first time in the Volunteer List between August and October 1917. One section at Kinross House, Kinross.

Kirkcudbrightshire

One heavy section at Firth Head, Dalbeattie.

Lanarkshire

Four heavy sections at Muirhall, Hamilton.

Lancashire

The Volunteer List for July 1917 shows heading only, no headquarters or officers are listed. The List for October 1917 gives location as 15 Piccadilly, Manchester and a commanding officer with commission dated 31st May 1917. Sixty heavy sections, ten light sections divided into five groups: Manchester Group, Liverpool Group, North Easter Group, North Western Group and Light Car Group.

Leicestershire

The Volunteer List for July 1917 shows headquarters as The Magazine, Oxford Street, Leicester. Ten heavy sections.

Lincolnshire

The Volunteer List for July 1917 shows headquarters as Old Barracks, Lincoln. First officer commissioned 30th May 1917. Thirteen heavy sections, three light sections, two field ambulance sections.

Linlithgowshire
One heavy section at 53 Hanover Street, Edinburgh.

London, City of
The Volunteer List for July 1917 shows headquarters as 83 Pall Mall, SW1. The List for October 1917 gives location as 39 Finsbury Square, EC2. Fifteen heavy sections divided into two groups: Group A, at 83 Pall Mall, SW1; Group B, at 225 Oxford Street, W1. The history of the City of London National Guard notes that its Mechanical Transport Column (the first heavy motor volunteer transport in the country) was formed as a result of Army Council Instruction No 90 of January 1917. The column consisted of two heavy squadrons of commercial motors and one light squadron of private motor cars under the title of 1st, 2nd and 3rd (National Guard) Squadrons, City of London Motor Volunteer Corps. They, after July 1917 (ACI No.1073) were designated Group No.1 'A', 'B' and 'C' (National Guard) Companies, City of London ASC, MT, (Volunteers). The strength of the group consisted of thirty three-ton lorries, twenty-four thirty-cwt. lorries; thirty-six fifteen-cwt. vans, and twelve motor cars.

London, County of
Headquarters, Polytechnic, Regent Street, W1. Officers' commissions dated 10th April 1917. The August 1918 Volunteer List gives location as Centre Block, Duke of York's Headquarters, Chelsea. There are thirty-three heavy sections and nine light sections divided into four numbered groups: 1 Group, at 11 Frogmore, Wandsworth, 2 Group, 27 Queen Victoria Street, EC4, 3 Group, 23 West Heath Drive, Hampstead, 4 Group, The Polytechnic Room 5, 309 Regent Street, W1.

Middlesex
The Volunteer List for July 1917 shows headquarters as 1 Muswell Rise, Muswell Hill, N10. The List for October 1917 gives location as 8 New Coventry Street, London, W1. In 1918 show as containing fifty-seven heavy sections and one light section divided into five groups: Central Group, at 19 Queen's Parade, Muswell Hill, N10; Northern Group, Market Chambers, Church Street, Enfield, Southern Group, 11 and 12 Silver Street, Wood Street, EC2; Eastern Group, Carmelite House, EC4, Western Group, 406 Euston Road, NW1. HQ remains at 8 New Coventry Street.

Midlothian
Five heavy sections at 53 Hanover Street, Edinburgh.

Monmouthshire
Four heavy sections at The Drill Hall, Stow Hill, Newport.

Morayshire
One heavy section at Drill Hall, Elgin.

Norfolk
Six heavy sections, one light section and six field ambulance sections at 21 Tombland, Norwich.

North Riding Motor Volunteer Corps
Appears for the first time in the Volunteer List between August and October 1917. No location or officers are listed.

Northamptonshire
Two heavy sections and one field ambulance section at Territorial Hall, Northampton.

Northumberland
The Volunteer List for July 1917 shows headquarters as Eldon Place, Newcastle-upon-Tyne. That for August 1918 has ten heavy sections, one light section, three field ambulance sections and one

composite section at Royal Grammar School, Eskdale Terrace, Newcastle-upon-Tyne.

Nottinghamshire

Nine sections at Drill Hall, Derby Road, Nottingham.

Oxfordshire

Two heavy sections and two light sections at Corn Market Street, Reading.

Perthshire

Two heavy sections at Drill Hall, Perth. .

Renfrewshire

Two heavy sections at 13 St James Place, Paisley.

Roxburghshire

One heavy section at Drill Hall, Paton Street, Galashiels.

Rutlandshire

The Volunteer List for July 1917 shows headquarters as Highfield House, Oakham.

Shropshire

Two heavy sections and two field ambulance sections at Kingston House, St Alkmund's Square, Shrewsbury.

Somerset

Two heavy sections at Lower Bristol Road, Bath.

Staffordshire

Nine sections at Artillery Barracks, Victoria Square, Hanley. .

Stirlingshire

One heavy section at Drill Hall, Princess Street, Stirling.

Suffolk

Six heavy sections at Ipswich.

Surrey

Nine heavy sections and one field ambulance section at Londesborough Lodge, Worcester Park.

Sussex

Appears for the first time in the Volunteer List between August and October 1917. Headquarters, 16 Highcroft Villas, Brighton. The List for August 1918 shows eight heavy sections at Drill Hall, Gloucester Road, Brighton.

West Riding

The Volunteer List for July 1917 shows heading only, no headquarters or officers are listed. The List for October 1917 gives location as 14 Park Square, Leeds and officers with commissions dated 23rd July 1917. In 1918 show as comprising twenty-nine heavy sections and twenty-three light sections divided into five numbered groups: No 1 Group, at Town Chambers, Huddersfield, No 2 Group, Valley Parade Drill Hall, Bradford, No 3 Group, Leeds, No 4 Group, Wakefield, No 5 Group, Sheffield.

Warwickshire

Two-and-a-half heavy sections, one motor ambulance line and one signal company at Drill Hall, Thorpe Street, Birmingham.

Worcestershire

Two heavy sections at The Shrubberies, Kidderminster.

Yorkshire, East
  Five heavy sections, one light section and four special sections at Wenlock Barracks, Anlaby Road, Hull.

Medical Volunteer Corps

Designated Royal Army Medical Corps (Volunteers)

Aberdeen (City of)
Aberdeen (County of)
Anglesey
Argyllshire
Ayrshire
Banffshire,
Bedfordshire
Berkshire
Berwickshire
Bristol (City of)
Buckinghamshire
Caithness and Sutherland
Cambridgeshire
Carmarthenshire
Carnarvonshire
Cheshire
Clackmannanshire
Cornwall
Cumberland
Denbighshire
Derbyshire
Devonshire
  One field ambulance)
Dorsetshire
  One field ambulance at The Secondary School, Alma Road, Weymouth.
Dumbartonshire
Dumfriesshire
Dundee, City of
Durham
  Two field ambulances)
Edinburgh, City of
Essex
Fifeshire
Flintshire
Forfarshire

Glamorganshire
 One field ambulance.
Glasgow, City of
 Three field ambulances at the RAMC Drill Hall in Yorkhill Parade,
Gloucestershire
Haddingtonshire
Hampshire
 Two field ambulances.
Herefordshire
Hertfordshire
 One field ambulance at 15 London Road, St Albans.
Huntingdonshire
Isle of Wight, Kent
 Two field ambulances, later six at 53 Bromley Common.
Kincardineshire
Kinross-shire
Kirkcudbrightshire
Lanarkshire, Lancashire
 Two field ambulances.
Leicestershire
Lincolnshire
 Two field ambulances at The Old Barracks, Lincoln.
London, City of
London, County of
Merionethshire
Middlesex
Midlothian
Monmouthshire
Montgomeryshire
Morayshire
Norfolk
 Six field ambulances.
North Riding
 One field ambulance.
Northamptonshire
 One field ambulance.
Northern Counties Highland
Northumberland
 Three field ambulances at Cambridge Hall, Newcastle-upon-Tyne.
Nottinghamshire
Oxfordshire
Peebleshire

Pembrokeshire

Perthshire

Renfrewshire

Rutlandshire

Selkirk

Shropshire
   Two field ambulances.

Somerset

Staffordshire

Stirlingshire

Suffolk

Surrey
   One field ambulance.

Sussex
   Two field ambulances.

Warwickshire

West Riding
   Two field ambulances.

Wiltshire

Worcestershire

Yorkshire, East
   Three field ambulances at Wenlock Barracks, Anlaby Road, Hull.

REFERENCES

Brinson, Daniel: *Military Insignia of Gloucestershire.* Colvithick, Bodmin, 2009.

County of London Royal Engineer Volunteers. The Electrical Press, London, 1918.

Disbrowe, Captain EJW: *History of the Volunteer Movement in Cheshire, 1914-1920.* Swain & Co Ltd, Stockport 1920.

Dorling, H: *The History of No 3 Hale Platoon, 'A' Company, 1st Volunteer Battalion The*

Cheshire Regiment 1914-1919. Manchester, 1920.

Endall Ivall, D and Charles Thomas: *Military Insignia of Cornwall.* Penwith Books, 1974.

Fisher, P: *The Brighton Volunteers in the Great War: The 1st Volunteer Battalion (1914-1919) The Royal Sussex Regiment.* Garnett, Mepham & Fisher Ltd, Brighton, 1932.

Gerring, Sergeant-Major C: *A Record of the Early Volunteer Movement and the Notts Volunteer Regiment (The Sherwood Foresters), 1914-1919.* Sisson & Parker, Nottingham, 1920.

Horn, Major GM: *The History of Group II, City of London RASC, MT (V).* 1920.

Kidston, JB: *The Glasgow Volunteers: Recollections, 1914-1918.* Hugh Hopkins, Glasgow, 1926.

Kipling, Arthur and Hugh L King: *Head-dress Badges of the British Army Volume One.* Frederick Muller Ltd, London 1973.

Lambert White, Colonel W: *Records of the East Yorkshire Volunteer Force (1914-1919).* Eastern Morning and Hull News Co, Ltd, Hull, 1920.

Legard, Colonel Sir James: *The North Riding of Yorkshire Volunteers, 1914-1919.* The Yorkshire Herald Co, York, 1919.

Manning Foster, AE: *The National Guard in the Great War, 1914-1918.* Cope & Fenwick,

London, 1920.

Martin, Ernest J: Article published in Volume 17 (1938) of the *Journal of the Society for Army Historical Research.*

Military Historical Society. Several articles in *The Bulletin.*

Potton, Edward: *A Record of the United Arts Rifle, 1914-1919.* Alexander Moring Ltd, London, 1920.

Quebec, John: *The C.L.V.C. A Short History of the City of London Volunteer Corps, August 1914-June 1915.* W Knott, London, 1917.

St Marylebone Volunteers: A pamphlet for recruiting.

Simpson, Frank: *The Chester Volunteers with special reference to 'A' Company, 3rd Volunteer Battalion The Cheshire Regiment.* The Courant Press, Chester, c1920.

Swan, Major-General JC: *The Citizen Soldiers of Buckinghamshire, 1795-1926.* Hazell, Watson & Viney, London, 1930.

The Volunteer Force and the Volunteer Training Corps During the Great War, Official Record of the Central Association Volunteer Regiments. PS King, London, 1920.

Tindall, John: *The Sidmouth Volunteers, No 9 Platoon, C Company, 1st Volunteer Battalion Devon Regiment, 1914-1918.* E Culverwell & Sons, Sidmouth, 1920.

Volunteer Force List July 1917

Volunteer Force List October 1917

Volunteer Force List January 1918

Volunteer Force List August 1918

Volunteer Force List October 1918.

Wray, Cecil J: *3rd Battn. (Old Boys) Central London Regiment (Volunteers). A List of Members.* Marchant, Singer & Co, London, 1915.

www.ingramcontent.com/pod-product-compliance
Lightning Source LLC
Chambersburg PA
CBHW061547010526
44114CB00027B/2951